Jesuit Writings of the
Early Modern Period, 1540–1640

Jesuit Writings of the Early Modern Period, 1540–1640

Edited and Translated by
John Patrick Donnelly, S.J.

Hackett Publishing Company, Inc.
Indianapolis/Cambridge

For further information, please address
Hackett Publishing Company, Inc.
P.O. Box 44937
Indianapolis, IN 46244-0937

www.hackettpublishing.com

Cover design by Abigail Coyle
Interior design by Elizabeth Wilson
Composition by Binghamton Valley Composition, LLC
Printed at Edwards Brothers, Inc.

Map on p. xx provided courtesy of Brill Academic Publishers. The reproduction of
Nadal's woodcut on p. 168, from the CD-ROM accompanying *Annotations and
Meditations of the Gospels, Vol. 1: The Infancy Narratives* (trans. Homann, ed.
Melion, 2003), is used by permission of St. Joseph's University Press. All other
images in this book are taken, with permission, from *Ars Jesuitica,* a CD-ROM
published in 2000 by the Institute of Jesuit Sources, 3700 West Pine Boulevard,
St. Louis, Missouri.

Library of Congress Cataloging-in-Publication Data

Jesuit writings of the early modern period, 1540–1640 / edited and translated by
John Patrick Donnelly.
   p. cm.
Includes bibliographical references and index.
ISBN-13: 978-0-87220-839-1 (pbk.)
ISBN-10: 0-87220-839-7 (pbk.)
ISBN-13: 978-0-87220-840-7 (cloth)
ISBN-10: 0-87220-840-0 (cloth)
1. Jesuits—History—Sources.   I. Donnelly, John Patrick, 1934—
BX3706.3.J47 2006
271'.53—dc22
                 2006007237

∞

CONTENTS

Acknowledgments   ix

Introduction   xi

Map   xx

Chapter 1: Writings of Ignatius of Loyola   1

Introduction   1
Autobiography   2
The Spiritual Exercises   8
Letter to Jerome Nadal: Suggestions for Charles V in Dealing
    with the Turkish Menace in the Mediterranean   16
Letter to João Nunes Barreto, Patriarch of Ethiopia   21

Chapter 2: Jesuit Education   32

Introduction   32
Letter from Juan Polanco to Antonio Araoz on Jesuit Schools   33
The Jesuit Constitutions   37
Juan Polanco, selections from *Chronicon,* on the Jesuit college
    at Messina   46
Joseph Simons, selections from *Vitus,* a drama   55

Chapter 3: Jesuit Missions in Asia and the Americas   64

Introduction   64
Francis Xavier's Letters   65
Writings of Matteo Ricci   88
    Nicholas Trigault, *The Christian Expedition Undertaken among
    the Chinese by the Society of Jesus, from the Commentaries of
    Father Matteo Ricci of the Same Society*   90
    Matteo Ricci, *The True Meaning of the Lord of Heaven*   95
Roberto de Nobili, *The Report on the Customs of the
    Indian Nation*   101

Antonio Ruiz de Montoya, *The Spiritual Conquest Accomplished
    by the Religious of the Society of Jesus in the Provinces of
    Paraguay, Parana, Uruguay, and Tape*   111
Jean de Brébeuf, "Important Advice to Those Whom It Shall Please
    God to Call to New France, Especially the Country of
    the Hurons"   121

Chapter 4: Jesuit Opposition to Protestantism   131

Introduction   131
Loyola's Letter To Canisius on How King Ferdinand Should
    Oppose Protestantism in Austria   132
Edmund Campion, "The Brag" or "Challenge"   138
Robert Bellarmine, *De Controversiis Christianae Fidei* (Selections
    on Scripture and tradition)   143

Chapter 5: Jesuit Spirituality   156

Introduction   156
Alfonso Rodriguez, *Practice of Perfection and Christian Virtues*   158
Jerome Nadal, *Annotations and Meditations on the Gospels*   166
Luis de La Puente, *Meditations on the Mysteries of Our
    Holy Faith*   174
Robert Bellarmine, *The Ascent of the Mind to God*   179

Chapter 6: Special Pastoral Ministries   188

Introduction   188
Juan Polanco, selections from *Chronicon,* on healing vendettas
    and caring for reformed prostitutes   189
Claudio Acquaviva, "Instruction for Those Going Out on Missions
    to Evangelize Peasants"   193
Friedrich Spee, *Cautio Criminalis*   198
Juan Polanco, selections from *Chronicon,* on the Jesuit opposition
    to bullfighting and carnival celebrations   205

Chapter 7: Jesuits and Politics   208

Introduction   208
The Fifth General Congregation of the Jesuit Order,
    Canons 12 and 13   209

Juan Mariana, *On a King and the Education of a King* 210

Claudio Acquaviva, Rules for the Confessors of Princes 216

Robert Bellarmine, *The Office of a Christian Prince* 221

Chapter 8: Jesuits in the Eyes of Their Enemies 231

Introduction 231

Juan Polanco, selections from *Chronicon* 234

Étienne Pasquier, *Le Catéchisme des Jésuites* 245

English Catholic Attacks on the Jesuits 250

    Christopher Bagshaw, *A Sparing Discoverie of Our English Jesuits* (1601) 251

    William Watson, "Preface to the Reader" in John Mush's *A Dialogue betwixt a Secular Priest and a Lay Gentleman* 254

Index 259

ACKNOWLEDGMENTS

"No man is an island." Though authors and editors have their names printed on a book's title page, books almost always depend on many people working in collaboration. As editor of this collection of documents illustrating early Jesuit history, I owe debts of gratitude to many people for their help and encouragement. Rick Todhunter of Hackett Publishing gave me steady encouragement and sage advice. Without the generous cooperation of the directors of the two main publishers of Jesuit primary sources—John Padberg, S.J., of the Institute of Jesuit Sources and George Lane, S.J., of Loyola University Press—this project would have been far more difficult. I am also grateful for the use of documents granted me by Paulist Press and E. J. Brill.

Robert Bireley, S.J., Thomas McCoog, S.J., and Eugene Merz, S.J., suggested sources that were valuable for this collection. Though my computer skills are very limited, I had help from Thomas Caldwell, S.J., Richard Sherburne, S.J., and Roland Teske, S.J.—all colleagues at Marquette University. I am indebted to two research assistants in Marquette's history department, Michael Sanders and Eric Otremba, as well as to Matthew Blessing, head of the Marquette University Archives, for scanning selections for me. Joseph Mueller, S.J., fine-tuned my translation of a 16th-century French document. John Paul, S.J., and Robert Lambeck, S.J., proofread parts of the text and helped me avoid many a slip. Without the help of them all, this project would have been impossible. Thank all of you!

John Patrick Donnelly, S.J.
August 1, 2005
Professor of History
Marquette University

INTRODUCTION

The Roman Catholic Church dominated religious faith and practice in Europe—from Ireland to Russia and the Balkans—from the fall of the Roman Empire until Martin Luther (1483–1546) challenged the Church's authority in 1517. Though the other Protestant leaders—such as Huldreich Zwingli (1484–1531) and John Calvin (1509–64)—who emerged in subsequent decades agreed with Luther on most theological points, their doctrinal differences from Luther gave rise to the different Protestant denominations that continue to thrive in Europe and America today. Because historians tend to highlight what is new in historical periods, scholars studying the Reformation have traditionally devoted most of their attention to the emergence of these Protestant churches, and rightly so; the Protestant challenge to Catholic doctrine had profound theological, cultural, and social repercussions. But in focusing on the work of the major Protestant reformers, historians tend to overlook the changes and developments that were simultaneously occurring in the Roman Catholic Church. Until 1517 the Church was one of the most powerful institutions in the world; its teachings and practices influenced the lives of millions of Europeans who looked to it to tell them how to live their lives in this world (and ensure their place in the next). Thus, though the changes enacted within the Church were not as novel or as dramatic as those proposed by Luther and his followers, they affected the lives of more people. When the dust settled after the last of the religious wars in 1648, two-thirds of Christians west of Russia and the Balkans remained Catholic (and Catholics still outnumber Protestants by roughly two to one).

During the century covered in this book, the Catholic Church underwent many changes, most of which reinvigorated it. It provided better training for priests in seminaries, increased its focus on preaching and the teaching of catechism, established thousands of religious confraternities for the laity, and provided more effective charity for the poor. The Council of Trent (1545–63) clarified Catholic doctrine, and the Church increased its efforts to evangelize rural villages and uproot superstition. All of these reforms contributed to a more vibrant Catholicism, as did a series of popes who devoted more attention to religious renewal (and less to politics and art patronage) than did their Renaissance predecessors.

During the 16th century, the Portuguese and Spaniards took the lead in exploring and establishing colonies in Asia, Africa, and the Americas. Catholic missionaries followed the explorers Christopher Columbus (1451–1506),

Hernan Cortes (1485–1547), and Vasco da Gama (1469?–1529). To many Catholics, gathering the inhabitants of these "new worlds" into the Catholic Church made up for those members lost to the Protestants in northern Europe.

Perhaps the best gauge of the Catholic Church's vitality in any era is the number of new religious orders formed during that period. These orders are usually founded by laymen and laywomen who see a need and answer a call; they are rarely founded by bishops, never by popes. Though no religious orders of historical significance were founded in the 15th century, some twenty orders for men and ten for women were founded during the Reformation (1517–1648). Not surprisingly, none of the new religious orders arose in Luther's Germany; Italy and Spain took the lead in forming new orders, followed by France after 1600. Such older orders as the Franciscans, Dominicans, and Carmelites embraced reform. Many of the roots of the Catholic Reformation reach back before 1517, but the challenge of the Protestant Reformation gave a new urgency to reforming the Catholic Church.

The Jesuits' impact on society and Church reform made them the most important of the new religious orders. They had two clear advantages over most of the new orders: first, they were founded in Rome and quickly established close ties with the papacy; second, their order was international in origin. Though the Capuchins, a new and austere branch of the Franciscans, outnumbered the Jesuits during the 16th century, they were generally confined to working with the peasants and the poor in Italy. The Jesuits, on the other hand, adopted an international perspective right from the start. The first men who helped Ignatius of Loyola found the Jesuit Order came from three nations; by Loyola's death in 1556 Jesuits from a dozen nations were working on four continents. Other new Catholic orders were much slower to branch out from their mother country. The Jesuits also worked primarily in cities, where their schools enrolled the sons of influential nobles, merchants, doctors, lawyers, and administrators.

Ignatius of Loyola (1491–1556), a Spanish nobleman of Basque descent, founded the Jesuit Order in 1540. After spending his youth as a page at the courts of two leading Spanish noblemen, he embarked on a promising career as a courtier. This career was cut short, however, when he volunteered to help defend the town of Pamplona, near Castle Loyola, from the invading French army. During the battle, a cannonball badly smashed one of his legs. The French soldiers, who quickly overtook Pamplona, were impressed by Loyola's valor and carried him back to Castle Loyola. There, during a long convalescence, he began to read religious books and experienced his first conversion. He turned away from his boisterous past as a courtier and determined to devote his life to serving God. Indulging his strong romantic streak, he shed his elegant clothing, discarded his sword, and set off as a pilgrim for Jerusalem. Along the way, he made an unplanned stop of nine months at the small town of Manresa, where he began to keep notes on his mystical religious experiences. These notes became the seeds of his most important book, *The Spiritual Exercises,* first published in 1548. Chapter 1 of this book includes Loyola's description of his conversion experience, two of his letters, and selections from *The Spiritual Exercises.*

From Manresa Loyola traveled to Barcelona, then to Rome and Venice, and finally to Jerusalem. Though he wanted to spend the rest of his life in Palestine, the Franciscan friars, who were in charge of Christian pilgrims in Jerusalem, would not allow him to do so. Upon returning to Barcelona, Loyola decided he needed a formal education if he was to devote the rest of his life to helping others find God. Since all university instruction in Europe was in Latin, he first enrolled in the 16th-century equivalent of a secondary school to learn the language. When he moved on to Alcalá and Salamanca, Spain's two leading universities, he ran into trouble with the Inquisition, which objected to his teaching laypeople before he had studied theology. Loyola then packed his bags for the University of Paris where, since he could not speak French, he would not be tempted to preach Christian living and would be able to focus on his studies. Thanks to the Paris curriculum, which was more structured than the curriculum at Spanish universities, he made good progress. (Later Jesuit colleges followed this "Paris method.") In Paris Loyola first met the students who were to become "the companions," the disciples he regarded as his cofounders of the Society of Jesus, the Jesuits. The most famous of these companions was St. Francis Xavier (1506–52), whom we will meet in Chapter 3.

Loyola shared his religious ideas and prayer methods with his companions in Paris, and they soon came to share his desire to go to Jerusalem. On August 15, 1534, Loyola and six companions took a vow to go to Jerusalem and spend their lives there helping pilgrims and working for souls. Because they planned to become priests, they also took vows of poverty and chastity. After finishing his master's degree in philosophy, Loyola returned to Azpeitia, his hometown, and nearby Castle Loyola. There he preached to the common folk and settled his affairs. This would be his last visit to Spain.

Loyola and his companions planned to gather in Venice to take ship for Palestine. Loyola and five of the other companions prepared for the trip by becoming ordained priests in Venice in 1537. But the war that had broken out between Venice and the Ottoman Empire, which controlled Palestine, spoiled their plans. Neither Loyola nor his companions ever saw Jerusalem again. The destruction of their plans was a blessing in disguise, however:

the Turks would never have allowed Loyola and his followers to proselytize in Palestine, and the young priests would probably have ended up rowing Turkish galleys, or worse. Luckily, the vows Loyola and his companions had taken in Paris included a back-up plan: if they could not go to Jerusalem, they would put themselves at the pope's disposal. Paul III (pope, 1534–49)[1] sent several of the companions to preach in northern Italian cities. But they wanted to give formal structure to their work for souls rather than be scattered individually across the countryside. So, in April 1539 Loyola and the companions gathered in Rome to discuss their plans. They decided that they could serve God and neighbor more effectively if they continued to work as a group. A group needs a leader, so the companions elected Loyola their superior. The companions had already made vows of poverty and chastity in Paris; in electing Loyola as their leader, they took a vow of obedience, the last of the three vows at the heart of any Catholic order. They also commissioned Loyola to draw up their plans for a new religious order and to present those plans to Pope Paul III for his approval. Despite opposition from some cardinals, that papal approval was granted on September 27, 1540. The Society of Jesus was born.

Loyola spent the rest of his life in Rome, leaving the city only briefly on a few short excursions. Meanwhile, the Jesuit Order began to grow: its members numbered one thousand by Loyola's death in 1556, three thousand by 1565. Loyola spent his last ten years writing letters and memos to Jesuits and their benefactors. (Some sixty-seven hundred of his letters have survived and been published.) He also drafted the Jesuit Constitutions, which were far more detailed than those of previous religious orders, and dictated his short autobiography.

This book presents primary documents written by or about the Jesuits from the foundation of the Jesuits, in 1540, until 1640. These documents illustrate the history, work, and mentality of the Jesuits during those years. The book is divided into eight chapters, each of which is focused on a different aspect of Jesuit history. Every chapter begins with a brief introduction of its subject; then three to six documents follow, usually in chronological order, each with its own introduction. Students should examine both the content of the documents and the context and mentality that shaped them. Footnotes explain difficult expressions in the texts, indicate the sources from which the documents are taken, and provide bibliographic information for those seeking more information.

People of the early modern era tended to be far more explicit about their values and prejudices than people would normally be today. Thus the letter

---

1. The dates for kings and popes give the years they reigned.

of Ignatius of Loyola to Peter Canisius (1521–97) included here makes clear Loyola's hatred of Protestantism. In turn, contemporary Protestants generally regarded the Jesuits as the shock troops of the papal Antichrist, servants of Satan; the more talented and energetic Jesuits were, the more evil and dangerous they seemed. The first seven chapters of this book offer documents in which Jesuits express their worldview and their enthusiasm for the religious order to which they had dedicated their lives. To balance that pro-Jesuit perspective, the eighth chapter prints documents illustrating how even many Roman Catholics loathed the Jesuits for a wide range of reasons.

The documents printed here illustrate the major themes and efforts of the early Jesuits. Unfortunately, limited space prevents me from including texts related to many other significant Jesuit ministries. Readers of this collection should bear in mind that the Jesuits served in many ways not addressed here. They worked in hospitals and prisons and served as military chaplains; they founded and supervised many confraternities and sodalities; they encouraged frequent confession and Communion. There is little here about Jesuit contributions to culture, art, and the sciences; fortunately, these are areas of much ongoing research.[2]

Loyola and his companions did not originally plan to teach academically or to operate schools. They planned, instead, to devote themselves to preaching, encouraging frequent confession and Communion, and administering the Spiritual Exercises to devout souls. To those ends, they planned to establish what they called Professed Houses where priests could live and work. These houses, attached to churches, would charge no fees for their services; they would depend entirely on freewill offerings for their maintenance. The idea of Professed Houses never caught on, however, and only a few were established. Meanwhile, Jesuit colleges flourished and multiplied. One hundred forty-four Jesuit schools had been established by 1580, 372 by 1615. These early Jesuit institutions taught teenage boys a curriculum advocated by Renaissance humanists: Latin and Greek language and literature, with some philosophy and catechism added. A few of the colleges became full universities. Relying on endowments from rich benefactors or local communities, the Jesuit colleges charged no tuition. Usually there was

2. See the wealth of articles in *Jesuit Science and the Republic of Letters*, edited by Mordichai Feingold (Cambridge, MA: MIT Press, 2003); *The Jesuits: Cultures, Sciences, and the Arts, 1540–1773*, edited by John O'Malley et al. (Toronto: Toronto University Press, 1999); *The Jesuits II: Cultures, Sciences and the Arts, 1540–1773*, edited by John O'Malley et al. (Toronto: Toronto University Press, 2005). For early Jesuit art, see Gauvin A. Bailey, *Between Renaissance and Baroque: Jesuit Art in Rome, 1565–1610* (Toronto: Toronto University Press, 2003).

a Jesuit church next to the colleges for preaching, celebrating Mass, hearing confessions, and teaching catechism. Many secular schoolmasters resented the Jesuit colleges; they claimed the Jesuits stole their students by not charging tuition. Established universities at Paris, Padua, Louvain, Kraków, and Lima felt that the new Jesuit colleges were encroaching on their territory by offering more advanced courses as the colleges expanded. These universities often resorted to legal maneuverings to force Jesuit schools to close completely or cut back their course offerings. Chapter 2 explores Jesuit education through four primary sources: a selection from the Jesuit Constitutions regarding education; some letters from Loyola and Juan Polanco (1510–76), Loyola's secretary, instructing Jesuits how to set up Jesuit colleges in Italy and Spain; Polanco's description of the first Jesuit college for lay students at Messina; and part of one of the thousands of dramas written and produced by Jesuits and performed by the students at their colleges.

Chapter 3, the longest in this book, is concerned with Jesuit missions in India, Japan, China, Latin America, and Canada. The selections included in this chapter record Jesuit missionaries' dealings with simple fishermen in southern India, the Guarani Indians of Paraguay, and the Hurons of Canada; some debates with sophisticated defendants of the Buddhist and Hindu traditions are also recorded here. As these selections make clear, Jesuit missionaries had to struggle to accommodate the customs and beliefs of non-Western cultures without betraying the basic tenets of the Christian faith they were trying to spread around the world.

The next chapter, Chapter 4, examines Jesuit opposition to Protestantism. Jesuit theological efforts to prevent the triumph of Protestant ideas took many forms: young Jesuit teachers left their colleges on weekends to teach catechism in the countryside; Jesuit scholars turned out books in which they challenged the tenets of Protestant theology. Robert Bellarmine (1542–1621) rejected Luther and Calvin's claims that the Bible is the sole criterion for Christian faith and practice; Bellarmine's rejection is included in Chapter 4.

Since both Protestantism and Catholicism recognized that the survival of their faiths depended, in large part, on who controlled the government, the battle between the two churches was often as political as it was theological. The documents in Chapter 4 illustrate some of the ways in which the Jesuits tried (and sometimes failed) to wrest political power away from the Protestants. In one of Loyola's harshest letters, he sent King Ferdinand (1531–64) of Bohemia and Austria suggestions on how to block Protestant influence in his lands. The Jesuits did not oppose the Inquisition; indeed, they supported it. But they tried to avoid serving as Inquisitors and often found themselves the victims of religious persecution at the hands of the

Protestants. After the Protestant English government made it an act of treason to serve as a Catholic priest in that country, dozens of English Jesuits died for their faith. One such martyr was Edmund Campion (1540–81), who challenged the English government to hold a theological debate in which he would take on all Protestant comers. Campion was captured following the publication of his challenge (which is included in Chapter 4). A rigged debate was staged, and he was executed.

Works of spirituality have always been far more popular than theological tracts. The invention of printing afforded a wonderful opportunity to deepen the faith of those who could read, and both Protestants and Catholics made good use of the printing press. Chapter 5 presents four Jesuit spiritual writings. In the first, Alfonso Rodriguez (1541–1616) defines the Jesuit identity for young Jesuits. Jerome Nadal (1507–80), Loyola's top assistant, arranged for the publication of an illustrated edition of Loyola's *Exercises* to be published with illustrations;[3] he also wrote meditations of his own, which were closely tied to superb engravings. In this chapter we will read Nadal's spiritual reflections on Christmas. The most popular bulky meditation book of the 16th century was written by Luis de La Puente (1554–1624); La Puente's meditation on Christ's parable of the sower is offered here. The chapter closes with Bellarmine's reflections on how nature—the sun, moon, and stars—can deepen our appreciation of God's grandeur.

Chapter 6 deals with special Jesuit ministries. The chapter begins with a selection from Juan Polanco's *Chronicon* in which Polanco offers ways in which Jesuits can end vendettas and help former prostitutes find a better life. Claudio Acquaviva (1543–1615), superior general of the Society of Jesus from 1581 to 1615, wrote a set of rules for Jesuits assigned to visit small towns and invigorate the faith of the peasants; these rules are printed here for the first time in English. (Acquaviva's rules for Jesuits assigned to the prestigious but difficult job of being royal confessors or spiritual advisers are found in Chapter 7.) The persecution of witches claimed far more lives during the Reformation than did persecutions based on faith. Most of the so-called witches were actually impoverished women who, once suspected of witchcraft, had no way to prove their innocence and escape torture and execution. In the selection included here from his *Cautio Criminalis,* Jesuit Friedrich Spee (1591–1635) denounces this dreadful injustice. The chapter ends with Jesuit opposition to bullfighting and wild celebrations at Mardi Gras.

Chapter 7 examines four Jesuit writings that illustrate Jesuit involvement in politics. The first document presents rules from the Fifth General

---

3. There is a recent edition of his illustrations: *The Illustrated Spiritual Exercises,* edited by Jerome Nadal (Scranton: Scranton University Press, 2001).

Congregation of the Jesuits (1593–94) forbidding Jesuits to meddle in politics. The second document is from Juan Mariana's book, *On a King and the Education of a King,* that he wrote for his pupil, the future Philip III of Spain. Its Chapter 6 discusses whether and when the assassination of tyrannical princes can be justified. Even though the Jesuits officially repudiated Mariana's book, it caused great hostility toward Jesuits, particularly in France. Jesuits served as royal confessors in several Catholic countries; this could easily lead to political involvement. In the third document, Claudio Acquaviva lays down rules restricting the work of confessors to moral and spiritual matters. The chapter closes with an excerpt from Bellarmine's *The Office of a Christian Prince,* which he wrote for the future king of Poland.

Few organizations have been praised as much as the Jesuits; few have been so bitterly condemned. The last chapter of this volume allows readers to see the Jesuits through the eyes of their Spanish, French, and English enemies. In each country the opposition took a different focus.[4] Protestants condemned all Catholic religious orders on theological grounds, of course. But they also condemned the Church because monks and friars seemed lazy and proud, were often badly trained, sometimes had wealth, or were given to sexual activity. In reality, few of these charges—except for the charge of pride—accurately described the Jesuits. The Jesuits also faced a great deal of opposition from within the Catholic Church itself. Members of other Catholic orders felt that the very title *Society of Jesus* was arrogant. Some members of older religious orders, especially the Dominicans, thought that the Jesuits had abandoned practices central to the life of religious orders. For instance, the Jesuits wore no distinctive uniform, such as the white and black robes of the Dominicans; they simply adopted the dress of the local parish clergy. Many Catholics thought that all members of religious orders should wear a distinctive habit or uniform that would identify them. Many bishops, parish priests, and friars resented the privileges given to the Jesuits by the pope. Other Catholics opposed the Jesuits because the Order seemed to be dominated by Spaniards, starting with Loyola himself. France and England were often at war with Spain, and so French and English Jesuits were frequently suspected by their countrymen to be potential or actual traitors. Many Catholics felt the Jesuits were too involved in politics, for

4. There are many histories of the Jesuit Order. Solid but a bit dry is William Bangert, S.J., *A History of the Society of Jesus,* 2nd ed. (St. Louis: Institute of Jesuit Sources, 1986); newer and more lively is Jonathan Wright, *God's Soldiers: Adventure, Politics, Intrigue and Power; A History of the Jesuits* (New York: Doubleday, 2004). The best book on the early Jesuits is John O'Malley's *The First Jesuits* (Cambridge, MA: Harvard University Press, 1993).

Jesuits often served as royal confessors in Paris, Lisbon, Vienna, and Munich. Others objected to the extreme centralization of the Jesuits, where a superior general, elected for life, personally appointed all of his major subordinates; to such critics, the Jesuit general seemed like a dictator. Most medieval Catholics went to Communion only once or twice a year, and the Jesuits came under fire for encouraging frequent confession and Communion. Chapter 8 contains documents illustrating such opposition to the Jesuits.

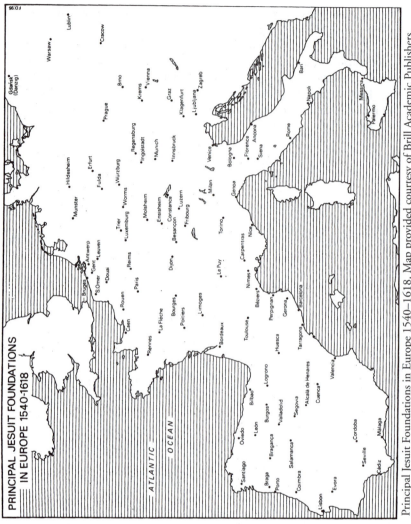

Principal Jesuit Foundations in Europe 1540–1618. Map provided courtesy of Brill Academic Publishers.

CHAPTER 1

WRITINGS OF IGNATIUS OF LOYOLA

INTRODUCTION

Ignatius of Loyola (1491–1556), whose life was briefly discussed in the Introduction to this book, was the founder of the Society of Jesus, popularly called the Jesuits. In his actions and writings, Loyola inspired the early Jesuits and served as the embodiment of the ideals toward which they were striving. Though he was not an eloquent writer (and the culture of the Renaissance valued nothing in a writer so much as eloquence), his writings are clear, sincere, thoughtful, and well organized. He wrote or dictated three books in his lifetime, the first and most important of which was *The Spiritual Exercises* (1548), a manual of directions and spiritual reflections for people who wanted to spend a month reorganizing their lives and learning to pray more effectively. It is the only one of his books published during his lifetime and has remained a best seller ever since. This chapter contains several meditations and directions for spiritual growth from *The Spiritual Exercises.*

Loyola's second book was *The Constitutions of the Society of Jesus,* which his early companions authorized him to write shortly after Pope Paul III approved the Jesuits as a religious order in 1540. Because Loyola wanted to learn from the experiences of his fellow Jesuits before laying down elaborate rules for them to follow, progress on the book was very slow for the first eight years. Though the basic Spanish text was finished by 1552, Loyola continued to make minor corrections and additions to the manuscript until his death in 1556. *The Constitutions* were then translated into Latin, officially approved by the First General Congregation, the highest governing body of the Society, and published in 1558. Loyola's *Constitutions* are far longer and more detailed than the rules of most other religious orders. (Chapter 2 contains a section from *The Constitutions* on how Jesuit schools should be organized.)

This chapter begins with a selection from Loyola's autobiography in which he describes the conversion he experienced while he was recovering from a wound he sustained during a battle with the French in Pamplona, Spain. Though he did not like to discuss his religious experiences with others, and did not want to write an autobiography, his early companions urged him to tell them more about his life before he joined them as a fellow student at the University of Paris. His autobiography stops abruptly in 1538.

Loyola kept detailed personal notes of his own private religious experiences but refused to share them with anyone except his confessor. Two bundles of his notes, covering some thirteen months (early February 1544 to late February 1545), somehow escaped his attempts to destroy them and were published in 1892. These notes reveal that the mystical revelations he experienced shortly after his conversion in 1522 came flooding back to him during his last sixteen years in Rome.

Loyola's responsibilities during those last years can be compared to the duties commonly held by the chief executive officer of a modern international corporation. He spent most of his time writing and dictating letters and memos, mostly to fellow Jesuits scattered around Europe or working as missionaries in Asia, Africa, and Latin America. Of the 6,742 extant items of his correspondence, 6,590 come from his last ten years. Two of Loyola's letters end this chapter: the first offers Loyola's suggestions on how Emperor Charles V (1519–56) might prevent Turkish ships from raiding his lands; the second presents Loyola's thoughts on how the new Jesuit patriarch in Ethiopia should deal with the king and people of that land. (Chapter 2 contains a letter from Loyola to Antonio Araoz on why Jesuits should work as teachers. Chapter 4 contains Loyola's letter to Peter Canisius on how to prevent the spread of Protestantism in Austria.)

Autobiography[1]

[In 1552 Loyola's health was declining, and his closest Jesuit coworkers feared he might die soon. Three of these colleagues—Pedro de Ribadeneira (1526–1611), Jerome Nadal (1507–80), and Luís Gonçalves da Câmara (1519–75)—wanted to know more about Loyola's life, so they began hounding him to write an account of his early years. Loyola's autobiography makes it clear that the greatest sin of his younger years was a thirst for glory, and he seemed fearful later in life that leaving an autobiography would be an act of self-aggrandizement.

Loyola finally yielded to his coworkers' requests and asked for help from Gonçalves—who was available in Rome and had a fine memory—to assist him in writing the book. Loyola related his life story to Gonçalves when his

---

1. These sections of Loyola's autobiography are taken with the publisher's permission from *Ignatius of Loyola: The Spiritual Exercises and Selected Works*, edited by George Ganss, S.J., et al. (New York: Paulist Press, 1991), pp. 68–73.

Loyola reads in bed during his recovery.

other work allowed him some free time: his autobiography was composed in August and September 1553, March 1555, and September and October 1555. Gonçalves would listen to Loyola's narrative and then write notes on what he had heard. Later Gonçalves would dictate his notes to a secretary. Like most 16th-century autobiographies, Loyola's is not written in the first person. Instead, Loyola refers to himself as "the Pilgrim," doubtless because he considered his life a pilgrimage to God and heaven, one with many twists and turns.

The section printed here relates Loyola's conversion from being a courtier whose life was dominated by a thirst for personal glory to a man dedicated to serving God and other people for the glory of God. Though Gonçalves periodically inserted marginal notes of his own into the text, his notes have been omitted here.[2]*]*

Chapter 1: Pamplona and Loyola
Mid-May 1521 to Late February 1522

1. Up to the age of twenty-six he was a man given to the vanities of the world; and what he enjoyed most was warlike sport, with a great and foolish desire to win fame. And so, whilst in a fortress that the French were attacking, when all were of the view that they should surrender, with their lives safeguarded—for they saw clearly that they could not offer resistance—he gave so many reasons to the commander that he actually persuaded him to resist, even against this view of all the officers, who drew courage from his spirit and determination. When the day came on which the bombardment was expected, he confessed to one of these companions in arms. And after the bombardment had lasted a good while, a shot struck him on one leg, shattering it completely; and as the cannon ball passed between both legs, the other also was badly injured.

2. The best study of Loyola's autobiography is Marjorie O'Rourke Boyle, *Loyola's Acts: The Rhetoric of the Self* (Berkeley: University of California Press, 1997), although it is more a literary and psychological study than a historical analysis.

2. So with his fall those in the fortress soon surrendered to the French, who on taking possession of it treated the wounded man very well—treated him with courtesy and kindness. And after he had been in Pamplona for twelve or fifteen days, they took him home in a litter. Here he felt quite unwell. All the doctors and surgeons who were summoned from many places decided that the leg ought to be broken again and the bones reset, saying that because they had been badly set the other time, or had got broken on the road, they were out of place, and this way he could not mend. And once again this butchery was gone through. During it, as in all the others he underwent before or after, he never said a word nor showed any sign of pain other than to clench his fists tightly.

3. Yet he kept getting worse, not being able to eat, and with the other symptoms that usually point to death. When St. John's day came, because the doctors were far from confident about his health, he was advised to confess. He received the sacraments on the eve of St. Peter and St. Paul. The doctors said that if he did not feel any improvement by midnight, he could be taken for dead. It happened that this sick man was devoted to St. Peter, so Our Lord deigned that he should begin to get better that very midnight. His improvement proceeded so well that some days later it was judged that he was out of danger of death.

4. And his bones having knit together, one bone below the knee was left riding on another, which made the leg shorter. The bone protruded so much that it was an ugly business. He could not bear such a thing because he was set on a worldly career and thought that this would deform him; he asked the surgeons if it could be cut away. They said that it could indeed be cut away, but that the pain would be greater than all that he had suffered, because it was already healed and it would take a while to cut it. And yet he chose on his own to make himself a martyr though his elder brother was shocked and said that he himself would not dare suffer such pain; but the wounded man bore it with his wonted endurance.

5. After the flesh and excess bone were cut away, remedial measures were taken that the leg might not be so short. Ointment was often applied, and it was stretched continually with instruments that tortured him for many days. But Our Lord kept giving him health, and he felt so well that he was quite fit except that he could not stand easily on his leg and had perforce to stay in bed. As he was much given to reading worldly books of fiction, commonly labeled chivalry, when he felt better he asked to be given some of them to pass the time. But in that house none of those that he usually read could be found, so they gave him a life of Christ and a book of the lives of the saints in Castilian.

6. As he read them over many times, he became rather fond of what he found written there. But, interrupting his reading, he sometimes stopped to

Ignatius of Loyola and the Jesuit Constitutions. Engraving by Hieronymus Wierx, 1556.

think about the things he had read and at other times about the things of the world that he used to think of before. Of the many foolish ideas that occurred to him, one had taken such a hold on his heart that he was absorbed in thinking about it for two and three and four hours without realizing it. He imagined what he would do in the service of a certain lady; the means he would take so he could go to the place where she lived; the quips—the words he would address to her; the feats of arms he would perform in her service. He became so infatuated with this that he did not consider how impossible of attainment it would be, because the lady was not of ordinary nobility, not a countess nor a duchess; but her station was higher than any of these.

7. Nevertheless Our Lord assisted him, by causing these thoughts to be followed by others which arose from the things he read. For in reading the life of Our Lord and of the saints, he stopped to think, reasoning within himself, "What if I should do what St. Francis did, and what St. Dominic did?"[3] Thus he pondered over many things that he found good, always proposing to himself what was difficult and burdensome; and as he so proposed, it seemed easy for him to accomplish it. But he did no more than argue within himself, saying, "St. Dominic did this, therefore I have to do it; St. Francis did this, therefore I have to do it." These thoughts also lasted a good while; then, other things coming in between, the worldly ones mentioned above returned and he also stayed long with them. This succession of such diverse thoughts lasted for quite some time, and he always dwelt at

3. St. Francis of Assisi (c. 1181–1226) was the most beloved of medieval saints; he founded the Franciscan religious order, which stressed a lifestyle of austere poverty. St. Dominic (1170–1221), a Spaniard, founded the Order of Preachers, known as the Dominicans. The Dominicans stressed theological learning and the ability to preach—skills most medieval parish priests lacked. (The Jesuits, on the other hand, stressed poverty, learning, and preaching.) Dominic himself preached against heresy in southern France.

length on the thought that turned up, either of the worldly exploits he wished to perform or of these others of God that came to his imagination, until he tired of it and put it aside and turned to other matters.

8. Yet there was this difference. When he was thinking of those things of the world he took much delight in them, but afterwards when he was tired and put them aside, he found himself dry and dissatisfied. But when he thought of going to Jerusalem barefoot, and of eating nothing but plain vegetables and of practicing all the other rigors that he saw in the saints, not only was he consoled when he had these thoughts but even after putting them aside he remained satisfied and joyful.

He did not notice this, however; nor did he stop to ponder the distinction until the time when his eyes were opened a little and he began to marvel at the difference and to reflect upon it, realizing from experience that some thoughts left him sad and others joyful. Little by little he came to recognize the difference between the spirits that were stirring, one from the devil, the other from God.

9. From this lesson he derived not a little light, and he began to think more earnestly about his past life and about the great need he had to do penance for it. At this point the desire to imitate the saints came to him, though he gave no thought to details, only promising with God's grace to do as they had done. But the one thing he wanted to do was to go to Jerusalem as soon as he recovered, as mentioned above, with as much of disciplines and fasts as a generous spirit, fired with God, would want to perform.

10. And so he began to forget the previous thoughts with these holy desires he had, and they were confirmed by a spiritual experience in this manner. One night while he was awake he saw clearly an image of Our Lady with the holy Child Jesus. From this sight he received for a considerable time very great consolation, and he was left with such loathing for his whole past life and especially for the things of the flesh that it seemed to him that his spirit was rid of all the images that had been painted on it. Thus from that hour until August 1553 when this was written, he never gave the slightest consent to the things of the flesh. For this reason it may be considered the work of God, although he did not dare to claim it nor said more than to affirm the above. But his brother as well as all the rest of the household came to know from his exterior the change that had been wrought inwardly in his soul.

11. Not worried at all, he persevered in his reading and his good resolutions, and all his time of conversation with members of the household he spent on the things of God; thus he benefitted their souls. As he very much liked those books, the idea came to him to note down briefly some of the more essential things from the life of Christ and the saints. So he set

Pope Paul III approves the Jesuit Order in 1540.

himself very diligently to write a book (because he was now beginning to be up and about the house a bit) with red ink for the words of Christ, blue ink for those of Our Lady, on polished and lined paper, in a good hand because he was a very fine penman.

12. And taking stock of what he might do after he returned from Jerusalem, so he could always live as a penitent, he thought he might enter the Carthusian house in Seville,[4] without saying who he was, so that they would make little of him; and there he would never eat anything but plain vegetables. But when he thought again of the penances he wished to do as he went about the world, the desire to enter the Carthusians cooled, with the fear that he would not be able to give vent to the hatred that he had conceived against himself. Still he instructed one of the household servants who was going to Burgos to get information about the rule of the Carthusians, and the information he obtained about it seemed good.

But for the reason mentioned above, and because he was wholly absorbed in the journey he was planning soon to make and that matter did not have to be dealt with until his return, he did not look much into it. Rather, finding now that he had some strength, he thought the time to depart had come; and he said to his brother, "Sir, the Duke of Nájera, as you know, is aware now that I am well. It will be good that I go Navarrete." (The duke was there at that time.)[5]

His brother took him to one room and then another, and with much feeling begged him not to throw himself away; also, to consider what hopes had

4. The Carthusians were considered the strictest and most austere of the monastic religious orders.

5. Loyola served as a courtier at the court of the duke of Nájera, who was viceroy of Navarre. Charles V was raised in Belgium, and several towns, including Nájera, opposed his becoming king of Spain in 1518. Loyola and other nobles at Charles' court helped the duke crush the rebellion at Nájera in September 1518. Loyola almost certainly helped the duke negotiate peace with his home region of Guipúzcoa, which rebelled against Charles V in April 1521. Loyola was wounded the next month.

been placed in him by the people, and how much he could achieve, and other such words, all with the purpose of dissuading him from his good intention. But he answered in such a way that, without departing from the truth, for he was now very scrupulous about that, he slipped away from his brother.

Chapter 2: Road to Montserrat
Late February 1522

13. And so, as he mounted a mule, another brother wished to go with him as far as Oñate. On the road he persuaded him to join in a vigil at Our Lady of Aránzazu. That night he prayed there that he might gain fresh strength for his journey. He left his brother in

Loyola writes the Constitutions and sends Jesuits on assignment.

Oñate at the house of a sister he was going to visit, and himself went on to Navarrete. . . .

14. On the way something happened to him which it would be well to record, so one may understand how Our Lord dealt with his soul, which was still blind, though greatly desirous of serving him as far as his knowledge went. Thus, he decided to do great penances, no longer with an eye to satisfying for his sins so much as to please and gratify God. So when it occurred to him to do some penance that the saints practiced, he determined to do the same and even more. . . .

The Spiritual Exercises

[Loyola's most important work, The Spiritual Exercises, *was first published in Rome in 1548. Though he never intended for people to read it as a literary work, the book has enjoyed more than five thousand editions in the past five centuries and remains a spiritual classic. Loyola wanted his* Exercises *to serve as a guidebook or manual for spiritual directors, mainly Jesuits, who were directing people through the thirty days of prayer and meditation called the "Spiritual Exercises." Loyola began collecting notes on his own spiritual experiences during the months of 1522 when he devoted himself to prayer at Manresa, in Spain, shortly after his conversion. He continued to add to his notes until he entered the University of Paris in 1528. In Paris he personally directed his first companions*

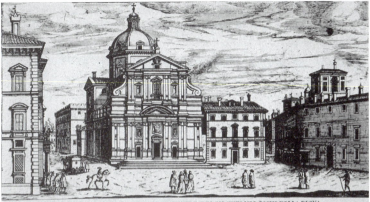

CHIESA DEDICATA AL NOME DI GIESV DE PADRI GIESVITI NEL RIONE DELLA PIGNA

The Gesù, mother church of the Jesuit Order. To its right is the Jesuit house where Loyola worked and died.

through this intense month of prayer. Later, new members of the Jesuits were required to make the Exercises, and many of them used their own notes on the experience in directing other retreatants or exercitants (the people making the Exercises) through the same experience. Sometimes exercitants were given a week-long condensed version. Sometimes a gifted nun would make the full Exercises under a Jesuit director—and would then direct the other nuns in her convent through the whole process. When the need for an official printed version of the Exercises finally became clear, Loyola had his Spanish notes translated into Latin; they were then submitted for papal approval and printed.

Loyola did not want The Spiritual Exercises *to be read by people who had not already completed the full thirty-day retreat because he feared that the book would seem like a confusing maze of meditations and directions. The main purpose of the Exercises was to teach people how to improve their prayer and reshape their lives to better follow God's will for them. Those who have only read the text of the* Exercises *will have little feel for their cumulative spiritual power.*

The Exercises are broken into four segments, or weeks. The first week largely dwells on our purpose in life and on sin. The second week focuses on the life of Jesus from his birth until Palm Sunday. The third week dwells on Christ's Passion and death; the fourth on his Resurrection. Interspersed among the meditations are many rules and concrete directions on how to pray and to better organize various aspects of one's life.

Sometimes Loyola assigns only a passage from the Gospels and expects the retreat director to craft a meditation on the passage suited to a particular retreatant's talents and needs; sometimes Loyola develops the meditations in considerable detail. Three of the latter meditations—the meditations on the First

Principle and Foundation of our lives, the Incarnation of Christ, and the Contemplation to Attain Love—are printed here. We begin with Loyola's introductory explanations or directions for those making the Exercises; we then move on to the three meditations and end with his practical directives for giving alms.[6]

Introductory explanations, to gain some understanding of the Spiritual Exercises which follow, and to aid both the one who gives them and the one who receives them

The First Explanation. By the term Spiritual Exercises we mean every method of examination of conscience, meditation, contemplation, vocal or mental prayer, and other spiritual activities, such as will be mentioned later. For, just as taking a walk, traveling on foot, and running are physical exercises, so is the name of Spiritual Exercises given to any means of preparing and disposing our soul to rid itself of all its disordered affections and then, after their removal, of seeking and finding God's will in the ordering of our life for the salvation of our soul.

The Second. The person who gives to another the method and procedure for meditating or contemplating should accurately narrate the history contained in the contemplation or meditation, going over the points with only a brief or summary explanation. For in this way the person who is contemplating, by taking this history as the authentic foundation, and by going over it and reasoning about it for oneself, can thus discover something that will bring better understanding or a more personalized concept of the history—either through one's own reasoning or to the extent that the understanding is enlightened by God's grace. This brings more spiritual relish and spiritual fruit than if the one giving the Exercises had lengthily explained and amplified the meaning of the history. For, what fills and satisfies the soul consists, not in knowing much, but in our understanding the realities profoundly and in savoring them interiorly.

The Third. In all the following Spiritual Exercises we use the acts of the intellect in reasoning and of the will in eliciting acts of the affections. In regard to the affective acts which spring from the will we should note that when we are conversing with God our Lord or his saints vocally or mentally, greater reverence is demanded of us than when we are using the intellect to understand.

---

6. The passages printed here are from *The Spiritual Exercises of Saint Ignatius,* translated by George Ganss, S.J. (St. Louis: Institute of Jesuit Sources, 1992), pp. 21–4, 32, 56–8, 94–5, 129–30. They are used with the permission of the Institute of Jesuit Sources.

The Fourth. Four Weeks are taken for the following Exercises, corresponding to the four parts into which they are divided. That is, the First Week is
devoted to the consideration and contemplation of sins; the Second, to the
life of Christ our Lord up to and including Palm Sunday; the Third, to the
Passion of Christ our Lord; and the Fourth, to the Resurrection and Ascen-
sion. To this week are appended the Three Methods of Praying. However,
this does not mean that each week must necessarily consist of seven or eight
days. For during the First Week some persons happen to be slower in finding what they are seeking, that is, contrition, sorrow, and tears for their sins.
Similarly, some persons work more diligently than others, and are more
pushed back and forth and probed by different spirits. In some cases, therefore, the week needs to be shortened, and in others lengthened. This holds
as well for all the following weeks, while the retreatant is seeking for what
corresponds to their subject matter. But the Exercises ought to be completed in thirty days, more or less.

The Fifth. The persons who receive the Exercises will benefit greatly by
entering upon them with great spirit and generosity toward their Creator
and Lord, and by offering all their desires and freedom to him so that his
Divine Majesty can make use of their persons and of all they possess in
whatsoever way is according to his most holy will.

The Sixth. When the one giving the Exercises notices that the exercitant is not experiencing any spiritual motions in his or her soul, such as
consolations or desolations, or is not being moved one way or another by
different spirits, the director should question the retreatant much about
the Exercises: Whether he or she is making them at the appointed times,
how they are being made and whether the Additional Directives are being
diligently observed. The director should ask about each of these items in
particular. . . .

The Seventh. When the giver of the Exercises sees that the one making
them is experiencing desolation and temptation, he or she should not treat
the retreatant severely or harshly, but gently and kindly. The director
should encourage and strengthen the exercitant for the future, unmask the
deceptive tactics of the enemy of our human nature, and help the retreatant to prepare and dispose himself or herself for the consolation which
will come.

The Eighth. According to the need perceived in the exercitant with respect to the desolations and deceptive tactics of the enemy, and also the
consolations, the giver of the Exercises may explain to the retreatant the
rules of the First and Second Weeks for recognizing the different kinds of
spirits.

The Ninth. This point should be noticed. When an exercitant spiritually inexperienced is going through the First Week of the Exercises he or

she may be tempted grossly and openly, for example, by being shown obstacles to going forward in the service of God our Lord, in the form of hardships, shame, fear about worldly honor, and the like. In such a case the one giving the Exercises should not explain to this retreatant the rules on different kinds of spirits for the Second Week. For to the same extent that the rules of the First Week will help him or her, those of the Second Week will be harmful. They are too subtle and advanced for such a one to understand.[7]

The first week: principle and foundation[8]

Human beings are created to praise, reverence, and serve God our Lord, and by means of this to save their souls. The other things on the face of the earth are created for the human beings, to help them in working toward the end for which they are created.

From this it follows that I should use these things to the extent that they help me toward my end, and rid myself of them to the extent that they hinder me. To do this, I must make myself indifferent to all created things, in regard to everything which is left to my freedom of will and is not forbidden. Consequently, on my own part I ought not to seek health rather than sickness, wealth rather than poverty, honor rather than dishonor, a long life rather than a short one, and so in all other matters.

I ought to desire and elect only the thing which is more conducive to the end for which I am created.

This first contemplation is devoted to the Incarnation[9]

It contains, after the preparatory prayer, three preludes, three points, and a colloquy.

The usual Preparatory Prayer.

The First Prelude is to survey the history of the matter I am to contemplate. Here it is how the Three Divine Persons gazed on the whole surface or circuit of the world, full of people; and how, seeing that they were all going down into hell, they decided in their eternity that the Second Person would become a human being, in order to save the human race. And thus, when the fullness of time had come, they sent the angel St. Gabriel to Our Lady.

---

7. In all Loyola gives twenty introductory explanations.

8. These short reflections on the purpose of life come at the start of the first week of the Exercises.

9. This meditation comes on the first day of the second week, which covers Christ's life from the Incarnation up to Palm Sunday.

The Second Prelude is a composition, by imagining the place. Here it will be to see the great extent of the circuit of the world, with peoples so many and so diverse; and then to see in particular the house and rooms of Our Lady, in the city of Nazareth in the province of Galilee.

The Third Prelude will be to ask for what I desire. Here it will be to ask for an interior knowledge of Our Lord, who became human for me, that I may love him more intensely and follow him more closely.

Note. It should be noted here that this same preparatory prayer, without any change, should be made throughout this and the following weeks, as was stated at the beginning. Similarly the same three preludes are to be made throughout this and the following weeks; but their content is changed in accordance with the subject matter.

The First Point. I will see the various persons, some here, some there. First, those on the face of the earth, so diverse in dress and behavior: some white and others black, some in peace and others at war, some weeping and others laughing, some healthy and others sick, some being born and others dying, and so forth.

Second, I will see and consider the Three Divine Persons, seated, so to speak, on the royal throne of their Divine Majesty. They are gazing on the whole face and circuit of the earth; and they see all the peoples in such great blindness, and how they are dying and going down to hell.

Third, I will see Our Lady and the angel greeting her. Then I will reflect on this to draw some profit from what I see.

The Second Point. I will listen to what the persons on the face of the earth are saying; that is, how they speak with one another, swear and blaspheme, and so on. Likewise, I will hear what the Divine Persons are saying, that is, "Let us work the redemption of the human race," and so forth. Then I will listen to what the angel and Our Lady are saying. Afterward I will reflect on this, to draw profit from their words.

The Third Point. Here I will consider what the people on the face of the earth are doing: How they wound, kill, go to hell, and so on. Similarly, what the Divine Persons are doing, that is, bringing about the most holy Incarnation, and other such activities. Likewise, what the angel and Our Lady are doing, with the angel carrying out his office of ambassador and Our Lady humbling herself and giving thanks to the Divine Majesty. Then I will reflect on these matters, to draw some profit from each of them.

Colloquy. At the end a colloquy should be made. I will think over what I ought to say to the Three Divine Persons, or to the eternal Word made flesh, or to our Mother and Lady. I will beg favors according to what I feel in my heart, that I may better follow and imitate Our Lord, who in this way has recently become a human being. Our Father.

Contemplation to attain love[10]

Two preliminary observations should be made.

First: Love ought to manifest itself more by deeds than by words.

Second: Love consists in a mutual communication between the two persons. That is, the one who loves gives and communicates to the beloved what he or she has, or a part of what one has or can have; and the beloved in return does the same to the lover. Thus, if the one has knowledge, one gives it to the other who does not; and similarly in regard to honors or riches. Each shares with the other.

The usual Preparatory Prayer.

The First Prelude. A composition. Here it is to see myself as standing before God our Lord, and also before the angels and saints, who are interceding for me.

The Second Prelude is to ask for what I desire. Here it will be to ask for interior knowledge of all the great good I have received, in order that, stirred to profound gratitude, I may become able to love and serve his Divine Majesty in all things.

The First Point. I will call back into my memory the gifts I have received—my creation, redemption, and other gifts particular to myself. I will ponder with deep affection how much God our Lord has done for me, and how much he has given me of what he possesses, and consequently how he, the same Lord, desires to give me even his very self, in accordance with his divine design.

Then I will reflect on myself, and consider what I on my part ought in all reason and justice to offer and give to his Divine Majesty, namely, all my possessions, and myself along with them. I will speak as one making an offering with deep affection, and say:

"Take, Lord, and receive all my liberty, my memory, my understanding, and all my will—all that I have and possess. You, Lord, have given all that to me. I now give it back to you, O Lord. All of it is yours. Dispose of it according to your will. Give me your love and your grace, for that is enough for me."

The Second Point. I will consider how God dwells in creatures; in the elements, giving them existence; in the plants, giving them life; in the animals, giving them sensation; in human beings, giving them intelligence; and finally, how in this way he dwells also in myself, giving me existence, life, sensation, and intelligence; and even further, making me his temple, since I am created as a likeness and image of his Divine Majesty. Then once again I will reflect on myself, in the manner described in the first point, or in any other way I feel to be better. This same procedure will be used in each of the following points.

---

10. This is the last and culminating meditation of *The Spiritual Exercises.*

The Third Point. I will consider how God labors and works for me in all the creatures on the face of the earth; that is, he acts in the manner of one who is laboring. For example, he is working in the heavens, elements, plants, fruits, cattle, and all the rest—giving them their existence, conserving them, concurring with their vegetative and sensitive activities, and so forth. Then I will reflect on myself.

The Fourth Point. I will consider how all good things and gifts descend from above; for example, my limited power from the Supreme and Infinite Power above; and so of justice, goodness, piety, mercy, and so forth—just as the rays come down from the sun, or the rains from their source. Then I will finish by reflecting on myself, as has been explained. I will conclude with a colloquy and an Our Father.

In the ministry of distributing alms the following rules ought to be followed

The First Rule. That love which moves me and brings me to give the alms should descend from above, from the love of God our Lord, in such a way that I perceive beforehand that the love whether greater or less, which I have for the persons is for God, and that God may shine forth in the reason for which I have a preferential love for these persons.

The Second. I will imagine a person whom I have never seen or known. Desiring all perfection for him or her in his ministry and state of life, I will consider how I would wish him to hold to a good mean in his manner of distributing alms, for the greater glory of God and the perfection of his soul. Then I, acting in the same way, neither more nor less will keep the rule and norm which I would desire and judge proper for this other person.

The Third. I will consider, as if I were at the point of death what procedure and norm I will at that time wish I had used in the duty of my administration. Then guiding myself by that norm, I will apply it in the acts of my distribution.

The Fourth. Imagining how I will find myself on judgment day, I will think well how at that time I will wish that I had carried out this office and duty of my ministry. The rule which I will then wish I had used is what I will follow now.

The Fifth. When I perceive myself inclined and affectionately attached to others to whom I want to distribute alms, I should delay and think over the four rules mentioned above. I should examine and test my affection by means of them and not give the alms until, in conformity with those rules, the inordinate affection has been completely removed and banished.

The Sixth. There is clearly no fault in accepting the goods of God our Lord in order to distribute them, when one has been called by our God and Lord to that ministry of distributing alms. However, there is place for doubt about culpability and excess in regard to the amount one takes and applies to oneself from what one holds for distribution to others. Hence one can reform one's way of living in his state, by means of the rules mentioned above. *The Seventh.* For the reasons already mentioned and many others, in regard to our own persons and household arrangements it is always better and safer to curtail and reduce our expenses. The more we do this, the more do we draw near to our high priest, model and rule, who is Christ our Lord. In conformity with this the Third Council of Carthage (at which St. Augustine was present) decided and ordered that the furniture of the bishops should be inexpensive and poor.

The same consideration should be applied to all the styles of living, in accordance with the person's condition and state. For example, in that of marriage we have Saints Joachim and Anne. They divided their possessions into three parts, gave the first to the poor, the second to the ministry and service of the Temple, and kept the third for their own support and that of their family.[11]

Letter to Jerome Nadal: Suggestions for Charles V in Dealing with the Turkish Menace in the Mediterranean[12]

[As noted at the beginning of this chapter, we have 6,590 letters to and from Loyola in the last ten years of his life. Most of Loyola's letters were concerned with offering spiritual advice or directives for Jesuit communities. Many of his letters were, in fact, drafted by his very able secretary Juan Polanco (1517?– 76) after the two men discussed what the letter should contain. Loyola would examine Polanco's draft letter and make revisions; finally a clean copy would be made and sent to the recipient. This letter to Jerome Nadal was drafted by Polanco. In it, he refers to Loyola several times. The letter was sent to Nadal so that he could propose the plans it contains to Emperor Charles V.[13] Loyola sent

---

11. *Joachim* and *Anne* are the names traditionally given to the father and mother of the Virgin Mary. Their names and the threefold division of their possessions were part of the popular piety of Loyola's time and are not found in the New Testament.

12. The translation of this letter is taken from *Letters of St. Ignatius of Loyola,* translated by William J. Young (Chicago: Loyola University Press, 1959), pp. 259–65. It is reprinted with the permission of Loyola University Press.

13. Charles V (1519–56) was the most powerful European ruler between the reigns of Charlemagne and Napoleon. His domains included Spain, Austria, the kingdom of Naples and Sicily, the duchy of Milan, the Netherlands, Peru, Mexico, and other scattered territories in Europe and the Americas. As Holy Roman Emperor, Charles was the nominal ruler of Germany, but his real power there was severely restricted. His main enemies were the Turks, the French, and the German Lutherans.

Nadal, his right-hand man, scurrying across Europe to negotiate with monarchs and leading churchmen and to organize Jesuit communities.[14]

In March 1536 Suleiman, the Turkish sultan (1520–66), entered into an alliance with Francis I of France against Charles V. The Turkish fleet operated out of Toulon in southern France. In January 1550 Henry II of France (1547–59) wrote the sultan to encourage him to break his truce with Charles. Three months later it was rumored that French envoys had been sent to Turkey and Algiers with offers of naval support for a Turkish attack on southern Spain. From 1551 to 1562 Suleiman was at war with Ferdinand, the brother of Charles V, who was king of Bohemia and imperial Hungary. In 1552 France entered into an alliance with the German Lutherans and forced Charles V to flee from Austria to Italy. This war led to the abdication of Charles V, who then turned over his German territories to Ferdinand in 1556.

The following letter, a very unusual one in Loyola's correspondence, must be read against this political background. It presents a grand strategy that urges Charles to build a fleet of ships for offensive operations in the Mediterranean. Such an offensive would force the Turks either to seek peace or to spend their resources in building defenses and stationing garrisons and squadrons along the enormous length of the Turk-controlled coastline stretching from Greece all the way to Algiers. This letter, which includes Loyola's suggestions on how to raise funds to pay for the fleet, illustrates his ability both to devise grand strategy and also to attend to the practical details of implementation.]

Rome, August 6, 1552
JESUS

In my former letter, which was more general in scope, I spoke briefly of how the zeal and charity of our father [Ignatius] were stirred, and how he also brought the light of reason to bear on the conviction that a large fleet should and could be prepared.[15] In this letter I will carry the argument further and show, first, that it ought to be prepared and that it is high time it was; second, that it can be done at little expense, even less in fact, than what is now spent by his majesty on maritime affairs.

The reasons I have for thinking it should be done are:

1. God's honor and glory suffer not a little when from nearly all parts Christians, great and small, are seized and carried off to live among the

---

14. Nadal's life is traced by William Bangert, S.J., and Thomas McCoog, S.J., in *Jerome Nadal, S.J., 1507–1580: Tracing the First Generation of Jesuits* (Chicago: Loyola University Press, 1992).

15. The first letter was written the same day and is quite short. It is translated in Young, *Letters of St. Ignatius of Loyola*, pp. 260–61.

infidels, where every day we see many of them denying their faith in Christ
to the great pity of those who retain some zeal for the preservation and advancement of our holy Catholic faith.

2. The conscience of those who fail in their duty to make suitable provision is burdened with the loss of so many who from childhood and in every
age become Moors[16] and Turks merely from the weariness of their toilsome
slavery and the countless evils they are made to suffer at the hands of the infidels. On the day of judgment our rulers will see whether they should have
held in so little esteem the bodies and souls of so many thousands who are
worth more than all their incomes and honors and patents of nobility, since
for each and every one of them Christ our Lord paid the price of His life's
blood.

3. Christendom will thus be rid of a great danger from these comings
and goings of the Turks, who up to the present have shown no warlike activity at sea. But now they are beginning to learn their lesson and to take
matters into their own hands. Beginning with what little is left of Christendom, they are employing the tactics which enabled them to take Constantinople;[17] that is, playing one prince against another, and then taking what
they please from both vanquished and survivor. They are now using this
strategy with France, and there is danger that later they will not only come
when called but will be able to apply pressure on Christian forces both by
land and by sea. This difficulty and those mentioned above will be obviated
if his majesty succeeds with the help of a strong fleet in getting mastery of
the sea.

4. This fleet will be able to free the kingdom of Naples in great measure
of the disturbances and uprisings which, if they had no help from the
Turks, these revolutionaries would have no reasonable hope of carrying
through to success. Not even France could offer them hope of help by sea,
and these rebels would then fear that the fleet would soon be upon them.
And not only would Naples be at peace, but all the rest of Italy and Sicily,
and all the other neighboring islands.

5. When the fleet is strong enough to deprive the king of France of any
hope of Turkish help in creating a costly diversion of your majesty's forces,
he would understand that it would be better to keep the peace. Even if he
were unwilling to remain within his own frontiers, he would have no opportunity of returning to Italy. Being always inferior in sea-power, and

16. The Moors were the Muslim people of Tunisia, Algeria, and Morocco.

17. With their excellent heavy cannons, the Turks conquered Constantinople in
1453. By then the Byzantine Empire was largely reduced to a band of territory west
of the city walls.

without any help coming by sea, he would be weaker, and consequently much more disposed for peace.

6. We should be freed from the losses which the Turks and the pirates are continually inflicting on all the coasts of Spain and Italy, and elsewhere, to say nothing of the costs of the garrisons which must be maintained in all ports, since we never know just where the Turkish fleet will strike.[18] How costly this is can easily be seen in the past two years in the kingdom of Naples and Sicily and elsewhere. A fleet, being a worldwide wall, would make these costs unnecessary.

7. The passage from Spain to Italy will be made safe, and it is known how important this is for the good of these kingdoms in general and for the individual good of many who have so much to suffer if this path of communication is broken.

8. If we have a powerful fleet and mastery of the sea, it will be very easy to recover what we have lost, and much more, on all the coasts of Africa and even Greece and the islands of the Mediterranean. We can even get a foothold on lands belonging to the Moors and other infidels, and open a way to their conquest and ultimate conversion. But without a fleet even other places of importance to Christendom, such as Tripoli, will also fall.

9. The reputation and honor of his majesty are involved, a reputation which must be sustained among the faithful and even the infidel. This will be vastly improved by a fleet which could seek honor and reputation in foreign parts and defend them at home without effort. As it is now, much credit and authority is lost. Even this authority can be a defense in many places to one's nationals even without the backing of arms.

These are the arguments from reason that convince our father [Ignatius] that a fleet should be raised.

And now for the second part. The following occurs to him as a possible method of procedure. It is taken for granted that his majesty has no shortage of man-power, for by God's grace he is better supplied with men than any known sovereign in the world. Funds can be raised from various sources:

18. The great historian Fernand Braudel writes about the situation in 1551: "But no one knew what the Turkish fleet would do next. Would it sail to Malta, Africa or Tripoli? Or would it sail westwards to rendezvous with the French galleys? What would the French do then, wondered Charles V at Augsburg." *The Mediterranean and the Mediterranean World in the Age of Philip II,* translated by Sian Reynolds (New York: Harper and Row, 1973), vol. 2, p. 919. The Turks did strike at Malta—where they took more than five thousand prisoners—and at Tripoli, which they captured after a short siege. Ibid., pp. 919–20.

1. An order could be issued that many of the rich Religious Orders in the estates of his majesty, which could get along with much less than they have, should provide a good number of galleys; for example, the Hieronymites so many; the Benedictines, so many; the Carthusians, so many, and so forth. Among them could be included the abbeys of Sicily and Naples which are without monks.

2. A second source would be the bishoprics and their chapters and beneficiaries, which taken all together could contribute a large sum of money with which to equip a good number of ships for the benefit of Christendom.

3. The four Orders of knights which, like that of St. John, are bound by their institutes to contribute men and money to the fleet against the infidel.[19] And that all be done in due form, the pope could give permission to make this levy, or to deal with superiors there in Spain and their other dominions, seeing that the universal good of Christendom is at stake.

4. A portion of the money which some of the grandees and nobles of their kingdoms spend in hunting and feasting and extravagant entertainment would be most justly used in equipping ships against the infidel and for God's glory. If they do not render personal service, they can render the service of their wealth and possessions. There are resources here for a large number of galleys.

5. Merchants surely among themselves could contribute a sum sufficient for a good number of galleys or ships, since over and above the good of Christendom, they stand to reap a benefit for their own interests.

6. The cities and towns of your kingdom and realms, especially those on the coast which suffer so many losses at the hands of the Turks and Moors and other pirates, have been robbed of much more than they would lay out in ships for the fleet to wipe out the robbers. Let them spend on the fleet what they have been accustomed to spend on defense. This would put an end to their expenditures and allow them to devote themselves entirely to their commerce without being worried by thought of defense. A heavier contribution could be expected from the regions that draw greater profit, such as Naples and Sicily.

7. Some help could be expected from the king of Portugal, who could apply to his kingdom this or a similar method for raising a certain number of galleys and other sailing vessels.

19. During the medieval crusades several religious orders of monk-knights were set up to fight the Muslims in The Holy Land. Later, four similar orders were set up in Spain to support crusades against the Muslims in Spain. After the fall of Granada in 1492, the Spanish kings had the pope appoint them superior general of all four orders, largely so they could siphon off the wealth of the orders for government needs. In 1522 Suleiman drove the Knights of St. John from Rhodes. Charles V gave them the island of Malta in 1530, after which they were known as the Knights of Malta.

8. There are the dukedoms. Genoa could provide a few galleys; Lucca and Siena will always help, now that Venice cannot.[20]

9. The duke of Florence,[21] who will reap some advantage over and above the general good to Christendom, might be able to help in some such way as was suggested for the king of Portugal, and from ecclesiastical and secular sources, as was pointed out above.

10. Some help could and should come from the pope and the states of the Church, if God will inspire them. If not, they will at least allow what has been outlined above, and this will be no small contribution.

From this you will see, dear father, what suggests itself to our father [Ignatius] as he examines the situation in the light of reason. Apart from what the emperor himself could contribute from his own income, which is large, it seems that from these ten sources enough could be collected to maintain a large fleet. And with the help also of the royal exchequer it seems that without much strain more than two hundred ships could be provided and maintained, and even three hundred, if necessary. The larger number of them, or nearly all of them, could be galleys. A great benefit would accrue to what is left of Christendom. It is hoped she could in this way even extend her boundaries, whereas now we see them dwindling and suffering considerable loss.

Give some thought to this and tell me what you think. If others, who could do so more properly, do not speak out, it might be that one of the poor members of the Society of Jesus should undertake to do so.

May God, who is eternal wisdom, grant to His majesty and to all of us the light to know His most holy will in all things and grace perfectly to fulfill it.

Letter to João Nunes Barreto, Patriarch of Ethiopia[22]

[The fastest-growing province in the early years of the Jesuit Order was Portugal, where King John III (1521–57) gave the Jesuits warm support and financial aid. The Portuguese had already built an empire that included Brazil; trading posts and naval bases in Angola, Mozambique, Goa, and southern India; and parts of Malaysia and modern Indonesia.

20. Genoa, Lucca, and Siena were Italian city-states allied with Charles V. Though Venice usually had the strongest Christian fleet in the Mediterranean, her fleet was badly beaten by the Turks in the battle of Prevesa in 1538. Venice had to pay the Turks a heavy indemnity and thereafter sought good relations with them for commercial reasons.

21. The Medici duke of Florence was an ally of Charles V.

22. This letter is also from Young, *Letters of Ignatius of Loyola*, pp. 381–90. Used with the permission of the press.

Beginning in the fourth century, the patriarchs of Alexandria sent Egyptian missionaries down the Nile; these missionaries gradually converted most Ethiopians to Christianity. The liturgy and theology of the Ethiopians were largely borrowed from the Coptic church of Egypt, and for centuries the patriarchs of Alexandria appointed the patriarchs of Ethiopia. In 1520 the Portuguese sent an embassy to the king of Ethiopia to seek an alliance with the Christian Ethiopians against their common Muslim enemies. This embassy accomplished very little, however, and in 1528 Ethiopian Muslims, with Turkish help, launched a decade-long attack on Ethiopia that conquered much of the country. In 1541 a Portuguese expeditionary force with muskets and cannons helped the Christian Ethiopian King Claudius (1540–59) defeat the invaders and drive them back. Claudius then wrote to King John III of Portugal to request more military aid and to proclaim the pope head of the universal church. Loyola saw this request as a marvelous opportunity to gain a Jesuit foothold in Black Africa. Pope Paul III and John III encouraged his hopes. Three Jesuits were consecrated bishops: João Nunes Barreto (c. 1519–71) as patriarch of Ethiopia and André de Oviedo (1518–77) and Melchior Carneyro (1516–83) as his coadjutors or assistant bishops. The three bishops and twelve other Jesuit missionaries sailed from Lisbon for India and then on to East Africa. The letter that follows contains Loyola's instructions for their work.

The mission of Barreto and his companions was an almost total failure. Claudius' proclamation that the pope was head of the universal church was simply a ploy to get Portuguese military aid. Barreto himself never reached Ethiopia. He sailed to Goa in India with the Portuguese ambassador to Ethiopia in 1556; there they learned that Claudius was becoming increasingly hostile to Catholicism. The Portuguese viceroy in Goa discouraged them from going to Africa. Oviedo, one of the two coadjutor bishops, and five other Jesuits were sent on to Ethiopia where they found Claudius polite but unhelpful. After leaving Claudius' court in 1559, Oviedo wrote a scathing letter denouncing Claudius and discouraging Rome from dealing with the schismatic Ethiopian church. Claudius, meanwhile, was killed in battle against the Muslims. Minas, his successor, forbade the Jesuits to preach and confiscated their churches. Barreto died in Goa in 1571. Oviedo remained in Ethiopia where he ministered to the Portuguese until his death in 1577.[23]

Aside from the mission's failure, Loyola's letter of instruction shows that he was flexible toward many Jewish practices retained by the Ethiopian Christians and felt that such minor local abuses as excessive fasting and corporal austerity should be tolerated but gradually corrected. Loyola wanted the missionaries to

---

23. The background here for Loyola's letter is taken from Philip Caraman, *The Lost Empire: The Story of the Jesuits in Ethiopia, 1555–1634* (Notre Dame: University of Notre Dame Press, 1985), pp. 11–5.

take advantage of the Ethiopian penchant for splendid ceremonies and vestments. He also wanted to help the Ethiopian people by importing European bridge builders and doctors and looked forward to opening Jesuit schools, perhaps even colleges and a university. His hopes anticipated actual developments in Black Africa by more than three centuries.

In his letter Loyola refers to the Ethiopian King Claudius as Prester John and shows considerable knowledge of the customs of Ethiopian Christians. Loyola had read True Relation of the Lands of Prester John, *a book published by Francisco Alvarez in 1540. Alvarez had been chaplain to the Portuguese ambassador to Ethiopia and had lived there from 1520 to 1526. He named the Ethiopian king Prester John, and Loyola followed his practice. Loyola also had several conversations with an Ethiopian monk who had been living in Rome since 1540.*[24]]

Rome, Circa February 20, 1555
JESUS

Some suggestions which may help to bring the kingdoms of Prester John[25] into union with the Catholic faith and Church.

Since, humanly speaking, the principal factor in this undertaking will be found primarily in Prester John, king of Ethiopia, and secondarily in the people, a few suggestions will be offered which may be of help in winning over Prester John. They will be followed by others which may help in dealing with the people and Prester John conjointly.

For the king

Besides the bulls which the pope addresses to him, the briefs which are written him from here will afford some help in winning over the heart of Prester John.[26] They recall to mind the submission which his father David sent to the Holy See and contain certain recommendations of those who are sent and accredited to him. They also make other friendly advances. But the principal and final help, after that of God our Lord, for winning the heart of Prester John must come from the king [of Portugal]. Not merely letters from his highness, but, if he will agree to it, a special ambassador will be required,

24. Ibid., pp. 7–15.

25. *Prester John* was the name given to a legendary medieval Christian ruler in Asia or Africa. Medieval Christians hoped they could join forces with him. Gradually these hopes focused on Ethiopia, a country with Christian roots dating to the fourth century. The Portuguese sent several hundred troops to help the Ethiopians fight Muslim invaders, who were encouraged by the Turks.

26. Bulls were formal major documents issued by the pope; briefs were less important letters of the pope.

who on the part of the king will call on Prester John and present the patriarch, the coadjutor bishops, and the other priests, and explain the order that will be followed, so that it will be no longer necessary to take patriarchs from Moorish lands or from schismatic Christians. The more solemnly this presentation is made on the part of his highness [the king of Portugal], the more authority it seems the patriarch will have for God's service.

It might be good to see whether his highness thinks that some presents should be sent, especially of things that are held in esteem in Ethiopia; and in offering them he could indicate that a true union of friendship will exist among Christian princes when they all hold the one religion. When this is recognized, he could send him every kind of official he desired, and God will give him the grace to overcome the Moors, so far as this will be for God's greater service.

Some letters from the king to individuals will also be of help, especially to those who are closer to Prester John and with whom he consults and whom he holds in esteem, notably the Portuguese. Other letters, if the king agrees, could be brought unaddressed, the proper addresses being supplied in Ethiopia. But whether by letter or otherwise an effort should be made to make such men friendly.

The [Portuguese] viceroy of India likewise could do much to add to the authority of the patriarch with Prester John, by letter or a personal representative, if the king does not send one.

The patriarch and those with him should try to be on familiar terms with Prester John and gain his good will by every honorable means. Should he be receptive and the opportunity present itself, give him to understand that there is no hope of salvation outside the Roman Catholic Church, and whatever she determines about faith or morals must be believed if one is to be saved. If you succeed in convincing Prester John of this general truth, you have already gained many particular points which depend on this fundamental truth and which can little by little be deduced from it.

If you can win over men of influence who have great weight with Prester John, or, on the other hand, if you can get him to make the [Spiritual] Exercises and give him a taste for prayer and meditation and spiritual things, this will be the most efficacious means of all to get them to think less of and even to abandon the extreme views which they entertain concerning material things.

Remember that the Ethiopians have a prophecy to the effect that in these times a king from this part of the West (apparently they have no other in mind than the king of Portugal) is destined to destroy the Moors. This is an additional reason for a closer friendship with him, and this in turn will be recommended by a closer uniformity. For if there is no opposition in the matter of religion, there will be a closer union of love between them.

You should also remember that up to this [time] Prester John holds both ecclesiastical and civil jurisdiction. Consider whether it would be good to let him know that kings and great princes of the Catholic Church usually have the right of presentation to important positions, but that the actual conferring of the dignity is done by the supreme pontiff and by bishops, archbishops, and patriarchs in their respective spheres of authority. Conforming himself in this matter with the Roman Church and her princes could be of much help to him.[27]

Take along with you the amplest faculties and see that you are able to explain them. The exterior appearance of the bulls or briefs should be as beautiful to the eye as possible. It will be all the better if they are translated into Abyssinian.

To the best of your ability you should have ready the proofs for the dogmas against which they err,[28] with the definition of the Apostolic See or the councils when there is any. For if they can be brought to admit this one truth, that the Holy See cannot err when it speaks *ex cathedra*[29] on matters of faith and morals, it will be easy to convince them of the others. You should be well prepared, therefore, to prove this thesis and you should approach this matter in a way that is accommodated to those people, or the understanding of anyone.

Concerning the abuses which exist, first try to bring over Prester John and a few individuals of wider influence, and then, without making a fuss over it once these are disposed of, see what can be done about calling a meeting of those in the kingdom who are held in high esteem for their learning. Without taking away from them anything in which they are particularly interested or which they especially value, try to get them to accept the truths of Catholicism and all that must be held in the Church, and encourage them to try to help the people to come to some agreement with the Roman Catholic Church.

After having removed the more substantial abuses—those which are in conflict with a sincere belief, such as the obligatory observance of the Old Law— it would be better to begin, with the support of Prester John, to remove or

---

27. At this time the kings of Portugal, Spain, and France had effective control of choosing the bishops in their countries.

28. The Coptic church in Egypt and its daughter church in Ethiopia adhered to Monophysite teachings on the relationship of the divine and human natures in Christ. These teachings were condemned by the Council of Chalcedon in 451. Roman Catholics, Eastern Orthodox, and the mainstream Protestants of Loyola's time all agreed with the council.

29. *Ex cathedra* statements (meaning "from the chair of St. Peter") are the most formal papal declarations and claim to be infallible. They are issued only very rarely.

lessen other abuses if it can be done. If this cannot be done, try at least to make it as plain as possible that there can be no obligation to observe such practices and that, even though they are tolerated, it would be better not to observe them. In this way they will lapse, especially if some of the leading men can be induced to give the example.

The austerities which they practice in their feasts and other corporal penances might be gently moderated, it seems, and brought within a measure of discretion. This could be done in four ways. The first would be to quote the testimony of Holy Scripture, to praise spiritual exercises over those that are corporal, since these latter are but of little avail [1 Tim. 4:8]. But you should not withdraw your approval from external exercises, which are necessary up to a certain point. Thus if they lose that esteem for things which they now hold in honor, these things will fall of their own weight, since they are rather repugnant to the flesh anyway. The second is rather to praise and prefer a golden mean to its extremes. The third means is taken from reason, which will convince them that it is against charity and the common good so to weaken themselves for good works by their fasting that their enemies invade their lands and put them to the sword, with so many offenses against God our Lord. This is an argument which will readily appeal to Prester John, and others too who have more than ordinary intelligence. The fourth means is that of example, which could be given by some of those whom they regard as holy, once you convince them that they should so act for God's greater service. It is quite likely that they will do so. Observe too that God calls some individuals to a life of penance and austerity; and when He does, praise what they do in this matter. But in general a measure of discretion is necessary if such austerities are to be praised.

Perhaps some exterior feasts would be a great help in getting rid of certain abuses. I am thinking of Corpus Christi processions and others which are in use in the Catholic Church. These would replace their [annual] baptisms, and so forth. Our own people, who are not so coarse, are helped by these feasts.[30]

Be very careful that public services such as Mass and Vespers are conducted in a way that will be edifying to the people. The recitation should be

---

30. The Ethiopians enjoyed elaborate religious ceremonies, some of which the Jesuits found objectionable. Here Loyola recognizes that the abolition of all such ceremonies would be met with resistance and that it would be better to replace them with similar ceremonies popular in Catholic Europe, such as that held on the Feast of Corpus Christi. In this ceremony, some sixty days after Easter, a priest in elaborate garments accompanied by a squad of altar boys and hundreds of people would march through town holding high the Eucharist in a golden container for all the spectators to see.

slow and distinct, since they do the opposite, and think that our way is more perfect. If the king approves having a choir with organ, this might be a help in the beginning. But let them be in charge of some non-Jesuits, as it is foreign to our rules.

Vestments of priest, deacon, and subdeacon, altar ornaments, chalices, altar stones, and equipment for making hosts ought to be of the best quality. Try to get them into the habit of making hosts for the Blessed Sacrament as they are made here. In bringing them to Communion let them know that confession should precede, and that Communion is not distributed any day one comes to the church. In the case of the sick who cannot come to the church, see that the Blessed Sacrament is brought to their homes.

It would be good to instruct them in the ceremonies of baptism. It must be conferred but once and not many times, accustomed as they are to baptize every year.

As they have never made use of confirmation, it ought to be administered to all the people after they have been prepared for the sacrament. You should also introduce the practice of extreme unction,[31] as they know nothing about it here.

At first you could hear the confessions of those who can understand you. For the others, it would be good for you to bend your efforts to learn the Abyssinian language. The confessors they have among them could be instructed in the proper procedure by means of interpreters. They should be told of reserved cases, which are restricted to bishops and patriarchs; and very severe penalties should be meted out to confessors who reveal matter of confession, something which they say is done there. Lastly, see that the abuses regarding these sacraments are diligently corrected.

With regard to holy orders, some reform is necessary with respect to age, integrity, competence, and other aspects in the candidate for orders, as far as circumstances which prevail there permit.

As to matrimony, and generally speaking the same must be said of all the sacraments, give heed to the form which must be observed. Ceremonies can be introduced gradually, in the measure in which they contribute to greater edification. These exterior rites should not be few in number, considering that the people are much given to ceremonies.

It would be a great help for the complete conversion of those lands, both at the beginning and throughout the rest of the time, to open a large number of elementary schools there, and secondary schools and colleges, for the education of young men, and even of others who may need it, in Latin and in Christian faith and morals. This would be the salvation of that nation.

---

31. Extreme unction is the sacrament of anointing the seriously sick and those close to death.

For when these youngsters grow up, they would be attached to what they have learned in the beginning and to that in which they seem to excel their elders. Before long the errors and abuses of the aged would lapse and be forgotten. If it appears hard to the people of that kingdom, habituated as they are to their old ways, to see their children properly trained, think about the advisability of Prester John's sending abroad a large number of those who have talent. A college could be opened in Goa and, if circumstances called for it, another in Coimbra, another in Rome, another in Cyprus, on the opposite side of the sea.[32] Then, armed with sound Catholic teaching, they could return to their lands and help their fellow countrymen. If they came to love the practices of the Latin Church, they would be all the more firmly grounded in her ways.

The patriarch could, by himself or through an interpreter or someone else, begin to give discourses and exhortations to the people within the limits of their capacity. The bishops and others could do likewise. Teaching the catechism in many different places by good teachers would also be of great importance.

Those among the native population who excel in talent and exercise some influence by reason of their good lives should be won over by making much of them. They could be given some ecclesiastical revenues and dignities, but only under the probability that they would turn out to be faithful ministers. You could even have some of these preach.

Some Portuguese who are acquainted with the Abyssinian language would be good as interpreters, should any of our [Jesuits] preach, and for conferences, after the manner of the Abyssinian preachers. Some could even be brought from Goa or other parts of India; and if there were children's catechism classes in India, they could serve as a beginning for a children's school in the kingdom of Prester John. This would seem to be very much to the point.

Take thought of beginning in the course of time some universities or liberal arts courses.

Consider the abuses or disorders which can be corrected gently and in a way that will give the people of the country a chance to see that a reform was necessary, and that it begins with them. This will furnish you with authority for the reform of other abuses.

Since Ours[33] have to lessen the esteem for corporal penance which the Abyssinians have, in the use of which they go to extremes, set before them

32. Goa was the Portuguese headquarters in India; Coimbra was the most important university town in Portugal; the island of Cyprus was a Venetian possession in the eastern Mediterranean.

33. The Jesuits used the term *Ours* to refer to fellow Jesuits.

charity in word and example. To this end it would be good to establish hospitals where pilgrims and the sick, curable and incurable, could be gathered, to give and cause others to give public and private alms to the poor, to arrange for the marriage of young girls, and to establish confraternities for the redemption of captives[34] and the care of exposed children of both sexes. They would thus see that there are better works than their fasts. It seems that Prester John, who is generous with his alms, should if possible have a finger in all these pious works.

In works of spiritual mercy also the people of the country should behold in you a tender solicitude for souls. This would be shown in teaching them virtue and their letters, all of which should be done without charge and for the love of Christ. These works should be praised in sermons and conversations and supported with texts from Holy Scripture and the example and sayings of the saints, as we indicated above.

Although you are ever intent on bringing them to conformity with the Catholic Church, do everything gently, without any violence to souls long accustomed to another way of life. Try to win their love and their respect for your authority, preserving their esteem of learning and virtue, without harm to your humility, so that they will be helped in proportion as they esteem those by whom they are to be helped.

Take along some good books, especially pontificals,[35] and others which explain the external rites of the Church, such as decrees of the Apostolic See and the councils with which they have to be made acquainted. They should know the number of bishops attending the councils (in Ethiopia much importance is attached to this point), and all this will be a very efficient help.

You should also take along some lives of the saints, and be well acquainted with them, especially the life of Christ our Lord and His miracles, for the reason given. You should have some calendars of the feasts. And lastly, it would be good for you to be well-versed in matters ecclesiastical, even the smallest items, because it is a branch of learning which they best understand there, and they have for this reason a higher esteem for it than for other branches that are more subtle, of which they understand nothing. It will also be a help for you to go well supplied with church ornaments for the altars, and vestments for priests, deacons, subdeacons, and acolytes; chalices, crosses, vessels for holy water, and other items which are used in external worship.

34. Confraternities for the redemption of captives were organizations of lay Catholics dedicated to raising the funds necessary to buy back Christians captured and enslaved by Muslims.

35. Pontificals were books of rules for celebrating Mass and other liturgical events.

You might think over and suggest to his highness in Portugal whether it would be a good idea to send along with you some men of practical genius to give the natives instructions on the making of bridges, when they have to cross rivers, on building, cultivating the land, and fishing. And other officials too, even a physician or surgeon, so that it may appear to the Abyssinians that their total good, even bodily good, is coming to them with their religion.

You should think also of the propriety of taking along with you a few well-chosen books on law and civil relations, so that they may have a sounder policy in their government and in the administration of justice.

Think also of the advisability of taking along some relics of the saints for the devotion of the people.

Recall that, according to their prophecies or traditions, their patriarchs were expected to come from Rome after a hundred had come from Alexandria. The Alexandrian line ended in Abimamarco, and so they received a pseudopatriarch who went to them in the name of the Apostolic See.[36] It would appear, therefore, that they are ready to give a good reception to the patriarch and, consequently, to his teaching. Be sure that you are informed in every respect of all that is known of the history of those kingdoms. It will be good to know this, for it will protect you from dangers and enable you to give greater help to the people.

Consider whether it would be well if the patriarch were able to dispose of abbeys and other revenues which become vacant, as a reward for the good ministers among them.

The bishops should set aside all pomp and circumstance and, as far as possible, personally discharge the office of pastors. They and their assistants should avoid all appearance of avarice.

The patriarch should have his council, which he should consult on matters of importance. After hearing their opinions he should come to a decision. The council should consist of four, and for the present among them shall be the two coadjutor bishops. As a rule they should live together,

---

36. For centuries the Ethiopians received their patriarchs or head bishop from the Coptic patriarch of Alexandria. The last of the Coptic patriarchs (or *Abuna,* as the head of the Ethiopian church was called) was named Marqos; Loyola calls him Abimamarco. He was more than one hundred years old when, in 1538, he consecrated as his successor João Bermudes, a Portuguese physician. Bermudes, who had come to Ethiopia in 1520 with the Portuguese ambassador, remained there when the ambassador returned home in 1526. Bermudes took for himself the title *papal legate.* Although the pope refused to recognize the validity of Bermudes' consecration as bishop, the Portuguese king did recognize him as patriarch. Later Bermudes worked to turn King Claudius away from union with the Catholic Church, not least because such a union could result in Barreto's replacing him as patriarch. Caraman, *The Lost Empire,* pp. 7–9.

except for temporary separations which may be required by some affair of importance, especially in the beginning. If one happens to be absent for a short time, the three, together with the patriarch, ought to choose another in his place.

If one of the four chosen in Portugal should die or be necessarily absent, the patriarch and the others of the Society [of Jesus] who were sent with him ought to choose as a substitute him who receives the largest number of votes.

Once the dioceses are set up, consider who of the natives would be suitable as bishops and archbishops. If there are any such, they could be consecrated. But if there is none, write to the king of Portugal and to Rome for others to be sent from here.

It also seems good to set up benefices for priests, and give them to persons of good lives and sound learning, as far as possible. Revenues should be assigned and conferred by the election of the bishops with the approval of the patriarch.

You will have to be very expert if you are going to neutralize the authority of the *Book of Abtilis*,[37] which, so they say, contains the canons of the apostles. It is the source of their abuses and excesses, and because they look upon it as part of the canonical Scriptures, from which there can be no dispensation, their errors, up to the present, have been as it were irremediable.

Consider whether it would not be better to eat apart by yourselves. The people, being much given to fasting, do not ordinarily eat before night. This will avoid giving them a bad example or making them suffer.

The churches of canons should be visited and also the monasteries of both monks and nuns. Find out what is in need of reform and make what provisions are possible.

Everything set down here will serve as directive; the patriarch should not feel obliged to act in conformity with it; rather [he should follow] whatever will be dictated by a discreet charity, considering existing circumstances and the unction of the Holy Spirit, who must direct him in everything. Thus with your own prayers, with those of the whole Society and the faithful everywhere, we must urge our petitions before the throne of God's kindness and goodness, so that, having compassion on these nations, He will deign to lead them back to the unity of His holy Church and the true religion and the way of salvation for their souls, to His honor and glory.

---

37. This book (entitled *Faith of the Fathers*), originally written in Arabic and translated into Ethiopic, was a collection of quotations from theologians running from the second century to the 11th century. Though it enjoyed great prestige among the Ethiopians, some of its contents opposed Catholic teaching and practice.

CHAPTER 2

JESUIT EDUCATION

INTRODUCTION

Loyola and his companions did not originally plan to become involved in education or teaching. After their efforts to go to Jerusalem collapsed, they assumed that they would primarily be preaching, administering the sacraments of confession and Communion, and directing people who were making the Spiritual Exercises. But new members of the Order often required long spiritual and intellectual training. Initially these new members, primarily young men, attended classes at such well-established universities as those in Paris and Padua while living in Jesuit residence halls (which were called "colleges"). These Jesuit residences offered only a few supplementary courses in philosophy and in the classical languages and literature. Duke Francis Borgia (1510–72), who greatly admired the Jesuits, established a seminary for young members of the Order on his estates at Gandia in Spain. Jesuits taught lay students for the first time in Europe at Gandia, where the sons of the local farmers were allowed to attend some classes.

The first real Jesuit college for lay students opened in 1548 at Messina in Sicily, thanks in large part to the support of the Spanish viceroy, Juan de Vega. Seizing the opportunity, Loyola sent a crack team of Jesuits to get the school off to a strong start. After seeing the Jesuits' success at Messina, other Sicilian towns asked for Jesuit colleges of their own. Then many Italian cities requested such schools. By 1615 there were 372 Jesuit colleges worldwide, and the number kept growing. The new schools emphasized a curriculum patterned partly on that of the University of Paris and partly on that pioneered by Renaissance humanists—though with more emphasis on religious content and practice than was found in either of these sources.

The first document in this chapter is a letter composed in 1551 by Juan Polanco under Loyola's direction. The letter was sent to Father Antonio Araoz (1516–73), who was canvassing possible locations for colleges in Spain; in the letter, Loyola reflects on the benefits that Jesuit colleges could bring to the Jesuits themselves, their students, and the local communities. He also suggests guidelines for student behavior.

In the next document in this chapter, a selection from the Jesuit Constitutions, Loyola lays out his regulations for colleges. In composing these regulations, Loyola drew on several years of actual experience in administering to, and teaching at, Jesuit colleges. He insisted that the early Jesuit schools should not charge tuition. Sometimes wealthy benefactors, such as Francis Borgia, funded the schools; sometimes town governments covered the school's expenses, as they did in Messina. The main benefactor of Jesuit schools in Portugal was King John III (1521–57). Then as now, the colleges had to carefully cultivate their benefactors, a point touched on by the letters printed here.

The new Jesuit schools faced considerable opposition. Much secondary education in Renaissance Europe was offered in small schools with only one schoolmaster. Such schools could hardly compete with the Jesuit institutions, which were bigger, better organized, and tuition free. When Jesuit schools began to lure students away from these smaller schools many schoolmasters were forced to leave the cities and set up shop in small towns where there were no Jesuit colleges. Major universities also resented the competition they faced from the Jesuit colleges, which were soon offering advanced courses in areas where the universities felt they had a legal monopoly. Sometimes professors encouraged their students to disrupt the Jesuit schools. In January 1591 university students at Padua invaded the city's Jesuit classrooms, shouted down the teachers, stripped, and marched naked back to the university. Sometimes the universities appealed to government officials to step in and reduce the number of courses offered by the Jesuits. Between 1591 and 1596, the three most prestigious universities in Catholic Europe—those in Padua, Louvain, and Paris—forced the Jesuit colleges in their cities either to close completely or to cancel their advanced courses.

The third document in this chapter traces the first eight years of the pioneer Jesuit college at Messina. One of the most popular of the student activities at Jesuit schools was the enactment of plays written by the Jesuit teachers. The last document in this chapter contains several scenes from one of the thousands of such plays that have survived.

Letter from Juan Polanco to Antonio Araoz on Jesuit Schools[1]

[Loyola commissioned his secretary Juan Polanco to write the following letter to Father Antonio Araoz, the Jesuit superior in Spain, to encourage Araoz's efforts

---

1. This letter of Polanco to Araoz is reprinted with the permission of the publisher from *Ignatius of Loyola: The Spiritual Exercises and Selected Works*, edited by George Ganss, S.J., et al. (Mahwah, N.J.: Paulist Press, 1991), pp. 361–65.

*to set up Jesuit colleges there. In this letter, Polanco explains in detail how the
schools could be financed and the advantages the Jesuits, their students, and the
towns might gain from the new schools.]*

Rome, December 1, 1551

The Peace of Christ. Seeing that God our Lord is moving his servants in
your region as well as here to start a number of colleges of this Society, our
Father [Ignatius] has thought it good to provide counsel about the procedure and advantages which have been learned through experience regarding
the colleges here (for those of the colleges there are already well known). He
wants this to be fully studied, so that, as far as the matter is in our hand,
nothing may be left undone for God's greater service and the aid of our
neighbors.

[1. The Procedure for Founding and Endowing a College]

The manner or method employed in founding a college is this. A city
(like Messina and Palermo in Sicily), or a ruler (like the King of the Romans[2] and the dukes of Ferrara and Florence), a private individual (like the
prior of the Trinità in Venice and Padua[3]), or a group of persons (as in
Naples, Bologna, and elsewhere) provide an annual sum of money—some
of them in perpetuity from the beginning, others not until they can test and
verify the value of this work.

A suitable building is procured, two or three priests of very solid doctrine
are sent, along with some of our own [Jesuit] students, who, in addition to
pursuing their own education, can aid that of other students and, through
their good example, personal contact, and learning, help them in virtue and
spiritual progress.

[2. The Steps in Opening a College]

The procedure in such places is this. At the beginning three or four
teachers in humane letters are appointed. One of the teachers starts off with
elementary grammar, accommodating himself to beginners; another is assigned to those on an intermediate level, another for those more advanced
in grammar. A different teacher is assigned to the students of the humanities who are further along in the Latin, Greek, and—if there is an inclination for it—Hebrew languages.

2. Ferdinand I, who ruled Austria in the name of Charles V, was given the title *King
of the Romans;* this title indicated that he was to become Holy Roman Emperor on
the death or abdication of Charles V.

3. Andrea Lippomano was prior of the Trinità monastery from which he drew
funds to support the Jesuits in Venetian territory.

When the school has been advertised, all who wish are admitted free and without receipt of any money or gratuity—that is, all who know how to read and write and are beginners in [Latin] grammar. However, being young boys, they must have the approval of their parents or guardians and observe certain conditions, as follows. They must be under obedience to their teachers regarding which subjects they study and for how long. They must go to confession at least once a month. Every Sunday they must attend the class on Christian doctrine [i.e., catechism] given in the college, as well as the sermon when one is delivered in the church. They must be well behaved in their speech and in all other matters and be orderly. Where they fail in this or in their duties, in the case of young boys for whom words do not suffice, a layman should be a hired as corrector to punish them and keep them in awe; none of our men is to lay his hand on anyone.

The names of all these pupils are registered. Care is taken not only to provide class instruction but also to have them do exercises in debating, in written composition, and in speaking Latin all the time, in such a way that they will make great progress in letters and virtues alike.

When there is a fair number of students who have acquired a grounding in humane letters, a person is appointed to inaugurate the course in the arts [i.e., philosophy]; and when there are a number of students well grounded in arts, a lecturer is appointed to teach theology—following the method of Paris,[4] with frequent exercises. From that point on, this whole arrangement is continued. For experience shows that it is inadvisable to begin by teaching arts or theology: lacking a foundation, the students make no progress. (This plan applies to places where there is a readiness for something more than humane letters—a readiness that does not always exist. In other places it is sufficient to teach languages and humane letters.)

Beyond this, the priests in the colleges will aid in hearing confessions, preaching, and all other spiritual ministrations. In this work the young men sometimes have grace that equals or exceeds that of the priests, God our Lord being greatly served thereby.

[3. The Accruing Benefits of Christian Education]

So much for the method. Now I shall mention the advantages which experience has shown to accrue from colleges of this type for the Society itself, for the extern [i.e., non-Jesuit] students, and for the people or region where the college is situated (although this can in part be gathered from what has already been said).

---

4. Ignatius of Loyola found that the haphazard courses he took at Spanish universities were far less effective than the organized sequence of courses he took at the University of Paris. He insisted that students at Jesuit schools follow the Paris model in which students progressed, step by step, from elementary courses to advanced ones.

[a. For the Jesuits Who Study or Teach in Such a College]
The advantages for our own men are these.

1. First of all, those who give classes make progress themselves and learn a great deal by teaching others, acquiring greater confidence and mastery in their learning.

2. Our own scholastics who attend the lectures will benefit from the care, persistence, and diligence which the teachers devote to their office.

3. They not only advance in learning but also acquire facility in preaching and teaching catechism, get practice in the other means they will later use to help their neighbors, and grow in confidence at seeing the spiritual harvest which God our Lord allows them to see.

4. Although no one may urge the students to enter the Society, particularly when they are young boys, nevertheless through good example and personal contact, as well as the Latin declamations[5] on the virtues held on Sundays, young men are spontaneously attracted, and many laborers can be won for the vineyard of Christ our Lord.

So much for the advantages for the Society itself.

[b. For Extern Students]
For extern students who come to take advantage of the classes the benefits are the following.

5. They are given a quite adequate education. Care is taken to ensure that everyone learns, by means of classes, debates, and compositions, so that they make great progress in learning.

6. The poor who lack the means to pay the ordinary teachers or private tutors at home here obtain gratis an education which they could hardly procure at great expense.

7. They profit in spiritual matters through learning Christian doctrine and grasping from the sermons and regular exhortations what they need for their eternal salvation.

8. They make progress in purity of conscience—and consequently in all virtue—through the monthly confessions and the care taken to see that they are decent in their speech and virtuous in their entire lives.

9. They draw much greater merit and profit from their studies, since they learn from the very beginning to make a practice of directing all their studies to the service of God, as they are taught to do.

---

5. A declamation was a public oration or address, usually made by students but sometimes by teachers. Declamations were most often delivered in Latin; sometimes they were delivered in vernacular languages. The audiences for these events were mainly fellow students and parents; the local elite would attend on more solemn occasions. Students making declamations would first rehearse with teachers. Successful performances would bring students as much local prestige as a star athletic performance would today; they also enhanced the school's reputation.

[c. For the Country or Region]

For the inhabitants of the country or region where these colleges are established there are in addition the following benefits.

10. Financially, parents are relieved of the expense of having teachers to instruct their children in letters and virtue.

11. Parents fulfill their duty in conscience regarding their children's formation. Persons who would have difficulty finding how to pay the teachers to whom they could entrust their children will find them in these colleges with complete security.

12. Apart from the schooling, they also have in the colleges persons who can give sermons to the people and in monasteries and help people through administration of the sacraments, to quite visible good effect.

13. The inhabitants themselves and the members of their households will be drawn to spiritual concerns by the good example of their children and will be attracted to going more often to confession and living Christian lives.

14. The inhabitants of the region will have in our men persons to inspire and aid them in undertaking good works such as hospitals, houses for reformed women, and the like, for which charity also impels our men to have a concern.

15. From among those who are at present merely students, in time some will emerge to play diverse roles—some to preach and carry on the care of souls, others to the government of the land and the administration of Justice, and others to other responsible occupations. In short since the children of today become the adults of tomorrow, their good formation in life and learning will benefit many others, with the spiritual profit expanding more widely every day.

I could elaborate this further. But this will suffice to explain our thinking here about colleges of this kind.

May Christ, our eternal salvation, guide us all to serve him better. Amen

The Jesuit Constitutions

[Loyola was commissioned by his first companions to write constitutions for the new Jesuit Order. Partly because he was occupied with his other responsibilities, and partly because he wanted to see how the Jesuit "way of proceeding" worked out in practice before establishing rules that would be hard to change, Loyola postponed work on the constitutions until 1547. The sections on education included here illustrate the need to learn by experience. The early Jesuit colleges mainly enrolled boys from ages ten to twenty and were roughly parallel, in terms of curriculum, to modern American high schools and junior colleges.

Roman college as rebuilt under Gregory XIII (1572–85).

In drafting his rules for Jesuit education, Loyola was strongly influenced by the scholastic tradition he experienced during his studies at the University of Paris. But he also borrowed from the humanist scholars of his day, as is evidenced by the stress Jesuit schools placed on eloquence in writing and speaking Latin, on the study of Latin and Greek literature, and on the acquisition of some skill in Greek and Hebrew among advanced students, especially those preparing for the priest-hood. The scholastic tradition influenced Loyola's decision to make Aristotle's writings central to philosophical studies at Jesuit schools and to make St. Thomas Aquinas the official Jesuit theologian. But the humanist tradition clearly influenced the role Loyola assigned to classical languages, biblical studies, and the works of the early Church Fathers, whose writings were more oriented toward pastoral application than were the treatises of the medieval scholastics.

The Jesuit schools enrolled more students and teachers than most contemporary schools; thus three Jesuits were usually teaching three different levels of Latin grammar, the most elementary subject at any given school. When a bright student mastered the material of the first level, he could immediately move up to the second level; slower students could proceed at their own pace. The Jesuit Constitutions required that their schools charge no tuition; costs would be covered by benefactors or city governments.

Loyola insisted that Jesuit schools adhere to strict morality and Catholic orthodoxy in the textbooks they used. Thus they avoided the writings of such Roman poets as Terence and Ovid, due to sexual content. Sometimes risqué passages were simply expurgated from books assigned in Jesuit classrooms.

Though Philip Melanchthon (1497–1560), the great Lutheran theologian, wrote many fine textbooks on grammar and rhetoric that did not contain Lutheran theology, Loyola still forbade their use lest students acquire a liking for Melanchthon. The same rule applied to the works of other prominent Protestant writers, including the writings of the great humanist Desiderius Erasmus (1466?–1536). The Jesuits wrote their own textbooks instead.

In Part IV, Chapter 16 of the Jesuit Constitutions—the last part of The Constitutions *to address the issue of education—Loyola discusses how Jesuit schools should inculcate good morals. Students were to attend daily Mass and a weekly catechism class. Once a week all students were required to listen to a gifted student from the upper classes give an exhortation on upright living. Classes began with a prayer. Students who scandalized other students were warned; they were dismissed from the school if they ignored the warning.]*

Part IV: Chapter 13. The method and order of treating the aforementioned branches.[6]

[453]. To give such treatment of both the lower branches and also of theology, there should be a suitable arrangement and order both for the morning and the afternoon.

[454]. And although the order and hours which are spent in these studies may vary according to the regions and seasons, there should be such conformity that in every region that is done which is there judged to be most conducive to greater progress in learning.

[455]. Concerning the hours of the lectures, their order, and their method, and concerning the exercises both in compositions, which ought to be corrected by the teachers, and in disputations within all the faculties, and in delivering orations and reading verses in public—all this will be treated in detail in a separate treatise, [approved by the general]. This present constitution refers the reader to it, with the remark that it ought to be adapted to places, times, and persons, even though it would be desirable to reach that order as far as this is possible.

[456]. Furthermore, there should be not only lectures which are delivered in public but also different masters according to the capacity and number of the students. These masters should take an interest in the progress of

6. The translation used here is from *The Constitutions of the Society of Jesus,* edited by George Ganss, S.J. (St. Louis: Institute of Jesuit Sources, 1970), pp. 215–25, used with the permission of the Institute of Jesuit Sources. The paragraph numbers, for example [453], are standard in modern editions of *The Constitutions.* Here *branches* refers to the level of a class, such as our freshmen, sophomores, etc.

each one of their students, require them to give an account of their lessons, and make them hold repetitions. They should also make those who are studying humane letters gain practice by ordinarily speaking Latin, and by composing in a good style and delivering well what they have composed. They, and much more those studying the higher branches, should engage in disputations often. Days and hours should be designated for this; and in these disputations the students should debate not only with the members of their own class, but those who are somewhat lower down should dispute about matters they understand with students who are more advanced, and conversely those who are more advanced should debate with those lower down by coming down to subjects which these latter are studying. The professors too ought to hold disputations with one another, always preserving the proper modesty and having someone preside to stop the debate and give the doctrinal solution.

[457]. Ordinarily, there will be three teachers in three different classes of grammar, another who is to lecture on humanities, and another on rhetoric. In the class of these last two groups there will be lectures on the Greek and Hebrew languages, and on any other [language] if it is to be learned. In consequence of this arrangement there will always be five classes. If there should be so much to do in some of them that one teacher alone does not suffice, a helper should be given to him. If the number of students makes it impossible for one teacher to attend to them even though he has helpers, the class can be divided into two sections so that there are two fifth classes or two fourth classes; and all the teachers, if possible, should be members of the Society, although there may be others according to necessity. If the small number or the arrangement of the students is such that so many classes or teachers are not required, discretion will be used in everything to adjust the number by assigning those who suffice and no more.

[458]. Whether in addition to the ordinary masters who have special care of the students there ought to be one or more teachers who in the capacity of public lecturers give lectures on philosophy or mathematics or some other branch with greater solemnity than the ordinary lecturers, prudence will decide, in accordance with the places and persons involved. But the greater edification and service of God our Lord will always be kept in view.

[459]. There will be repetitions not merely of the last lesson, but also of those of the week and of a longer time when it is judged that this ought to be the case.

[460]. Likewise, it will always be the function of the rector to see to it himself or through the chancellor that the newcomers are examined and placed in those classes and with those teachers that are suitable for them.

Furthermore, it is left to his discretion (after he has heard the counsel of those deputed for this purpose) to decide whether they ought to be retained longer in the same class or to advance into another. So too in regard to the study of the languages other than Latin, he is to determine whether it should precede the arts and theology or follow them, and how long each should study these languages. The same holds true for the other higher branches. According to the difference of abilities, ages, and other circumstances that must be considered, it will be the rector's function to investigate how far each student should progress into these branches and how long he should apply himself to them, although it is better for those who have the age and ability to advance and distinguish themselves in all these areas for the glory of God our Lord. . . .

[462]. Just as steady application is necessary in the work of studying, so also is some relaxation. The proper amount and the times of this relaxation will be left to the prudent consideration of the rector to determine, according to the circumstances of persons and places.

[463]. At least one day during the week should be given to rest from dinner on. On other points the rector should consult with the provincial[7] about the order to be observed in regard to the vacations or ordinary interruptions of the studies.

Chapter 14. The books which should be expounded.

[464]. In general, as was stated in the treatise on the colleges, in each faculty those books will be lectured on which are found to contain more solid and safe doctrine; and those which are suspect, or whose authors are suspect, will not be taken up. But in each university these should be individually designated.

In theology there should be lectures on the Old and New Testaments and on the scholastic doctrine of St. Thomas [Aquinas]; and in positive theology those authors should be selected who are more suitable for our end.

[465]. Even though the book is without suspicion of bad doctrine, when its author is suspect it is not expedient that it be lectured on. For through the book, affection is acquired for the author; and some part of the credence given to him in what he says well could be given to him later in what

---

7. Within the Jesuit Order there were usually three levels of superiors: the general, who had charge of the whole Society and resided in Rome; the provincial, who had charge of a whole country (e.g., Portugal) or a large region of a country with many Jesuits (e.g., Spain); and the rector, who had charge of a local community.

he says un-soundly. Furthermore, it rarely occurs that some poison is not mixed into what comes forth from a heart full of it.

[466]. The Master of the Sentences[8] will also be lectured on. But if in time it seems that the students will draw more help from another author, as would be the case through the writing of some compendium or book of scholastic theology that seems better adapted to these times of ours, it will be permitted to make this book the subject of the lectures, after much weighing of counsel and examination of the matter by the persons deemed fit in the whole Society and with the superior general's approval. In regard to the other branches and humane letters too, if some books written in the Society are adopted as being more useful than those commonly used, this adoption will be made after much consideration, with our objective of greater universal good always kept in view.

[467]. For example, in connection with some section of canon law, the councils, and so on.

[468]. In regard to the books of humane letters in Latin or Greek, in the universities as well as in the colleges, lecturing to the adolescents on any book which contains matters harmful to good habits of conduct should be avoided, as far as possible, unless the books are previously expurgated of the objectionable matters and words.

[469]. If some books, such as Terence,[9] cannot be expurgated at all, it is better that they should not be lectured on, in order that the nature of the contents may not injure the purity of the minds.

[470]. In logic, natural and moral philosophy, and metaphysics, the doctrine of Aristotle should be followed, as also in the other liberal arts. In regard to the commentaries, both on these authors and on those treating humanities, a selection should be made. Those which the students ought to see should be designated, and also those which the masters ought to follow by preference in the doctrine they teach. In everything which the rector ordains, he should proceed in conformity with what is judged throughout the whole Society to be more suitable to the glory of God our Lord.

8. Peter Lombard's (1100?–64?) *Sentences* was the standard medieval textbook in theology. It was mainly a compilation of short passages (or "sentences") from the early Church Fathers on theological issues. During the 16th century the *Summa Theologiae* of St. Thomas Aquinas gradually replaced *Sentences* as the standard textbook.

9. Terence (Publius Terentius, c. 185–c. 159 B.C.) was a Greek-born Roman slave who became one of the best-known Roman comedic playwrights. Loyola and the Jesuits considered his plays too risqué for classroom use.

Chapter 15. The terms and degrees.

[471]. In the study of humane letters and the languages a definite period of time for their completion cannot be established, because of the difference in abilities and knowledge of those who attend the lectures, and because of many other reasons which permit no other prescription of time save that which the prudent consideration of the rector or chancellor will dictate for each student.

[472]. In the case of beginners of good ability, an effort should be made to discern whether a semester in each of the four lower classes would be enough, and two semesters in the highest class spent in studying rhetoric and the languages. But a definite rule cannot be given.

[473]. In the arts, it will be necessary to arrange the terms in which the natural sciences are to be lectured upon. It seems that less than three years would be insufficient for them. Another half year will remain for the student to review, perform his academic acts, and take the degree of master in the case of those who are to receive degrees. In this way the whole curriculum enabling a student to become a master of arts will last three years and a half. Each year with the help of God one such cycle of treatises will begin and another will come to its end.

[474]. If someone has attended the lectures on some part of the arts elsewhere, this can be taken into account. But ordinarily, in order to be graduated one must have studied for the three years mentioned. This holds true also for the four years of theology, in regard to being admitted to the acts[10] and receiving a degree in it.

[475]. If because of insufficient personnel or for other reasons facilities for that arrangement are lacking, the best that will be possible should be done, with the approval of the general or at least of the provincial.

[476]. The curriculum in theology will be one of six years. In the first four years all the matter which must be lectured on will be expounded. In the remaining two, in addition to the reviewing, the acts customary for a doctorate will be performed by those who are to receive it.

Ordinarily, the cycle of the curriculum will be begun every fourth year and the books which are to be lectured on will be arranged in such a sequence that a student can enter the curriculum at the beginning of any one of the four years. By hearing the lectures on what remains of the four-year curriculum, and then on the matter immediately following until he reaches

---

10. *Acts* here refers to the disputations and public examinations required for the degree.

the point where he began, he will hear the lectures of the entire curriculum within four years.

[477]. If in some college or university of the Society the situation is such that it appears better to begin the cycle of subjects every two years, or somewhat later than every four, with the consent of the general or of the provincial that which is found to be more suitable may be done.

[478]. In the matter of the degrees, both of master of arts and of doctor of theology, three things should be observed. First, no one, whether a member of the Society or an extern, should be promoted to a degree unless he has been carefully and publicly examined by persons deputed for this office, which they should perform well, and unless he has been found fit to lecture in that faculty. Second, the door to ambition should be closed by giving no fixed places to those who receive degrees; rather, they should "anticipate one another with honor" [Rom. 12:10], without observing any distinction which arises from places. Third, just as the Society teaches altogether gratis, so should it confer the degrees completely free, and only a very small expenditure, even though it is voluntary, should be allowed to the extern students, that the custom may not come to have the force of law and that excess in this matter may not creep in with time.[11] The rector should also take care not to permit any of the teachers or other members of the Society to accept money or gifts, either for themselves or for the college, from any person for anything he has done to help him. For according to our Institute, our reward should be only Christ our Lord, who is "our reward exceedingly great" [Gen. 15:1].

[479]. If it appears, for sufficiently weighty reasons, that someone ought not to be examined publicly, with the permission of the general or provincial that may be done which the rector judges will be for the greater glory of God our Lord.

[480]. Thus, banquets should not be permitted, nor other celebrations which are costly and not useful for our end. Neither should there be any conferring of college caps or gloves or any other object.

Chapter 16. What pertains to good moral habits.

[481]. Very special care should be taken that those who come to the universities of the Society to obtain knowledge should acquire along with it good and Christian moral habits. It will help much toward this if all go to confession at least once every month, hear Mass every day and a sermon

---

11. Many universities of Loyola's time charged a high fee for the actual conferral of a degree even if a candidate had already completed all academic requirements.

every feast day when one is given. The teachers will take care of this, each one with his own students.

[482]. Those who can be easily constrained should be obliged to what has been said about confession, Mass, the sermon, Christian doctrine,[12] and declamation. The others should be persuaded gently and not be forced to it nor expelled from the schools for not complying, provided that dissoluteness or scandal to others is not observed in them.

[483]. Furthermore, on some day of the week Christian doctrine should be taught in the college. Care should be taken to make the young boys learn and recite it; also, that all, even the older ones, should know it, if possible.

[484]. Likewise each week, as was said about the colleges, one of the students will deliver a declamation about matters which edify the hearers and lead them to desire to grow in all purity and virtue. The purpose is not only practice in literary style but also the encouraging of moral habits. All those who understand Latin ought to be present.

[485]. Ordinarily the one who must deliver this declamation should be a member of the highest class, whether he is one of the scholastics of the Society or one of the non-Jesuits. However, at times someone else could give it or deliver what another has composed, according to the rector's judgment. But no matter who makes the presentation, since the performance is public, it ought to be such that it will not be judged unworthy of being given in that place.

[486]. In the schools no curses, nor injurious words or deeds, nor anything immoral, nor dissoluteness on the part of the students who come to the school from without should be allowed. The masters should make it their special aim, both in their lectures when occasion is offered and outside of them too, to inspire the students to the love and service of God our Lord, and to a love of the virtues by which they will please Him. They should urge the students to direct all their studies to this end. To recall this to their minds, before the lesson begins, someone should recite some short prayer which is ordered for this purpose, while the master and students are attentive and have their heads uncovered.

[487]. The prayer should be recited in a manner which furthers edification and devotion, or else it should not be said, but the teacher should uncover his head, make the sign of the cross, and begin.

[488]. For those who in some regard fail to attain to the proper diligence either in their studies or in what pertains to good moral habits, and for whom kind words and admonitions alone are not sufficient, there should

---

12. *Christian doctrine* was the usual term for catechism classes.

A Jesuit college during a recreation period. Note the two Jesuits in the foreground.

be a corrector[13] from outside the Society. He should keep in fear and should punish those who need chastisement and are fit for it. When neither words nor the corrector avail and some student is seen to be incorrigible and a scandal to others, it is better to dismiss him from the schools, rather than to keep him where he himself is not progressing and others are receiving harm. This decision will be left to the rector of the university, that everything may proceed in a manner conducive to glory and service to God our Lord.

[489]. If a case should arise in which dismissal from the schools is not enough to remedy the scandal, the rector will take care to provide what is more suitable. However, as far as possible he ought to proceed in a spirit of leniency and to maintain peace and charity with all.

Juan Polanco

Selections from *Chronicon,* on the Jesuit college at Messina

[Juan Polanco (1517–76) was the son of a wealthy merchant in Burgos, Spain; after earning a master's degree at the University of Paris in 1538 he worked in the papal curia for three years before entering the Jesuits in 1541. In 1547 Loyola appointed Polanco Secretary of the Society of Jesus; Polanco

---

13. The corrector was a layman who administered physical punishment to wayward students. Loyola forbade Jesuits from ever laying a hand on a student.

worked as Loyola's right-hand man until Loyola's death in 1556. Polanco continued to serve as secretary under the next two generals, Diego Laínez (1512–65) and St. Francis Borgia (1510–72), finally relinquishing the position in 1572. From 1573 to 1575 he prepared his Chronicon, *a year-by-year history of the Jesuits from 1539 to 1556. The* Chronicon *related Jesuit history chronologically, country by country, town by town, in some forty-five hundred pages of Latin text. Polanco was a gifted writer with a superb memory, and his book is an unsurpassed goldmine for scholars tracing the history of the Jesuits during Loyola's lifetime. Nobody knew the details of early Jesuit history as well as Polanco did. Though he planned to carry his chronicle down to 1573, an assignment to Sicily, and his subsequent death, cut short his work.*

This section gathers Polanco's account of the Jesuit college at Messina in Sicily, which became the model for the hundreds of Jesuit colleges founded throughout the 16th and 17th centuries. Students who wanted more advanced education after finishing their work at the local Jesuit college went on to universities. Some Jesuit colleges did include more advanced courses, including professional training in theology and law.]

The Year 1547: *201. Preparations at Messina for the first Jesuit college for lay students.*[14]

At the suggestion of Ignatius Lopez, a medical doctor, and with the advocacy of Lord Didaco de Cardona, a leading magistrate of the Kingdom, serious negotiations about setting up a college at Messina began. The viceroy [Juan de Vega] and his wife were strongly supportive of this project. The viceroy judged that colleges could be set up not just at Messina but also at Palermo, Catania, and Calatafimi, but he wanted the city of Messina itself to make a request before he himself wrote to Father Ignatius. The proposal gained favorable and very easy approval when Lord Didaco brought it before the city council. . . . What was quickly obtained when the request was made to the city was that [the city] would give an appropriate residence and church and a solid and secure annual income of five hundred gold pieces for establishing the college. The city considered setting up a Studium Generale or university at Messina but asked for only four teachers from the

---

14. Polanco's chronicle is arranged year by year; each passage in the original Latin edition is listed by year and is numbered. These designations allow readers to check the original Latin text. The passages printed here are taken from *Year by Year with the Early Jesuits, 1537–1556: Selections from the* Chronicon *of Juan de Polanco, S.J.,* edited and translated by John Patrick Donnelly, S.J. (St. Louis: Institute of Jesuit Sources, 2004), pp. 64–5, 72, 75–6, 91–2, 122–3, 221–2, 280–2, 330–1, 427–8. They are used with the permission of the Institute of Jesuit Sources.

Society. Of them, one would lecture on grammar, the second on philosophy, the third on scholastic theology and the fourth on cases of conscience [i.e., moral problems]. A certain confraternity of noblemen, which had a chapel dedicated to Saint Nicholas with a house attached, gladly offered their church, which was quite beautiful and large, for the good of the city and of such a pious work. It was on one of the city's main streets and in a healthy location, with a garden and a residence adapted for studies and rather quiet. At length the city magistrates came to the viceroy, Juan de Vega, and easily obtained his consent (which was necessary) and letters requesting both Father Ignatius and the ambassador of Emperor Charles V at Rome to obtain from the Supreme Pontiff the approvals necessary for a university. At this time they were already thinking about expanding the college, and they decided to ask for an abbey from the rather large number of them in Sicily [whose income] was sometimes applied to hospitals and pious works. Therefore the city and Lord Juan de Vega wrote to Father Ignatius and requested that a college be set up at Messina for its great benefit. This was gladly granted them at the start of the next year. Their request was made toward the end of 1547.

The Year 1548: *231. Origins of the college at Messina.*

Toward the start of this year the viceroy of Sicily and the city of Messina acted diligently by sending letters to the Supreme Pontiff and to Father Ignatius about a college at Messina. It was brought to pass. Colleges of this sort began to be established in these regions at the time when Ours[15] undertook the profession of teaching. For Ours had already begun to teach at Goa in India and Gandia in Spain. Before those destined to begin this college had left Rome, Father Ignatius asked everybody in the community to respond on four points and required an answer from each person. First, were individuals prepared and ready to go to Sicily or not, and would they embrace that role as the more dear which would be assigned to them by the superior, who held the place of Christ? Second, would the person who should be sent there be prepared for any external ministry (if he were uneducated); and if he was educated, would he be prepared to interpret texts in any discipline as he was commanded under obedience, whether it be in scholastic theology or sacred scripture or philosophy or the humanities (for these were the four lectures that were to be presented)? Third, would a person sent as a student devote himself to whichever discipline [Ignatius] wanted, according to the command of obedience? Fourth, besides obedience in carrying out what had been said, would they regard what the superior would show them as the better course by submitting their own

---

15. Polanco and many other Jesuits used the term *Ours* to refer to their fellow Jesuits.

judgment and will to holy obedience? When all gave the right answers, he assigned those who were to be sent. Among them were Father André des Freux, a Frenchman; Father Peter Canisius, a German; Father Benedetto Palmio, an Italian; Father Jerome Nadal, a Spaniard; and Annibal de Coudret, a Savoyard.[16] Thus did charity and obedience join together very diverse nations. There was a problem about the teaching methods of some or those being sent. [Ignatius] wanted this handled in his presence. Finally he wanted to bring the college [faculty] before Pope Paul III, who received them kindly and sent them off with an apostolic blessing and fatherly exhortation in which he responded to a very devout address of Peter Canisius.

243. Starting the college at Messina.

Father Jerome Nadal with the others mentioned earlier left Rome for Sicily as spring drew near. On their journey they moved many souls to devotion, sometimes by preaching, sometimes by hearing many Confessions. They also tried successfully by disputations or private conversation to bring to a more sound mind some people who did not think rightly about the faith. They finally arrived safely at Messina right on the octave of Easter of this year 1548. They were welcomed with great evidence of humanity and charity not only by the viceroy and Lady Eleonora, his wife, a woman of supreme virtue, but also by the city itself which manifested the strong support in their hearts for the foundation of this college. Although the church of Saint Nicholas and a house were set aside for Ours, still Ours lived in a rented house for some months because much rebuilding was required on the decorum of the church and for outfitting our dwelling and the schoolrooms. While [Ours] opened the school and began zealously to benefit their neighbors, a neighboring house was purchased and a garden acquired and the surroundings of Saint Nicholas were nicely arranged at considerable expense to the city. It spent this year almost 2,500 gold pieces over and above the 500 annual income for supporting Ours which had been assigned by the unanimous consent of the city council and ratified by the viceroy. A public ceremony was also held before the viceroy himself in which the land of Saint Nicholas was turned over to the Society.

The city entrusted a certain nobleman with the care of the building who employed an outstanding architect and built six interconnected classrooms outside the dwelling place of the college. Although the citizens of their own accord favored this project, the authority and support of Didaco de Cordoba, a major magistrate of the Kingdom of Sicily, and of the viceroy himself, encouraged them not a little. Almost beyond belief was the constant warmth with which the viceroy embraced our Society. The number of [students] who attended the classes for beginners was large enough right from

16. All five of these became prominent Jesuits. Their roles at Messina are discussed later.

the start; fewer were those who came to the upper classes, as is usual. The college offered not just the lessons [in those subjects] which the city had requested in its letters but many others out of charity or to help young men. The teaching method of the University of Paris was gradually introduced there. Father Nadal assigned three teachers for grammar: Father Benedetto Palmio was in charge of the first class, Annibal de Coudret of the second, and Giovanni Battista [Passeri] of the third. Father Canisius taught the art of oratory. Master Isidore [Bellini] taught dialectic. Father André des Freux taught Greek literature, and Father Nadal [taught] Hebrew but left the lectures to Father André, for although he divided his time with administering the college, he taught scholastic theology in the morning and gave lessons on cases of conscience in the afternoon.

Year 1549: *350. The college at Messina goes forward.*

Since the lowest class had a high enrollment Father Nadal judged that it should be divided and for the greater progress of the students a new class should be added which would be between the lowest and the second lowest. Thus grammar began to be taught in five classes. At that time Father [Benedetto] Palmio taught rhetoric in the top class. This took place at the renewal of studies in Fall. At this time Father André des Freux undertook teaching logic with good results (it seemed good to start a class of philosophy each year); he continued this till he had a successor. For during this second year Master Isidore [Bellini] continued with natural philosophy [i.e., physics]. Father Antoine Vinck Durandi took over scholastic theology. Nadal himself taught three different subjects, namely Euclid[17] in mathematics and various authors in Greek and Hebrew literature. In accord with a regulation of Father Ignatius, they had to write every week in detail and inform him even about the number of students in every class. Thus during November Father Nadal writes that there were seventy-eight students in the lowest class, fifty-six in the second lowest, forty-two in the third class, fourteen in the fourth class which is called humanities (over which Father Annibal [Coudret] had charge), and fifteen or sixteen in the fifth class, that is, rhetoric. Father André [des Freux] had sixteen in logic, Isidore [Bellini] had thirteen in philosophy, and Father Antoine had only three in scholastic theology (since there was almost no mature student among the lay students, and the religious[18] were not as yet coming to our schools). Father Nadal had ten for his Greek course and three or four for Hebrew and ten or twelve for mathematics. Presentations were added to the individual lectures, following the Paris method, so that the college seemed to have some appearance of a

---

17. Euclid was a Greek mathematician who taught in Alexandria around 300 B.C. His geometry book remained in use for more than two thousand years.

18. Members of religious orders.

university. God preserved the health of the teachers despite these considerable labors undertaken from dawn to dusk.

351. Public presentations to start the school year.

This reopening of classes, which was done in October, was proceeded by three days of public disputations involving all the disciplines they were going to teach. This was carried through to the great edification of the spectators and added to the great enthusiasm and ardor of the young men to take up their studies. The more advanced courses were delayed somewhat until negotiations about university [status], which at that time had not yet been finished, were completed in the viceroy's presence, as happened shortly thereafter (he was in attendance at the disputations along with the judges and all the leading men of the city, and he heard the orations and poems related to the reopening of studies).

The Year 1550: 57. *Problems in setting up a university at Messina.*

This year negotiations about a university were long and hard, and in the larger council of Messina citizens it was finally decided that revenues of 5,500 gold pieces be applied to setting up the aforesaid university. Apostolic letters obtained at Rome made the whole university subject to the Rector of the college of the university, and thus the Society took over possession of it since the viceroy had also added letters for carrying this out. The university was magnificently proclaimed throughout the city with the sound and mighty display by the fleet and the cannons. The next day lectures in law and medicine began. But since the people of Messina were ill disposed to having the professors of law and medicine subject to Ours, Father Nadal with the assent and approval of Father Ignatius arranged for separate faculties so that one body, which contained courses in theology, philosophy and humanities, was left to the Society; another body was established from the faculty of canon and civil law and medicine with its own Rector. This the people of Messina welcomed so gratefully that it hardly seemed possible to them to commend highly enough this solution of the aforesaid Father Nadal, and they kept calling him a friend and father of the city. But when it came to dividing the revenues actions spoke louder than words: 4,000 scudi were assigned to the other faculties; they applied only 1,500 scudi of the annual revenue to our college, while they imposed the burden of having fifteen teachers. Indeed, this money was to be paid by the officials of the city itself, and they wished this whole donation to depend on the discretion of the same city. Since the minimal income and the conditions seemed intolerable, it was easy to see that the hearts of the citizens were angry with the viceroy whom they thought responsible for this work. When the affair was brought to Father Ignatius, it seemed to him that these conditions were completely unacceptable. A reasonable solution seemed that the revenues be divided evenly between those two bodies. If a larger contribution could not be obtained, the Society should be obliged to fewer teachers. And if what was hoped for could not be obtained, it was preferable for the college to be as it was with the donation remaining at only 500 scudi rather than its taking on such heavy burdens with increased revenues.

Because the viceroy was already preparing himself for the expedition to Africa,[19] the question of the revenues was postponed until his return, and so the time for this year gradually ran out. Dealing with this business was made very difficult because of some of the magistrates, whom they call the sworn ones [*jurati*], had been thrown into prison, aside from the previous sworn ones whom [the viceroy] had sent into exile. Ours never gave their assent, but in accord with the mind of Father Ignatius they reserved the whole business to the viceroy. After he had set out for Africa he wrote from a certain island that Ours should obtain from the city what they could, but [the city officials] would not contribute anything.

The Year 1552: *311. Developments at the college of Messina.*

I will also add this about the studies of Ours: since the professor of philosophy had no students the course in philosophy was wholly discontinued. Only men in our house attended the course in Hebrew. The course in rhetoric had only four extern students besides Ours. Still there were about 270 students in the lower classes. But Ours who lived in the college and the house of probation provided Father Annibal [Coudret] with a good harvest. This year eleven of the novices, as is the custom in the Society, began wearing ankle-length cassocks, to the great satisfaction of the whole city and especially of their parents and even of the viceroy. His heart took great comfort in seeing those new saplings taking on the Society's ways. Among the novices Don Fernando de Vega, the viceroy's nephew, had already left. Earlier he had indicated that he aspired to the Society and obtained his enrollment among the novices, but it is thought that this inclination of his heart was not real or at least that Fernando backed away from it easily and returned to the court. The viceroy's daughter, Isabel de Vega, took this very hard.

The Year 1553: *407. The reassignment of Ours at Messina stirs resentment.*

As regards sermons: Father Benedetto Palmio, who was greatly beloved in that city, went to Palermo on February 11 so that he along with others could go from there to Rome. Initially this brought considerable anguish to our spiritual friends. They complained that, after financing had been taken care of, gradually all our best men left there, and they tearfully begged Father Antoine [Vinck, the new Rector] to lecture them on something profitable until the promised arrival of Father Girolamo Otello. He began to do this with the approval of the consultors, and every day of Lent he began to explain the

---

19. The "expedition" was an attack on Turkish bases in Tunisia.

penitential psalms in addition to the day's gospel. They listened beyond our expectations since it turned out that both he in his lectures and Father Giovanni Filippo [Casini] in his sermons on feast days and Sundays were satisfactory.

409. The fears die down that funding for the college would be cut off. That rumor which had arisen over the departure of Father Benedetto therefore died down. It had gotten to the point that the city councilmen were discussing forbidding the treasurer to pay funding credited to the college on the grounds that the Society in the college in Messina did not have the workers which the amount of funding required. But they did nothing, perhaps fearing to anger the viceroy. But if he left office, some action was to be feared. Finally when Father Otello got to be known the cause of the problem disappeared.

426. Candidates leave Messina for Rome. On September 18, eleven of Ours set out from Messina for Rome. Among them were five young men of Messina, almost all of whom were nobles and trained in Latin and Greek literature, students of Father Annibal [Coudret]. They all went as a group to the viceroy, Juan de Vega, to greet him at their departure. Seeing them brought him great consolation; he embraced each one of them with tears of joy and said, "These are the plants which carried to another place will bear rich fruit." The previous day the same viceroy attended some Latin orations which the Messina students delivered in our church. Some other orations were given in Greek and Hebrew. The viceroy, who was eager to keep the college going, listened to them all with great pleasure and approval.

The Year 1554: *451. Ignatius decides about censorship and corporal punishment at Messina.* Among other things, Father Annibal [Coudret] asked the advice of Father Ignatius about whether [the writings of Juan] Luis Vives and Terence[20] should be excluded in our classes since it was difficult to find [alternative] readings for teaching the Latin language suitable in the lower classes. He also asked whether it was permitted at least to strike students on the palm of the hand without using a whip, for it seemed this would be useful for the students and approved by their parents. But the response from Rome was that Father Ignatius did not want the aforesaid authors to be read and that in the future the same readings were going to be prohibited in the other colleges. Still, they were not prohibited. But until other useful books could be

---

20. Juan Luis Vives (1492–1540) was the most prominent Spanish humanist. Terence (c. 185–c. 159 B.C.) was a Roman playwright whose comedies were popular in the Renaissance for their racy dialogue. Six of his plays survive.

found that were not written by suspect authors Ours in Sicily could use the usual books. Father Ignatius would not permit [Ours to administer] any sort of physical punishment in the colleges of Italy, not even on the palm of the hand. Henceforward they should punish boys through a lay corrector.

The Year 1556: *1032. The progress of the college in Messina.*

The number and progress of the students in the college kept growing daily, and the reputation and respect for its classes even increased to the point that some of the elite were moved to switch their sons from the education given by others and turn them over to Ours. Among others this was the case of a judge of the highest royal court who entrusted to Ours the training of his three sons in letters and morals. So did another nobleman with his five young sons. This showed that outstanding talents were going to come from those classes to the great benefit of the state. These talents, developed by piety and good training, were recognized as very suited for public employment. The diligence of the professors and their skillful work brought it about that those who wanted bright prospects for their sons entrusted them to Ours for their training.

1036. Teaching catechism at Messina.

Ten of our [Jesuit] collegians kept on teaching catechism in ten parishes of this city, something they had started doing the previous year. But when the Cardinal of Messina [Giovanni Andrea de Mercurio], who stayed at Messina this Summer, transferred this way of instructing children to his pastors to experiment (as he put it) on whether they could carry on this task without so much labor by Ours, for a time [Ours] ceased going to the aforesaid parishes for the aforesaid task. But when the same Cardinal found out that in almost all the parishes the spiritual edifice, which our labor built up very happily, was collapsing, he ordered Father Provincial to visit him and asked that once again he direct the work of the Society to this task. So in the month of August Ours began to instruct youths with no meager profit for them in the aforesaid parishes in the same way and order as before.

College of Louis-le-Grand, Paris. Its students included the French authors Molière and Voltaire.

Joseph Simons

Selections from *Vitus,* a drama

*[In addition to regular class work, the new Jesuit colleges of the Renaissance of-
fered students a range of extracurricular activities. Athletics were unimportant
in the Jesuit schools; instead most of the extracurricular activities were tied to
the religious and academic goals of Jesuit education. Thus Catholic students,
who made up the vast majority in Jesuit schools, were expected to attend Mass
regularly, often every school day. Students were encouraged to make frequent
use of confession and Communion and to join sodalities (youth confraternities
directed by the Jesuits) to encourage devotion to Mary, the mother of Jesus. Student volunteers often helped the Jesuits teach catechism in rural areas.*[21]

*Public disputations and orations were often used to begin the school year;
see, for instance, those at Messina in 1549 described in the introduction to the
preceding selection. Many of the city's elite and the parents of the students attended these performances. Such public events were designed to raise support
for the schools by displaying both the skill of the teachers and the academic
progress of the students. Parents usually returned home proud of their sons,
even if they understood little of the Greek and Latin orations and disputations.*

*Following the staging of the first play at Messina in 1551, the Jesuits in-
creasingly made drama the main extracurricular activity in their colleges. Performances attracted an upper-class audience and encouraged public support for
the colleges, much as sports do today. The dramas also served to inculcate religious orthodoxy and sound morality. Hundreds of these plays were later published; the texts of thousands more are extant in manuscript form. Although
the plays were originally designed to improve the skill of students in speaking
Latin, vernacular languages were gradually incorporated into the plays—first
in Spain, then across the rest of Catholic Europe. Many plays mixed Latin and
vernacular; some scenes were in poetry but others in prose, just as in Shake-
speare's plays. Tragedies were far more common than comedies. Biblical stories
and the lives of the saints often furnished the plots—thus in 1580 students at
Pont-à-Mousson staged a play about Joan of Arc in French. All the students
were young men, and male actors played female parts—as was common practice among professional theater groups. Eventually music and dancing were introduced into the plays, and sheer spectacle often overshadowed the religious*

---

21. For a fine study of the Jesuit sodalities, see Louis Châtellier, *The Europe of the
Devout: The Catholic Reformation and the Formation of a New Society,* translated by
Jean Birrell (Cambridge: Cambridge University Press, 1989). By the mid-18th century there were some twenty-five hundred sodalities, largely made up of students
and former students of the Jesuit colleges.

message. The dramas sometimes included elements that seemed to presage the development of classical ballet and opera. In small cities the school dramas were often the most important entertainment events of the year. But Jesuit drama also could draw huge crowds in large cities. Louis XIV and the royal family often attended presentations at Paris where "for summer ballets and tragedy [the] audience generally range between thirty-five hundred and seven thousand."²² Ballet rarely commands such crowds today.

Two scenes from Vitus *by Father Joseph Simons (1594–1671) are printed here as examples of Jesuit drama. Simons, originally named Emmanuel Lobb, was born and raised in Portsmouth, England. When he turned eleven, his mother sent him to Portugal to learn Portuguese as a step toward a business career; while there he converted to Catholicism. He first attended the Jesuit college for Englishmen at St. Omers, Belgium, then the English College in Rome where he studied for the priesthood. In 1619 he entered the Jesuit Order in Belgium. He enjoyed a career of some distinction as a teacher and administrator at the Jesuit colleges in St. Omers, Rome, Liège, and Ghent before returning to England, where he served as provincial superior from 1667 until his death in 1671.*

Vitus *was written and first performed in 1623 in St. Omers. The text of the play was published, along with four of Simons' other plays, in 1656 in Rome; three later editions were printed in the 17th century. Like Simons' other tragedies* Vitus *was written in Latin verse; the ancient Roman dramatists who most influenced him were Terence and Seneca.²³ Another of Simons' tragedies,* Zeno, *was produced in Rome, Naples, Parma, Seville, and St. Omers.²⁴*

The story of Vitus *takes place during the reign of the Roman Emperor Diocletian (284–305), who brought law and order back to the Roman Empire after half a century of chaos. Unfortunately, Diocletian's reform program included a bitter persecution of the Christians; their refusal to worship the traditional Roman gods was, Diocletian felt, a major cause for Rome's decline. When Diocletian's son Valerius was attacked and tortured by an evil spirit, Diocletian ordered that Vitus, a fourteen-year-old Christian boy famous for*

---

22. Judith Rock, *Terpsicore at Louis-le-Grand: Baroque Dance in the Jesuit Stage in Paris* (St. Louis: Institute of Jesuit Sources, 1996), p. 116.

23. Seneca (c. 4 B.C.–A.D. 65) was a Stoic philosopher who also wrote nine surviving tragedies in a florid Latin style that influenced Simons and many Baroque tragedians.

24. *Jesuit Theater Englished: Five Tragedies of Joseph Simons,* edited by Louis Oldani and Philip Fischer, translated by Richard Arnold et al. (St. Louis: Institute of Jesuit Sources, 1989), pp. vii–ix. For an overview of Jesuit drama, see William H. McCabe, *An Introduction to the Jesuit Theater: A Posthumous Work,* edited by Louis Oldani (St. Louis: Institute of Jesuit Sources, 1984). The scenes from *Vitus,* printed here with the permission of The Institute of Jesuit Sources, are from pp. 311–15, 322.

performing miracles, be brought to Rome to help Valerius. Though Vitus cured Valerius (to Diocletian's delight), the emperor then commanded Vitus to abandon his Christian faith, promising him great rewards if he did so and threatening horrible tortures if he refused. When Vitus refused, Diocletian had him tortured with molten lead—to no avail. When Vitus was placed on the rack and faced death, an angel carried him off and returned him to his homeland, where he later died peacefully. Scene 4, printed here, largely deals with Diocletian's threats to torture Vitus and his father Hylas.[25]

SCENE 4

[After vainly trying every device in order to subvert Vitus, the emperor finally hands him over to be tortured with melted lead.]

THE CAST: DIOCLETIAN, VITUS, HYLAS, LUPUS, PAPINUS, VALERIUS, OTHO, PULCHERELLUS, URBANUS, MODESTUS, ANGEL [26]

DIOCLETIAN: Tell me, most attractive of lads, in what direction does your mind now incline?

VITUS: Caesar, misfortunes have restored my mind to better bent.

DIOCLETIAN: A welcome answer. At last you will be playing again through the palace, a glory dear to the Caesars. But explain the manner of your conversion.

VITUS: Inaction had depressed my spirit. I was too languid in my love. The prison gave new life to the fires of love that had lain so long banked and bound me yet more closely to the Christian God. Love is changed into flames. Christ, I yearn for you alone. To the whole world I proclaim that you are God.

25. Simons' plot largely follows the popular legend of St. Vitus, who was greatly revered in medieval Germany as one of the Fourteen Holy Helpers, saints who were to be invoked by people with special needs—Vitus was the patron saint of actors and was invoked to cure epileptics and those afflicted by St. Vitus dance, a disease named after him. The names and roles of most of the persons in Simons' drama are taken from the legend.
26. The roles of Diocletian, Vitus, and Hylas are described in the headnote. Lupus is a courtier; Papinus is a slave of Hylas; Valerius is Diocletian's son; Otho and Pulcherellus are pages; Urbanus is the chief priest of Jupiter, king of the Roman gods.

DIOCLETIAN: A figment sprung from a brain!

VITUS: Doubtless you mean Pallas Athena sprung from the pregnant brain of Jove.[27] No, our God is ruler of the universe, the one who sowed the stars and humankind, the sure salvation of a tottering world. To his divinity I witness with the blood that I have shed.

DIOCLETIAN: Just live, I beg you, worthy of Jove's Augustus.[28] Enjoy youth, and as long as the breeze of verdant young manhood favors you, minister wine cups to me, a lesser Jove, for you are more pleasing to me than Trojan Ganymede, who was Jove's young wine steward.[29] Put Christ outside your thoughts, and by the swamp of Styx[30] I swear, as the gods swear oaths, that none will ever rise higher in my love than you and no one will displace you. Though you ask for a scepter equal to Caesar's own,[31] you will obtain it. But if you refuse to yield, then every kind of bloody, painful, savage torture awaits you. And now that you may believe my words, look to each side of you within those twin shrines to see illustrative examples. [Here the doors of two shrines on the stages are opened.] Terror dwells in this home, in that one Honor. Terror lies in wait for Christ's followers, together with dread devices to inflict pain, punishment, and long-drawn-out death. There, fastened to the walls, you see fearful reminders of cruel doom. But follow Jove and the gods; then Honor will welcome you within its mansion so rich with gold and gems. Surrounding Honor you see many glorious things: wealth, scepters, robes of state blazing with scarlet, purple raiment, amusements, pleasures, and every blessing that exists anywhere. Now decide which you prefer.

VITUS: The pathway to my choice is easy, I admit. Terror motivates lowly minds and honor exalted ones.

DIOCLETIAN: Vitus, now at last you show good sense!

VITUS: [*Walking toward the shrine of Terror.*] But true honor dwells within this shrine of yours. Here kingship shines with its hallmarks. To me, the forceps is my scepter, swellings from beatings are my robe of state. The

---

27. Pallas Athena was the goddess of wisdom; Jove is another name for Jupiter, king of the gods. Here Simons alludes to the Greek myth that claimed that Athena was born directly from the head of Jove, without a mother.

28. Augustus was another name for the Roman emperor. Diocletian is claiming that Jove is the emperor's special patron.

29. Ganymede was the young cup bearer for the Olympian gods and goddesses.

30. The Styx was the river the dead had to cross to reach the underworld of Greek mythology.

31. The scepter was a symbol of royal power.

gridiron is my throne, and deadly wheels my diadems.[32] Blood poured from my veins will supply the purple, and the torturer will be my entourage of nobles. How dear and welcome to me is this kingship. Thus do I set aside the examples of your cruelty, bloodstained prince, and turn them into majestic wealth. Strike me, butcher me, cut me to pieces—I am a Christian. My only prayer is to suffer, professing Christ.

Augustus, don't offer me togas drenched with scarlet, for they are reddened with the blood of innocent men. God sees that they have been slain by your hand. God, who alone wields the thunderbolt, sees you and in his justice is preparing avenging change of fortune. Diocletian, the God who has brought back booty from vanquished hell and who, when it pleases him, smashes the royal crowns that are the envy of the common throng, that God has ordered me to speak these things to you. Haughty man, why do you exalt yourself and bid that you be worshiped as a god throughout the world? You cannot halt the rushing chariot of the sun god, can you?[33] By your nod you cannot bridle the capricious winds or put reins upon the fates, can you? But if you cannot do these things, then how can you be a god? What an empty thing is the human mind's excessive pride!

DIOCLETIAN: And can your Christ do these things for Caesar? As messenger, carry this news to Christ in hell: I am a god, although he howl against me. I am the lightning bolt and terror of the Christian flock, which one day I shall destroy root and branch. I do not want to be a god if your Christ is to become a god!

VITUS: Whoever hurls rebellious thunderbolts against heaven should fear lest they fall upon his own head. Crime turns back upon its author. Vent your crazed anger in every direction; devise novel ways of savage torture. Still, you yourself will perish. Christ will rule your empire, and as long as time shall roll its swift wheels, as victor he will proclaim his ordinances throughout the willing nations.

DIOCLETIAN: Insolent wretch! Lictor, drag him away to the flames.[34]

---

32. Here Vitus is claiming that by dying for his Christian faith, even being roasted alive on a gridiron, will gain him a heavenly reward greater than a royal throne, a king's crown, or an emperor's purple robes.

33. Vitus here points out the limits to Diocletian's power: he cannot stop the sun in its course. In classical Greek mythology Apollo, the sun god, was often depicted as driving a glowing chariot across the heavens.

34. The highest Roman officials were traditionally accompanied by several lictors, bodyguards who carried *fasces*, a bundle of rods and an axe symbolizing the official's power to have his subjects beaten with rods or beheaded. The word *fascism* is derived from this Roman practice.

HYLAS: [*Kneeling.*] Caesar, be slow to act! Stay your avenging hand. I am Hylas, illustrious for my noble descent, a wealthy man from the isle of Sicily. I implore you suppliantly. I, who have never bowed before the feet of any other man, lie prostrate at your knees. Have pity upon a father. If you do so, may your fortunate son surpass all your prayers for him, vigorous in years and dominance. This boy here is the sole consolation of his afflicted father. When I disguised myself in garments not my own in order to give him sound advice, I was dragged off into a rocky prison. No Christian corruption has infected my heart.

DIOCLETIAN: Architect of deception, craftsman of shameful deeds. Is this the way you trick the court, you who sham a father's look but at heart are a Christian priest? With magic potion and bewitching spell you bound Vitus and drew him to Christ.

VITUS: On both counts you are mistaken, Caesar. I gladly proclaim that this man is truly my own father. He opposed me because he could not tolerate Christ. The poor man worships blocks of wood and stones, following the customs of the Trojan people.

LUPUS: Papinus, come here!

PAPINUS: [*With extended arms and eyes turned toward the sky.*] I swear by you, torches of the sky and fires of heaven, by you gods in the citadel of the skies. If I lyingly speak falsehood, may Chaos gape wide with inexorable jaws and swallow me, the liar. Hylas is pretending to be the boy's father. While he openly adores the Roman gods secretly Christ is his delight. As a priest he worships Christ with Panchaean incense.[35] I bear witness that he imbued the boy with hellish venom. He was the first to teach him Christ and drive out Jove.

HYLAS: Why does the earth still now stand firm and not belch out vindictive flames in anger?

PAPINUS: It proves the truth of what I swore!

DIOCLETIAN: Why waste words upon the winds? Whether Vitus obeys you as his father or his master in Colchian magic,[36] I care not. I swear by hell's river Acheron[37] that, unless you unweave your magic spell and restore the boy you stole away from Jove, you will be burned to ashes as a practitioner of black magic. This is my firm decision.

---

35. Panchaia was a mythical island east of Arabia famous for its incense. Virgil (*Georgics,* 2:138, 4:378) and other Roman authors refer to its rich incense.

36. Colchis was a province of Asia on the east coast of the Black Sea. It was famous as the home of the witch Medea and her magical powers.

37. Acheron was a famous mythical river in the underworld often mentioned by ancient writers (e.g., Virgil, *Aeneid,* 6:295).

HYLAS: Where is the fidelity of the gods, the veracity of men? I call to witness all the justice of the world: you are punishing an innocent man.

DIOCLETIAN: Lictor, quickly reduce Hylas to ashes. Let him go to the stake.

HYLAS: [*Running back to VITUS' side.*] Son, save your father! You are your parent's safety. All rests in your hands. You alone can rescue your father from a frightful death. If there be any part of me surviving in you, if any filial affection sways you, have pity on your father, son. But if your heart is set upon injustice, then turn me over to the flames.

VITUS: May God forbid! I acknowledge I owe my father gratitude. The principles that your good character impressed upon me long ago, those do I still bear deep within my heart, never erased. If my blood can ransom my father's life, look, I lay bare my heart. Let Caesar turn his anger here.

HYLAS: Reject Christ and honor Jove, then neither of us goes to death.

VITUS: Father, spare me this! My heart is set on Christ forever.

HYLAS: I am the unhappy father of a detestable son!

LUPUS: Do you value your father less than Christ?

VITUS: I value man less than God.

OTHO: Will you allow the one who gave you life to be led to the fire?

VITUS: The crime is his who gives the order. Caesar is burning an innocent man. I shall not avert crime by doing greater crime.

DIOCLETIAN: Let both of them burn. Let flame consume doers of sacrilege.

HYLAS: [*Prostrate before the emperor.*] By the sacred glory of your august person, by the holy scepter of your kingship, by your hand that is kindly toward the wretched, I beseech you. Pardon this boy. Let the punishment fall upon me alone.

VITUS: Rather, forbid the slaughter of this innocent man and let a son save his father from death by becoming a victim for Christ.

DIOCLETIAN: Forswear Christ, offer devout incense to Jove, and I will preserve your father's life.

VITUS: What! Should my disloyalty save my innocent father? Far be that from me, tyrant. My heart is set eternally on Christ.

DIOCLETIAN: Stubborn fool! Chief priest, let fiery liquid consume him as he lives and watches. Offer up to Jove his scalded body. Let that obstinate scoundrel die. I pardon Hylas. His emotions have betrayed the fact of his fatherhood.

HYLAS: Prince, how lenient you are!

VALERIUS: Caesar, this crisis forces me to plead with you. Father, curb your fatal thunderbolt. Through my entreaty let this boy live, who brought health to your son when he was dying. Shall one so handsome perish in the flames? This face that shines with the splendor of the stars? Shall this great grace of youth be turned into ashes?

VITUS: Do you plead on my behalf, you who have betrayed your faith? Leave off your efforts. The moment has no need of your entreaties. When one confesses Christ, his chief prayer is to die. How I long to wear in happiness the laurels that the Christian faith bestows.

DIOCLETIAN: I'll answer your prayer: Burn!

VALERIUS: Die, obstinate one!

HYLAS: Ingrate, your heart is bound with oak and triple steel. Go, lictor, hand him over to the flames. I shall be present to assist at your execution and will offer you up to Jove.

LUPUS: Go, parricide, suffer the death that you deserve.

OTHO: Go, unyielding rock, disgrace to the human race.

PULCHERELLUS: Go, filthy monster, who bring ruin on your father.

URBANUS: This is the answer to my prayer. Vitus is condemned to the flames.

SCENE 8 [FINAL SCENE]

[VITUS and MODESTUS,[38] *rescued from torture by an angel, are carried to LUCANIA whence they had come. There they die peacefully. ANGEL, MODESTUS, VITUS, standing amid clouds.]*

ANGEL: Now at last you may gaze down upon the earth below and see the dwellings of Rome. Those torturers' hands have been vanquished, their racks and gallows destroyed. The fury of angry Diocletian has been tamed.

MODESTUS: But the glorious palm of victory has been snatched away from us!

VITUS: Where do you hurry us along through these spaces of the sky? Why do you not permit our contest to be closed in violent death?

---

38. Modestus is Vitus' companion and tutor.

Dear guardian, allow us to return to the bloodstained homes of Aeneas's race.[39]

ANGEL: Your contest has ended, Modestus. You have borne witness to the holy faith with your devoted blood. Victorious, now you will direct your steps toward the eternal citadel. Vitus, do not think that your efforts to win a martyr's red robe have been in vain if death by utmost suffering be denied you, eager though you be. The laurel wreath awaits those who have borne their grievous pain bravely. It was the will of God that you both be rescued from the tyrant's hands and end your lives in peaceful death. Now that we are carried in a cloud across the radiant sky, we shall be wafted to the spot from which you came to the city seated upon her seven hills. There it is destined for you to complete your last day of life and be conveyed in triumphal chariot to the stars. One who defends his faith by suffering has not suffered in vain. The palm of victory awaits those who struggle in the fight.

THE END

39. Modestus and Vitus want the angel to return them to martyrdom at Rome. Ancient Romans believed that Aeneas' descendants founded that city.

CHAPTER 3

JESUIT MISSIONS IN ASIA
AND THE AMERICAS

INTRODUCTION

Though Ignatius of Loyola and his companions in Paris vowed in 1534 to go to Palestine and work for souls, war between the Venetian republic and the Ottoman Turkish Empire made the trip impossible. Instead, the young men put themselves at the disposal of the pope who sent several of them to work as missionaries. Paragraph 92 of the later Jesuit Constitutions states, "Further still, in conformity with our profession and manner of proceeding, we should always be ready to travel about in the various regions of the world, on all occasions when the supreme pontiff or our immediate superior orders us."[1] Though the Jesuit superior general had the power to assign any Jesuit to foreign missions in any land, the vast majority of those who set out as missionaries were volunteers.

St. Francis Xavier (1506–52) was the first Jesuit missionary. He worked in India, Malaysia, Indonesia, and Japan. This chapter contains four of Xavier's letters in which he describes his work and formulates guidelines for other Jesuit missionaries in Asia. The second great pioneer of mission work was Matteo Ricci (1552–1610), whose knowledge of Western science and ability to translate Western writings into Chinese won him the esteem of Chinese intellectuals and gained him access to the imperial court in Beijing. Two documents printed here illustrate Ricci's work: the first is a summary of his writings; the second is a dialogue between Ricci and a Buddhist scholar on the topic of life after death. The next document is by Roberto de Nobili (1577–1656), who adopted the dress and habits of a Brahmin scholar while serving in India; his contribution here discusses the delicate topic of which Hindu practices Indian converts to Christianity could retain.

The final two documents address the Jesuits' interaction with the native people of South and North America. In the Americas the Jesuits faced chal-

---

1. *The Constitution of The Society of Jesus* (St. Louis: Institute of Jesuit Sources, 1970) p. 104.

lenges very different from those presented by Chinese mandarins and Indian scholars. When compared to the cultures of Asian civilizations, life among the native peoples of the Americas seemed less sophisticated but more demanding and dangerous. To protect Native Americans in Paraguay, the Jesuits gathered them into communities called "reductions," taught them catechism, and baptized them. But Brazilian slave traders destroyed the reductions and enslaved tens of thousands of Christian Indians. Here we will read Antonio Ruiz de Montoya's account of life in the reductions and their destruction by the merciless slave traders. Jean de Brébeuf describes the hardships and joys Jesuits experienced in ministering to the Hurons of Canada. He and many of his converts were later killed by raiding Iroquois.

Francis Xavier's Letters[2]

[Many Catholics regard St. Francis Xavier (1506–52) as the greatest Christian missionary since St. Paul. A Spanish nobleman, Xavier was Loyola's roommate at the University of Paris. It is said that Loyola directed Xavier away from worldly values and toward a higher calling by repeatedly asking Xavier a question first posed by Jesus in Mark 8:36: "What does it profit a man to gain the whole world and suffer the loss of his soul?" Xavier was one of Loyola's six companions in Paris who vowed to go to and work in Palestine. To prepare himself for this calling, Xavier began studying theology in 1534. After the first Jesuits started working in Italy, King John III of Portugal asked Pope Paul III for two Jesuits to serve as missionaries in the Portuguese colonies of India. Xavier volunteered, and together with the Portuguese Jesuit Simão (Simon) Rodrigues (1510–79), he headed for Lisbon, where John III welcomed them. Rodrigues soon became a favorite of the king and a tutor to the crown prince, and Xavier had to go on to India without him.

Xavier sailed from Lisbon in 1541. As he boarded the ship he was handed a letter from Paul III appointing him a papal nuncio with authority over Catholic clergy in India. The trip to India was long and arduous and lasted more than a year, including six months spent in Mozambique. Xavier's missionary career began in earnest when he disembarked at Goa, the Portuguese headquarters in India. First he preached to the Portuguese colonists; then he journeyed down India's west coast and worked, through interpreters, among the pearl fishermen. Xavier considered himself a pioneer in spreading Christianity to new lands, not only in India but also in East Asia. He sailed around India

---

2. The four letters of Francis Xavier printed here are taken from *The Letters and Instructions of Francis Xavier*, edited and translated by M. Joseph Costelloe, S.J. (St. Louis: Institute of Jesuit Sources, 1992), pp. 63–74, 195–9, 344–8, 383–7. The letters are printed with the permission of the Institute of Jesuit Sources.

to Madras on the east coast. In 1546 he pushed on to Malacca, the main Portuguese base in Malaysia that guarded the passage from the Bay of Bengal into the Pacific Ocean. His next stop was the Moluccas, the fabled Indonesian Spice Islands. Other Jesuits followed in his wake. Xavier returned to Goa to organize the Jesuits there. Then, with a few other Jesuits, he decided to visit Japan, a land almost completely unknown to Europeans.

When no Portuguese captain dared to take him to Japan, Xavier hired a Japanese pirate and eventually landed at Kagoshima in August 1549. Accompanying him was Anjiro, a Japanese nobleman and Christian convert, whom Xavier had befriended in Malacca. Anjiro, a native of Kagoshima, arranged a meeting with the local ruler, who granted Xavier permission to preach in his territory. But the harvest of converts there was meager. Xavier, who always reached for the more, sought to achieve the Jesuit goal of "God's greater glory." Xavier hoped to meet the Japanese emperor and convert him. Though Xavier and a Jesuit companion reached the imperial capital (today's Kyoto) in 1551, they could not obtain an audience with the emperor. Gradually Xavier learned that the emperor was largely a revered figurehead; in feudal Japan real power lay with the local lords, the daimyos. *Xavier put aside his badly worn cassock, donned bright silk robes, and sailed to Yamaguchi, the headquarters of the strongest daimyo. Xavier offered the daimyo music boxes, a clock, and other wonders from Europe. The daimyo granted Xavier's request to preach the Gospel and allowed his subjects to become Christians. Xavier's new strategy was successful, and he soon baptized five hundred Japanese Christians. Xavier was deeply impressed by the Japanese, especially by their sense of honor and their high rate of literacy.*

Eventually, Xavier felt he must return to India to reorganize the work of his fellow Jesuits in mainland Asia. He barely survived a typhoon on the trip. He reached Goa in 1552 but was determined to open a mission in China, the largest, most populous, and most cultured land in Asia. Because Japan had received much of its culture from China, Xavier felt that Japanese prejudices against Christianity would melt away if Christianity could gain a foothold in China. Europeans, however, were forbidden to enter China. Xavier settled on an island off the Chinese coast and tried, in vain, to persuade smugglers to land him on the mainland. He contracted a fever, lapsed into a coma, and died on December 1, 1552.[3] The publication of his letters in Europe created a sensation, inspiring many young men to follow in his footsteps.]

---

3. For a popular biography of Xavier, see James Brodrick, *Saint Francis Xavier* (New York: Wicklow, 1952). The most detailed biography is that of Georg Schurhammer, *Francis Xavier: His Life, His Times,* translated by M. Joseph Costelloe, S.J. (Rome: Jesuit Historical Institute, 1973–82), 4 vols.

Letter 20. To Xavier's companions living in Rome, from Cochin,[4] India, January 15, 1544

May the grace and love of Christ our Lord ever assist and favor us. Amen.

1. Two years and nine months ago I sailed from Portugal, and, including this letter, I have written to you three times since then. During the time that I have been in India, I have received only one letter from you, written on January 13, 1542; and God our Lord knows how much consolation I received from it. The letter was given to me around two months ago. It was so late in arriving in India because the ship which brought it wintered in Mozambique.

2. Micer Paulo, Francisco de Mansilhas, and I are in good health. Micer Paulo is at the College of the Holy Faith in Goa and has charge of the students there. Francisco de Mansilhas and I are with the Christians of Cape Comorin. I have been with these Christians for more than a year and can tell you that there are many of them, and that many more are being converted each day. As soon as I arrived here on this coast, I sought to learn from them what they knew about Christ our Lord. When I asked them what they believed about the articles of the faith or maintained more firmly now that they were Christians than when they were pagans, the only answer that I could get from them was that they were Christians and that, since they did not understand our language, they did not know our law or what they should believe. Since they did not understand me nor I them, their native language being Malabar and mine Basque, I assembled those who were more knowledgeable and sought out individuals who understood both our language and theirs. After they had helped me with great toil for many days, we translated the prayers from Latin into Malabar, beginning with the Sign of the Cross, confessing that there are three persons in one sole God, then the Creed, the Commandments, the Our Father, Hail Mary, Salve Regina, and the Confiteor.[5] After I had translated these into their language

---

4. Cochin is a leading city of Kerala in southwest India; Vasco da Gama started a Portuguese settlement there in 1502. Many inhabitants of the region were Christians who claimed they could trace their Christian roots back to the apostle St. Thomas.

5. These, the most common Catholic prayers, were also said by European Catholics in Xavier's day. The "Creed" is the Apostles' Creed; the "Commandments" are the Ten Commandments given to Moses in the biblical books of Exodus and Deuteronomy; the "Our Father" is the Lord's Prayer found in Matthew's Gospel; the "Hail Mary" weaves together statements about Mary from Luke's Gospel; and the "Salve Regina" (Hail, Queen) was another popular prayer to Mary. The "Confiteor" was a confession of one's sinfulness recited by the congregation at the start of Mass.

and had learned them by heart, I went through the entire village with a bell in my hand in order to assemble all the boys and men that I could. After they had been brought together, I taught them twice a day. Within the space of a month, I taught them the prayers and ordered the boys to teach their fathers and mothers and all those of their house and their neighbors what they had learned at school.

3. On Sundays I brought all the villagers together, both men and women, young and old, to recite the prayers in their own language. They were obviously pleased and very happy to come. Beginning with the confession of one sole God, three and one, they recited the Creed in a loud voice in their own language, and continued to repeat after me what I said. When we had finished the Creed, I repeated it by myself. Reciting each article by itself, I paused at each of the twelve [articles] and advised them that being a Christian means nothing more than to firmly believe without doubting any of the twelve articles. After they had professed that they were Christians, I asked them if they firmly believed in each of the twelve articles. They then all together, both men and women, young and old, would, at each one of the twelve articles, answer me that they did in a loud voice with their arms folded over each other upon their breasts in the form of a cross; and I had them recite the Creed in this way more frequently than any other prayer, since only by believing in the twelve articles is a man called a Christian. The first thing that I taught them after the Creed was the Commandments, telling them that the law of the Christians has only ten Commandments, and that one is called a good Christian if he keeps them as God commands, and that, on the contrary, one who does not observe them is a bad Christian. Both Christians and pagans are astonished to see how holy is the law of Jesus Christ and its complete conformity with natural reason. After the Creed and the Commandments, I recite the Our Father and Hail Mary, and they repeat them just as I have said them. We recite twelve Our Fathers and twelve Hail Marys in honor of the twelve articles of the faith,[6] and after these we recite ten more Our Fathers and ten more Hail Marys in honor of the Ten Commandments, observing the following order: We begin by reciting the first article of the faith; and after we have recited it, I say in their language, and they with me: "Jesus Christ, Son of God, give us the grace to firmly believe without any doubt the first article of the faith"; and so that he may grant us this grace, we say an Our Father. After finishing the Our Father, we all say together: "Holy Mary, Mother of Jesus Christ, obtain for us from your son Jesus Christ the grace to firmly believe,

---

6. The Apostles' Creed has twelve short statements of faith; these were traditionally attributed to the twelve Apostles of Jesus. The same creed is used in Roman Catholic, Eastern Orthodox, and most Protestant churches today.

and without any doubt, the first article of the faith"; and so that she may obtain for us this grace, we recite the Hail Mary. We keep this same order for all the other articles.

4. After we have finished the Creed and the twelve Our Fathers and Hail Marys as I have said, we recite the Commandments in the following way: I begin by reciting the First Commandment, and all recite it after me. After it has been recited, we all say together: "Jesus Christ, Son of God, grant us the grace to love you above all things." After we have asked for this grace, we all recite the Our Father. After we have finished this, we say: "Holy Mary, Mother of Jesus Christ, obtain for us the grace from your Son so that we can keep the First Commandment." After we have asked this grace from Our Lady, we all recite the Hail Mary; and we keep this same order for all the other nine Commandments. In this way we recite twelve Our Fathers and twelve Hail Marys in honor of the twelve articles of the faith, asking God our Lord for the grace to firmly believe them without any doubt, and ten Our Fathers with ten Hail Marys in honor of the Ten Commandments, asking God our Lord that he may grant us the grace to observe them. These are the petitions which I teach them to make in our prayers, telling them that if they ask these graces from God our Lord, he will grant them, all the rest more fully than they could ask for them by themselves. I have them all recite the Confiteor, especially those who are to be baptized, and afterwards the Creed; and at every article I ask them if they firmly believe. After they have answered me that they do and I have spoken to them about the law of Jesus Christ which they must keep in order to be saved, I baptize them. We recite the Salve Regina when we wish to end our prayers.

5. I hope in God our Lord that the boys will be better men than their fathers, since they manifest much love and affection for our law and for learning and teaching the prayers. They have such a great abhorrence for the idolatries of the pagans that they frequently quarrel with them; they reproach their fathers and mothers when they see them worshiping idols, and they denounce them by coming to tell me about it. When they tell me about idolatries that are being practiced outside the villages, I collect all the boys of the village and go with them to the place where the idols have been erected; and the devil is more dishonored by the boys whom I take there than he was honored by their fathers and relatives when they made and worshiped them, for the boys take the idols and smash them to bits. They then spit upon them and trample them under their feet; and after this they do other things which, though it is better not to mention them by name, are a credit to the boys who do them against one who is so impudent as to have himself worshiped by their fathers. For four months I remained in a

large Christian village translating the prayers of our language into theirs and teaching them.

6. During this time there were so many who came and asked me to come to their homes to recite some prayers over their sick, and others who came in search of me because of their infirmities, that the mere reading of the Gospels, the teaching of the boys, baptizing, translating the prayers, answering their questions, which were never failing, and then the burial of the dead left me no time for other occupations. I was thus extremely busy in complying with the devotion of those who summoned me or came to visit me, and I could not deny their holy requests lest they lose their faith in our religion and Christian law. Since matters had come to such a state that I could not satisfy them all, nor avoid hurting their feelings over whose house I should visit first, seeing the devotion of the people, I found a way to satisfy them all. I ordered the boys who knew the prayers to go to the homes of the sick, and all those of the house and of the neighborhood to assemble there, and all to recite the Creed many times, and to tell the sick person that he should believe and that he would recover; and after this to say the other prayers. In this way I satisfied them all and had the Creed, the Commandments, and the other prayers taught in the houses and squares. God our Lord thus granted many favors to the sick, giving them health in soul and in body through the faith of those of the house, of their neighbors, and their own. God showed them great mercy in their sufferings, since he called them through their infirmities and brought them by force as it were to the faith.

7. Leaving one in this village who could continue with what had been begun, I went to visit the other village and proceeded in the same way, for there are never lacking holy and pious occupations in these regions. I could never come to an end in describing to you the harvest that is being gained by baptizing newborn children and teaching those who are old enough to learn. I leave a copy of the prayers in the villages which I visit, and I order those who know how to write to copy them, to learn them by heart, and to recite them every day. And I give them orders on how all should be assembled on Sundays to recite them. I therefore leave someone in the villages to see that this is done.

8. Many fail to become Christians in these regions because they have no [missionary] who is concerned with such pious and holy matters. Many times I am seized with the thought of going to the schools in your lands and of crying out there, like a man who has lost his mind, and especially at the University of Paris, telling those in the Sorbonne[7] who have a greater regard

---

7. The Sorbonne is the college of theology at the University of Paris.

for learning than a desire to prepare themselves to use it in helping others: "How many souls fail to go to glory and go instead to hell through their neglect!" And thus, as they make progress in their studies, if they would study the accounting which God our Lord will demand of them and of the talent which has been given to them, many of them would be greatly moved and, taking means and making spiritual exercises to know the will of God within their soul, they would say, conforming themselves to it rather than to their own inclinations, "Lord, here I am! What would you have me do? Send me wherever you will, and if need be, even to the Indies!" With how much greater consolation would they then live! And they would have great hope in the divine mercy at the hour of their death, when they will encounter that particular judgment which no man can escape and will say on their own behalf: "Lord, you gave me five talents. Behold, here are another five that I have gained with them!"

I fear that many who study in the universities study more to obtain honors, benefices, or bishoprics with their learning than with the desire of adapting themselves to the demands of these honors and ecclesiastical states. Those who study are accustomed to say: "I wish to become learned so that I can thus obtain a benefice or ecclesiastical honor and then serve God with such an honor." They therefore make their decision according to their own inordinate affections, fearing that God might not desire what they desire; for their inordinate affections do not let them leave this choice to the will of God our Lord. I was almost moved to write to the University of Paris, or at least to our Master de Cornibus and to Doctor Picard,[8] how many millions of pagans would become Christians if there were laborers, so that they may take pains to find persons who seek not what is their own but what is of Jesus Christ. There is such a great multitude of those who are being converted to the faith of Christ in this land where I am that it frequently happens that my arms become exhausted from baptizing, and I can no longer speak from having recited so often the Creed and the Commandments in their language, and the other prayers, along with an exhortation which I know in their language, in which I explain to them what it is to be a Christian, what paradise is, and what hell is, telling them what kind of people they are who go to the former and what kind to the latter. I recite the Creed and the Commandments more frequently than the other prayers. There are days when I baptize an entire village, and on the coast where I now am there are thirty Christian villages.

The [Portuguese] governor here in India is a great friend of those who become Christians. He makes a donation of four thousand pieces of gold each year, and these are only to be used for, and paid to, those persons who

---

8. These two were eminent professors of theology at the University of Paris.

are very diligent in teaching Christian doctrine in the villages which have been recently converted to the faith. He is a great friend of all those of our Society; he has a great desire that some of our Company come to these regions, and I believe that he is writing to the king in this regard.

9. Last year I wrote to you about a college that is being built in the city of Goa. There are already many students in it, who speak different languages and were all born of pagan parents. Among those in the college, for which many buildings have already been erected, there are many who are learning Latin, and others who are learning how to read and write. Micer Paulo is with the students of this college. He says Mass for them every day and hears their confessions, and he never ceases to give them spiritual instructions. He has care of the physical needs of the students. This college is very large: more than five hundred students could be housed in it, and it has the revenues to support them. The college receives many alms, and the governor is very generous in its regard. All Christians have reason for giving thanks to God our Lord for the holy founding of this house, which is called the College of the Holy Faith. Through the mercy of God our Lord, I hope that before many years have passed the number of Christians will have been greatly increased, and that the boundaries of the Church will be extended by those who are studying in this holy college. . . .

13. I can tell you nothing more about these regions than that the consolations which God our Lord gives to those who go among these pagans and convert them to the faith of Christ are so great that, if there is ever any joy in this life, this can be said to be it. Many times it happens that I hear a person who goes among these Christians exclaim: "O Lord, do not give me many consolations in this life! Or, now that you in your infinite goodness and mercy give them, take me into your holy glory, for it is most painful to live without seeing you after you have communicated yourself so intimately to your creatures!" Oh, if those who pursue knowledge employed the same great efforts in helping themselves to relish these consolations, how many toils would they endure by day and night in order that they might know them! Oh, if those joys which a student seeks in understanding what he is studying, he should seek to find in assisting his neighbors to appreciate what is necessary for them so that they may know and serve God, with how much greater consolation and readiness would they prepare themselves for the accounting which they must give when Christ bids them: "Give an account of your stewardship!"

14. In these regions, my dearest brothers, my recreations consist in frequently calling you to mind and the time when, through the great mercy of God our Lord, I knew you and conversed with you. I know interiorly and feel within my soul how much through my own fault I lost of the time that

I conversed with you, since I did not appreciate the many insights which God had given you about himself. God has granted me a great grace through your prayers and the constant remembrance which you have of me when you commend me to him. I know that God our Lord, despite your physical absence, lets me perceive through your help and assistance my infinite multitude of sins and gives me the strength to go among the infidels, for which I give great thanks to God our Lord and to you my dearest brothers. Among the many graces which God our Lord has granted me in this life, and continues to grant me every day, is one which I greatly desired to see fulfilled during my lifetime, that is, the confirmation of our rule and way of life. Thanks be to God our Lord for all eternity that he deemed it well to manifest in public what he gave to his servant Ignatius, our Father, to experience in secret. . . . I bring this to a close asking God our Lord that, since he in his mercy brought us together, and for his service has again separated us so far from each other, he may also unite us again in his holy glory. . . .

[Your dearest brother in Christ, Francisco.]

Letter 63. To Father Simão Rodrigues in Portugal from Cochin, India, January 20, 1548[9]
May the grace and love of Christ our Lord ever help and assist us. Amen. Dearest brother in Christ:

1. For the love and service of God our Lord, brother Master Simão,[10] I urge you to be busy about sending some preachers of our Society, since there is a great need of them in India. Of all those whom you have sent, I have only seen Juan de Beira, Father Ribeiro, and Nicolau, a layman, who are in Maluco, and Adam Francisco, who is in Cochin. I asked about the others; they told me that there is not a preacher among them.

I also earnestly beseech you for the love and service of God our Lord that when you arrange for the sending of some of the Society who are not preachers to these regions of India to convert the infidels, they be persons who have been well tried in the Society and have had much experience in gaining victories over themselves during the course of some years, and that

9. Rodrigues was the superior of the Portuguese Jesuit province, by far the largest province at that time. He enjoyed considerable influence with the Portuguese king. All Jesuits sent to Asia had to pass through Lisbon and could depart only with the king's approval.

10. Xavier addresses Rodrigues as "Master" since Rodrigues had a master's degree from the University of Paris. Men of the 16th century were very careful about the use of such titles.

they not be of poor health, since the labors in India require physical strength, even though spiritual strength is more important. The king[11] would do a very great service to God our Lord if he sent many preachers of our Society to India, since the people of India, as you should know, are very poorly instructed. I am telling you this from my own experience.

2. If the increase of our holy faith among the infidels in these regions encounters many difficulties, do not be surprised, since the chief and strongest opposition to it is to be found within ourselves. I am consequently of the opinion that we must first take care of ourselves and then of the pagans. For the service of God our Lord, you should do all that you can this coming year to send preachers. I am not writing to you about affairs in India, since I arrived here from Malacca only eight days ago and know nothing about them; and I am distressed by some things that I have come to know. I believe that our companions are writing at length to you about all that is happening here.

Those of our Society whom you send here for the conversion of infidels should be so reliable that any one of them could be sent either alone or with a companion to any region where there is hope of the greater service of God our Lord, for example, to Maluco, China, Japan, or Pegu,[12] and so forth. Even if they did not have much learning, if they had much virtue as their companion, they could go to any of these regions and do much for the service of God our Lord.

3. To relieve the conscience of the king, to whom the whole Society is greatly indebted because of his great friendship for it, he is first seriously obliged to assist his subjects in spiritual things and then the infidels. I earnestly desire, for the honor and service of God our Lord and the relief of the king's conscience, that he provide all the fortresses of India with preachers of our Society or of the order of St. Francis,[13] and that these preachers should have no other occupation more serious or significant than that of preaching on Sundays and feast days to the Portuguese and, after dinner, to the male and female slaves and the free Christians of the land on the articles of the faith; and on one day a week they should also preach to the wives and daughters of the Portuguese about these same articles of the faith and the sacraments of confession and Communion, since I know from experience the great need that they have of this.

---

11. King John III of Portugal was a strong supporter of the Jesuits. At the time Xavier was writing Portugal was the only European nation with bases in East Asia.

12. Pegu is a district of south central Burma.

13. Friars of the order of St. Francis are also known as Franciscans.

For the relief of the king's conscience, strive to influence him in this regard; for it seems to me, and I pray to God that I may be mistaken, that this good man will at the hour of his death find himself greatly indebted with respect to India; for I fear that in heaven God our Lord and all his saints are saying of him: "Through his letters the king shows his good desires for the increase of my honor in India, since it is only on this title that he holds it in my name; but he never punishes those who fail to execute his letters and commands, though he arrests and punishes those to whom he has committed his temporal interests if they fail in any way to increase his estates and revenues."

4. If I were convinced that the king knew the sincere love which I have for him, I would ask him for a favor through which I might render a service to him, namely, that every day he should spend a quarter of an hour in asking God our Lord to grant him to comprehend and to feel more keenly within his soul the saying of Christ: "What does it profit a man if he gain the whole world and suffer the loss of his own soul?" [Mk. 8:36]. He should also adopt the pious practice of adding at the end of all his prayers: "What does it profit?" etc. It is time, dearest brother Master Simão, to disillusion the king, for the hour is nearer than he thinks when God our Lord will call him to give a reckoning with the words: "Give an account of your stewardship" [Lk.: 16:2]. He should therefore take care to provide India with spiritual foundations.

5. My dearest brother Master Simão: From the experience which I have had, I know of only one way and route for the great increase of the service of God our Lord in these regions of India. I know of no other, and this is it: that the king send an instruction to the governor of India, whoever he may be, in which he tells his governor that he does not rely so much upon any Religious Order in India (naming in the first place our Society) as he does upon him for the increase of the faith of Jesus Christ in these regions of India. He therefore orders him to make the island of Ceylon [modern Sri Lanka] Christian and to increase the number of Christians on Cape Comorin. In order to do this, the governor should look for members of Religious Orders in these regions, and he should be given all power over our Society so that he might dispose of it and give orders to it and do with our men and with all the others whatever he desires and deems to be good for the increase of our holy faith. If he does not undertake to make the whole of the island of Ceylon Christian and greatly increase our faith, he, the king, promises—and in order to intimidate governors and to convince them that he is speaking the truth, he should take an oath and keep it (since he will obtain great merit by doing so, and more by fulfilling it)—that if

they do not relieve his conscience by making many Christians in these regions, he will, when they return to Lisbon, put them in irons and keep them in prison for many years and confiscate all their possessions. If the king gives such an order and the governors do not comply with it and are severely punished for their failure to do so, these regions will in this way become Christian, but in no other way.

6. This is the truth, brother Master Simão. I say no more. In this way the thefts and injuries to which these poor Christians are subject will come to an end; and those who are in a position to bring this about will be greatly encouraged to do so; for, if the king entrusts this matter of making Christian converts to any other person than the governor, he should have no hopes of producing any harvest. Believe me that I am speaking the truth from what I have experienced here; and there is no need for me to tell you how I know it. I am anxious to see two things in India: the first, that governors be subject to this law; the second, that there be preachers of our Society in all the fortresses of India; for this would, believe me, contribute much to the service of God, both in Goa and in all the other regions of India. May God our Lord watch ever over us. Amen.

From Cochin, January 20, 1548. Your dearest
brother in Christ,   Francisco.

Letter 64. Instruction for those of the Society who are on the Fishery Coast and in Travancore.[14]
From Manapar, India, February, 1548

The following is the order which you should observe in the service of God, and you must be most diligent in keeping it.

1. First of all, in the villages which you visit or which are under your care, you must be very diligent in baptizing the newborn infants, since this is the most important thing that can be done in these regions at the present time. You should therefore go from house to house in the villages which you are visiting and ask if there are any children to be baptized, and you should take with you some boys of the village to help you with your questions.

2. Do not trust that the local police or others will come to tell you that a child has been born, since they are careless and the infants run the risk of dying without baptism.

3. In the villages in which you are staying, or which you visit, or for which you are responsible, take great care that the children are taught Christian doctrine, and that they are brought together with great diligence.

---

14. Travancore is on the east coast of India south of Madras.

Order the villagers to be very diligent in teaching them and in doing their duty. Take account of how many know the prayers so that you may gain a richer harvest at your next visit, since they will know the accounting that you will exact from them; and the main harvest is that which is being produced among the children.

4. On Sundays, in the village or villages which you have to visit, take care that the men come to the church to recite the prayers; and in the villages which you do not visit on Sundays, you should ask the local policeman if the chiefs and the others of the village are going to church.

In the village where you happen to be, you should give an explanation of the prayers after they have been recited; and you should condemn the vices that are found among the people with clear examples and comparisons, always speaking so clearly that they understand you, telling them that if they do not amend their ways, God will punish them in this life with sicknesses, and shorten their days through the tyrannies of the king's village chiefs; and that after their death they will go to hell.

5. You should also inquire about those in the village who are quarreling with each other; on Sundays you should strive to make them friends when they come together in the church, and you should do the same on Saturdays with women who are quarreling with each other.

6. The alms which you receive from men and women on Sundays and Saturdays, and the alms which are offered in the church or were promised by the sick, should all be distributed among the poor, so that we do not take anything for ourselves.

7. You should visit those who are sick and order the villagers to come and tell you when someone is ill. When you visit them, have them recite the Confiteor and the Creed; and ask them if they truly believe in each article; and take with you a boy who knows the prayers for this so that he may recite them; and read a Gospel over them. On Sundays and Saturdays advise the men and the women that they should inform you when a person is ill, warning them that if they do not do so, you must not bury them in the church nor where the Christians are buried.

8. On Saturdays and Sundays, when the men and women come together in the church, explain to them the articles of the faith, following the norm which I left in writing with Father Francisco Coelho, so that he might translate it from Portuguese into Malabar. When the translation of these articles has been made, do what I have written about them, so that you have them read every Saturday and Sunday in the church where you are and in those which you are obliged to visit.

9. When anyone dies, you must bury him, going to his house with a cross, the boys reciting the prayers along the way; when you have reached

the house, you should recite a responsory. After removing the body, you should bring it to the place of burial; and all the boys should recite the prayers. At the place of burial, recite another responsory. And, after you have buried the body, give a brief exhortation to those who are present, reminding them that they must die and that, if they wish to go to paradise, they must prepare themselves for doing so by living well.

10. On Saturdays and Sundays urge the men and women to bring any child that has fallen ill to the church so that you may read a Gospel over it. You should do this so that the adults may be strengthened in their faith and in their love for the church, and so that their infants get better.

11. When there are quarrels and disputes among the people, you should strive to settle them, but entrust those that are serious to the captain or to Father Antonio,[15] so that you can be engaged as little as possible in examining their disputes. Do not neglect spiritual works of mercy in order to busy yourself with hearing complaints. If the complaints which you receive from the people are of little importance, order them to be settled by the chiefs of the village after the prayers have been said on Sunday.

12. Be very kind in your dealings with the captain, and do not quarrel with him on any account. Strive to live in peace and love with all the Portuguese on this coast; and do not be at odds with anyone, even though they may wish to be so. Reproach them with love for the wrongs which they do to the Christians. If they fail to amend their ways, tell the captain about it. To repeat, I again advise you not to be at odds with the captain on any account.

13. Your conversations with the Portuguese should be about the things of God. Speak to them about death, the day of judgment, and the pains of hell and of purgatory; and you should therefore advise them to confess their sins, to receive Communion, and to keep the Ten Commandments of God. If you speak to them of these things, they will not hinder you in what pertains to your office; and those who speak with you will do so of spiritual things, or they will leave you alone.

14. You should assist the native priests in spiritual matters, telling them to confess their sins, to say Mass, and to give a good example by their way of life. You should not write anything bad about them to anyone. All you can do is to give an account of it to Father Antonio, who is the superior of this coast.

15. Antonio Criminali (1520–49) was an Italian missionary and superior of the Jesuits on the Fishery Coast. He became the first Jesuit martyr when he was clubbed to death by Hindus angered by the tollgate erected by Portuguese officials on the road to the Hindu temple.

When you baptize infants, first read a Gospel of St. Mark or the Creed, and then baptize them with the intention of making them Christians, saying the words that are essential for baptism: "I baptize you in the name of the Father and of the Son and of the Holy Spirit" [Mt. 28:19] pouring the water as you say the words. When you have baptized them, read a Gospel or recite a prayer according to your own devotion. When you baptize adults, have them first recite the Confiteor and the Creed; at each article ask them if they believe in it; and after they have said that they do, baptize them.

15. Be careful not to say anything bad about the Christians in the presence of Portuguese, but always support and defend them when speaking about them; for if the Portuguese would take into account the little learning of these people and the short time that they have been Christians, they would be surprised that they were not worse than they are.

16. Strive with all your might to make yourself loved by the people, for if you are loved by them, you will gain far richer harvest than if you are despised by them.

17. Do not punish any of them without first consulting Father Antonio; and if you are in a place where the captain is, do not punish or arrest anyone without his approval.

18. When anyone makes a pagoda,[16] whether it be a man or a woman, you should, as a punishment, banish him, with the approval of Father Antonio, from the village in which he is living to another.

19. Show much love for the children who come to the prayers, and avoid offending them, overlooking the punishments which they deserve.

20. When you write to the priests and brothers in India, you should give a detailed account of the harvest you have gathered. You should also write to the lord bishop with great respect and reverence, as to our superior, so that he recognizes our obedience to him.

21. You should not go to any land at the request of any king or lord without the approval of Father Antonio, giving the excuse that we are not allowed to go there.

22. I again earnestly recommend that you strive to become loved in the villages which you will visit and in those where you will live so that, because of your good works and kind words, we may be loved by all rather than be despised, for in this way you will do much good, as I have already said. May the Lord grant this to us and be with us all. Amen.

February 1548.   Entirely yours,   Master Francisco.

---

16. A pagoda is an East Asian temple or shrine.

Letter 97. To Father Ignatius of Loyola, in Rome from Cochin, India. January 29, 1552

May the grace and love of Christ our Lord ever help and assist us. Amen.

1. My true Father: I recently received a letter from your Holy Charity[17] in Malacca when I was returning from Japan; and God our Lord knows how much my soul was consoled on receiving news of your life and health, which I cherish so highly. And among the many other very saintly words and consolations which I read in your letter were these last, which said "Entirely yours, without my being able to forget you at any time, Ignatius;" and, just as I then read them with tears, so I am now writing these with tears, as I recall times past and the great love which you ever had, and still have, for me; and as I also reflect upon the many toils and dangers of Japan from which God our Lord freed me through the intercession of your Charity's holy prayers.

2. I would never be able to describe the great debt that I owe to the people of Japan, since God our Lord, through respect for them, gave me a great knowledge of my infinite iniquities; for, being apart from myself, I did not recognize the many evils that were within me until I saw myself amidst the toils and dangers of Japan. God our Lord made me clearly feel the great need which I had of one who would take great care of me. Your Holy Charity may now see the burden that you are giving me in the care of so many holy souls of the Society who are here, since I clearly know, apart from the mercy of God, my great inadequacy in this regard. I was hoping that you would commend me to those of the Society and not them to me.

3. Your Holy Charity has written to me that you have a great desire to see me before you leave this life. God our Lord knows what an impression these words of great love made upon my soul, and how many tears they have cost me whenever I recall them; and it seems to me that I shall have this consolation, since nothing is impossible to holy obedience.

4. For the love and service of God our Lord, I am asking a kindness from you; and, if I were in your presence, I would kneel down before your holy feet [and ask you to send a Jesuit] . . . to be the rector of the college of Goa, for the college of Goa has the greatest need of something from your hand.

5. The reason why priests of the Society must be sent to the universities of Japan is the fact that the laity defend their errors by saying that they are also held by their schools and scholars.

17. Xavier usually addresses Ignatius of Loyola as "Your Holy Charity." Such honorific titles were very common in the 16th century. A few still survive: kings are called Your Majesty; popes are called Your Holiness; judges are called Your Honor.

6. And those who go there will suffer great persecutions, for they will have to oppose all their sects, and also to manifest and explain to the world the wily ways and means employed by the bonzes[18] to relieve the laity of their money.

7. But the bonzes will not tolerate this, especially when the priests say that the bonzes cannot rescue souls from hell, for this is how they gain their livelihood; moreover, when they condemn the sin against nature,[19] which is so common among them, they will have to endure tribulations on this account and for many other reasons; and they will suffer great persecutions. I am writing to Father Master Simão [Rodrigues] and, in his absence, to the rector of the college of Coimbra,[20] that they should not send persons from there to these universities unless they have been seen and approved by your Holy Charity.

8. They will suffer greater persecutions than many think; they will be pestered by visits and questions at all hours of the day and during part of the night; and they will be called to the homes of important people who cannot be refused. They will have no time for prayer, meditation, and contemplation, or for any spiritual recollection; they will not be able to say Mass, at least in the beginning; they will be continuously occupied with answering questions; they will lack the time to recite the office, and even to eat and sleep. These people are very demanding, especially with strangers, whom they hold of little account and are always ridiculing.

9. What, then, will happen when they speak ill of all their sects and their open vices, and especially when they say that those who go to hell cannot be helped? Many will become furious when they hear this about hell, that there is no remedy for it. Others will say that we know nothing, since we cannot rescue souls from hell. They have no knowledge of purgatory.

10. There is a need for trained scholars, especially for good *artystas,* to answer their questions, and for those who are *sophystas*[21] to catch them up as soon as they contradict themselves. These bonzes are deeply ashamed when they are caught in contradictions, or when they are unable to reply.

11. They will have to endure great colds, since Bandu, which is the most important university of Japan, is far to the north, as are also the other universities; and those who live in cold lands are more acute and intelligent.

18. Bonzes were Buddhist monks.

19. "Sin against nature" refers to same-sex activity.

20. Coimbra was the site of a Portuguese university and the largest Jesuit community outside Rome.

21. Xavier is asking Loyola to send good philosophers and logicians, respectively, to India.

There is, moreover, nothing but rice to eat. There are also wheat and other kinds of plants, and other things of little sustenance. They make wine from rice but have nothing else, and this is rare and costly. But the greatest trial of all are the constant and obvious dangers of death.

12. It is not a land for the elderly because of its many hardships, nor for those who are very young, if they have not had much experience; for they will otherwise ruin themselves instead of helping others. It is a land that is open to all kinds of sins, though the people

Loyola sends St. Francis Xavier to India.

are themselves scandalized by every little thing they see in those who reproach them. I am writing this detailed report to Master Simão, or, in his absence, to the rector of Coimbra.

13. I would be greatly consoled if your Holy Charity would send an order to Coimbra that those whom they intend to send to Japan should first go to Rome. I am of the opinion that Flemings or Germans who know Spanish or Portuguese would be good for Japan, since they could endure the many physical labors and also the great colds of Bandu; and I believe that there are many of these persons in the colleges of Spain and Italy. Moreover, though they lack a facility in the languages for preaching in Spain or Italy, they would be able to reap a rich harvest in Japan.

14. also believe that I should tell your Holy Charity that those of the Society who are to come to live in India should be individuals who have been chosen for the colleges of Spain and Coimbra, even though no more than two came each year; and they should be such as are required in India, men of sufficient perfection, who can later preach and hear confessions; and, if it should seem good to you, they should first make a pilgrimage to Rome and discover by themselves, through their travels, how much they are, so that they do not find themselves like novices in these regions, where there are very great dangers of falling for lack of strength.

15. This is why they must be well tried; and also, so that we who are here, instead of being consoled by them, are not saddened by their dismissal. Your Holy Charity should see if it would be good to advise Master Simão in this regard.

16. It does not seem to me that those of the Society who are in Yamaguchi, and those here who are to go there either this year and in the following years, if God so wills, have the qualifications for being sent to the universities, but rather those for learning the language and the teachings of the sects, so that they may serve as interpreters for the priests coming from Europe and faithfully translate everything that is told them.

17. It seems to me that there will be a great increase in what is being done in Yamaguchi, since there are many Christians in that city, and among them there are many fine persons; and others are being converted every day. I live with great hopes that God our Lord will preserve Father Cosme de Torres and Juan Fernández from being slain, since the greatest dangers are now past, and also because there are many Christians, including persons of high rank, who are taking great care to protect them by day and night. Juan Fernández is a lay brother and can already speak Japanese very well. He translates everything that Father Cosme de Torres tells him. With their constant preaching, they are now engaged in explaining all the mysteries of the life of Christ.

18. Since the land of Japan is well disposed for Christianity to be perpetuated by itself among the people there, all the efforts that are being made are well employed. I am consequently living with great hopes that your Holy Charity will send holy persons from there to Japan, since of all the lands that have been discovered in these regions, the people of Japan are the only ones who could by themselves perpetuate Christianity, even though this will require very great labors.[22]

19. China is an extremely large land, peaceful, and ruled by grand laws. It has only one king, and he is readily obeyed. It is a very rich kingdom and has a great abundance of all kinds of provisions. From China to Japan it is only a short crossing. These Chinese are very talented and dedicated to studies, especially with respect to the human laws pertaining to the governing of a state. They have a great desire for knowledge. They are a white race, without beards and with very small eyes. They are a generous people and, above all, very peaceful. There are no wars among them. If there should be no obstacles here in India to prevent me from leaving this year, 1552, I hope to go to China for the great service of our God which can be rendered both in China and Japan; for, if the Japanese learn that the Chinese have accepted the law of God, they will more

22. Xavier was far more impressed by the intellectual ability of the Japanese compared to that of the other nations he visited. He felt that the Japanese would make better priests and Jesuits than men from the other nations in which he worked. But he overestimated the Order's ability to gain a significant foothold in that country. Today more Jesuits come from India than from any other nation.

quickly lose their faith in their sects. I have great hopes that both the Chinese and the Japanese, through the Society of the name of Jesus, will abandon their idolatries and worship God and Jesus Christ, the Savior of all nations.

20. It is a remarkable fact that, though the Chinese and Japanese do not understand each other when they speak, since their languages are very different from each other, Japanese who know the Chinese characters can make themselves understood in writing, though not by speaking. These Chinese characters are taught in the universities of Japan, and the bonzes who know them are regarded by others as learned men; and the Chinese manner of writing is such that each character indicates one thing. Consequently, when the Japanese are learning it, when they write a Chinese letter, they paint over it what it means. If the character means "man," they paint over it the figure of man; and they do the same with all the other characters. The characters thus correspond to words; and when a Japanese reads these letters, he reads them in Japanese, and when a Chinese reads them, he reads them in Chinese. Thus, when they speak, they do not understand each other; but, when they write, they understand each other only through the letters, since they know their meaning, even though the languages themselves always remain different.

21. We composed a book in Japanese which dealt with the creation of the world and with all the mysteries of the life of Christ; and we then wrote this same book in Chinese letters, so that when I go to China I can make myself understood until I am able to speak Chinese.

22. For the love and service of God our Lord, may your Holy Charity, with all of the Society, continuously commend me to God. . . .

> From Cochin, January 29, 1552.   Least son and farthest exile,
> Francisco

Letter 110. To Father Ignatius of Loyola in Rome, from Goa, April 9, 1552

May the grace and love of Christ our Lord always help and assist us. Amen.

1. In the year 1552, in the month of February, I wrote to your Holy Charity on how I came to India from Japan, and about the harvest which was gained there through the conversion of pagans to our holy faith, and on how Father Cosme de Torres and Juan Fernandez remained in Yamaguchi, a leading city of Japan, with the Christians who had already been converted and the many who were being converted every day. This present year two of the Society are going to Yamaguchi to assist Father Cosme de Torres and to learn the language, so that when priests of great trust come from there to go to the universities of Japan, they will find there members of the Society who can accurately translate what the priests will tell them. Through the mercy of God there is already in Yamaguchi a house of the Society; this is so far

from Rome that from Goa to Yamaguchi it is more than fourteen hundred leagues, and from Rome more than six thousand.

2. Six days from now, with the help and favor of God our Lord, three of us of the Society, two priests and one lay brother, are going to the court of the king of China, which is near Japan, a land that is extremely large and inhabited by a very gifted race and by many scholars. From information which I have received, they are greatly devoted to learning; and the more learned one is, the more noble and esteemed he is. All the paganism of the sects in Japan has come from China. We are going with great confidence in God our Lord that his name will be manifested in China. May your Holy Charity take special care to recommend us to God, both those who are in Japan and those of us who are going to China. God willing, we shall write to you in great detail about what we shall have experienced in China—about how we were received, and also about how disposed it is for the increase of our faith.

3. After I returned to the college of Goa, I had to dismiss some persons from the Society.[23] I was greatly distressed to discover ample reasons for doing so; but, on the other hand, I was much relieved to dismiss them. I appointed Father Master Gaspar [Berze] the rector of the college, a Fleming by birth, a very reliable person, who has received many virtues from God. He is a very great preacher, very well received by the people, and greatly loved by those of the Society. He moves the people so much to tears when he preaches that it is something for which many thanks can be given to our Lord. I am leaving all in these regions, both priests and brothers, under his obedience. Those who could be a source of disedification during my absence I have dismissed for things in the past. All those who now remain are such that I am well content to go to China. But if God our Lord should take Master Gaspar from this life, I have left a document written and signed by my own hand in which I state who will succeed him as rector of this college, in order to avoid any trouble that might arise in the election of a rector before your Holy Charity provided a rector for these regions. Because of the great distance from here to Rome, I did this to avoid difficulties which might occur, both in the election of a rector and in the long time that it would take for a letter to go from here to Rome and for a reply to return.

4. It seemed to me that God our Lord would be greatly served if, before I departed for China, I left an order that a brother of the Society should go next year to Portugal, and from there to Rome, with letters for your Holy Charity to let you know the need that these regions have for priests who have been well tried and proven in the world, for men of this kind reap a

---

23. Xavier does not give the precise reasons for their dismissal.

rich harvest in these regions; whereas those who are learned but have had no experience and have not been tried by persecutions from the world produce a meager harvest in these regions; and those whom I dismissed were such.

5. From what I have experienced in Japan, the priests who are to go there to profit souls spiritually, especially those who are to go to the universities, have need of two things: the first is that they have been much tried and persecuted in the world and that they have had much experience and have acquired a great interior knowledge of themselves, since they will be more persecuted in Japan than they ever were perhaps in Europe. The land is cold and has few resources. The people do not sleep in beds, since there are none. There is a shortage of food. They have a contempt for strangers, especially for those who come to preach the law of God; and they retain this until they have acquired a taste for God. Those who go there will always be persecuted by the priests of Japan; and I do not think that those who are to go to the universities will be able to take with them what they would need for saying Mass, since there are many thieves in the lands through which they must pass. Since in the midst of such great difficulties and persecutions, they will be deprived of the consolation of the Mass and of the spiritual nourishment which persons obtain from receiving their Lord, your Holy Charity may see the virtue that will be required in the priests who are to go to the universities of Japan.

6. They must also be learned in order to be able to answer the many questions that are posed by the Japanese. It would be well if they were good Masters of Arts, and it would certainly be no loss if they were dialecticians, so that they could catch the Japanese in contradictions when they dispute with them. It would also be good if they knew something about the celestial sphere, since the Japanese are delighted with learning about the movements of the heavens, the eclipses of the sun, the waxing and waning of the moon, and how rain, snow and hail, thunder, lightning, comets, and other natural phenomena are produced. The explanation of such matters is a great help in gaining the good will of the people. I thought it well to give your Holy Charity this account of the people of Japan, so that you might appreciate the virtues that must be possessed by the priests who are to go there.[24]

7. I have frequently thought that a number of Flemish and German priests of the Society would be good for those regions, since they can endure great labors and put up with the cold; and there, both in Italy and in

---

24. Fifty years later Matteo Ricci used his knowledge of Western science and geography to win favor with Chinese intellectuals and the imperial court in Beijing. See the selection later in this chapter.

Spain, they would be less missed, since they do not have a command of the language that is needed for preaching. But, if the brothers in Japan are to understand them, they must be able to speak Spanish or Portuguese; but even if they do not know much, they can learn it on the way, since it will take them at least two years to reach Yamaguchi from there.

8. I believe that I should inform your Holy Charity about the need that these regions have for one who is conversant with the things of the Society, a person who has had experience in them and has been associated for some time with your Holy Charity. This college [in Goa] and all the members of the Society who are here in India have a great need for such a person, so that they may be well instructed according to the holy Rules and Constitutions of the Society. Even if this person should have no talent for preaching, he will not on this account fail to be useful and needed in these regions. For the service of God our Lord, send someone from your hand to be rector of this college; for whoever he may be, even if he is not very learned, if you send him from your hand, he will be such a one as is needed in this house, since the priests and brothers in these regions wish to see someone from Rome who has conversed much with your Holy Charity. . . .

11. A great service will be rendered to God our Lord if the priests who are to come to these regions are thoroughly tried, since this land has need of them. I am also writing to Father Master Simão [Rodrigues], or to the rector of the college of Coimbra in his absence, that he should not send priests here who would not be missed there, since such are not needed

Xavier writes to Loyola from India.

here, and it will be a great boon if your Holy Charity would issue an order that no priest of the Society is to come to these regions who has not first made a pilgrimage to Rome and comes to India with the permission of the superior general. Most of all, it seems to me to be very important that no person from Portugal, or from any other country, should come as rector to these regions of India who has not first gone to Rome and been sufficiently examined by our superior general, and that he comes here with his permission and decree, but in no other way. I say this from the experience which I have had of those who came from Portugal to be rectors of this college. And since I fear that one may come next year as in the past, I am leaving an order that none of those who come from there to be the rector of this house are to be accepted as such if they have not been so ordered by our superior general and do not have a document from him to this effect. I have done this to avoid some things which I forebear to put in writing.

12. I would be greatly consoled if your Holy Charity would ask a person in the house to write to me at great length news about the priests who came with us from Paris, and about all the others, and about how the things of the Society are prospering, both about the colleges and houses, and also about the number of professed priests, and about some very distinguished persons who had excellent qualities before they entered into the Society, and about some great scholars who are in it, since such a letter will refresh me in the midst of numerous trials on both sea and land, in China and Japan.

May our Lord join us together in the glory of paradise, and also, if it will be to his service, in this present life. This could be easily accomplished if I were so ordered by obedience. All tell me that one can go from China to Jerusalem. If this should be so, as I am told, I shall write it to your Holy Charity, and how many leagues it is, and how long it would take to go.

From Goa, April 9, 1552.   Your least son and farthest exiled,
                                                                    Francisco.

WRITINGS OF MATTEO RICCI

[Matteo Ricci (1552–1610) entered the Jesuits in 1571. He received the usual Jesuit training at the Roman College and also studied mathematics under a leading scholar, Christopher Clavius, S.J. (1537–1612). Ricci then volunteered to work as a missionary in Asia. He studied theology for three years after reaching India in 1578. Because of his excellent language skills he was sent to Macao, the Portuguese colony near Hong Kong where he studied Chinese with Michele Ruggieri, the pioneer of Jesuit efforts to penetrate China. In 1583 Ricci and Ruggieri settled in Chaoking and dressed like Buddhist monks. They wanted to use their skills in Western science to ingratiate themselves with Chinese scholars. Ricci produced a world map that won the admiration of Chinese intellectuals. Later he translated into Chinese treatises on Western mathematics, philosophy, and theology and a catechism. Ruggieri returned to Italy in 1588 to try to persuade the pope to send an ambassador to Beijing. Ricci moved northward to Guangdong in 1589 where he exchanged the clothing of a Buddhist monk for that of a Confucian scholar. In

1597 Ricci became superior of all Jesuits in China. Though his first efforts to set up a Jesuit house in Beijing, the capital, ran afoul of hostile officials, the emperor summoned him to the capital in 1601. In Beijing Ricci and his Jesuit assistant presented the emperor with Western scientific gifts; in return they were granted the right to reside in the capital, where the emperor subsidized their work in mathematics and astronomy. The Mandarin scholars who controlled much of the government held Ricci's work—and that of later Jesuits who continued his scholarly work in Beijing for the next 150 years—in high esteem. The Jesuits hoped to convert an emperor so that a Chinese Constantine would lead the world's most populous nation to Christianity. Though this never happened, the imperial favor enjoyed by the Beijing Jesuits provided a shield for Catholic missionaries working elsewhere in China. Ricci and his Jesuit successors at Beijing also served as the main intellectual link between Europe and China; this link led to almost two centuries in which knowledge in literature, philosophy, mathematics, science, and art was shared between the two regions.[25]

The two documents offered below illustrate Ricci's work. The first selection is taken from Nicholas Trigault's De Christiana Expeditione apud Sinas *(The Christian expedition among the Chinese) published in Augsburg in 1615, five years after Ricci's death. Trigault, a Belgian Jesuit, joined the Jesuit community in Beijing and had access to Ricci's diaries and private papers. He reworked Ricci's writings slightly to make them more accessible and attractive to European readers in the hope that they would be moved to offer support and financial help for Jesuits working in China. Prior to the publication of Trigault's book, Europeans were largely dependent upon Marco Polo's writings, composed three centuries earlier, for their understanding of China. Public interest in the current state of Chinese affairs turned Trigault's book into an immediate success. Not the least of Ricci's accomplishments was convincing Europeans that the "Cathay" described by Marco Polo was in fact China. Between 1615 and 1623 Trigault's book went through four editions in Latin, three in French, and one each in German, Spanish, and Italian.]*

25. See Donald Lach, *Asia in the Making of Europe* (Chicago: University of Chicago Press, 1965–), 3 vols. The discoveries beginning in the 1490s opened Asia, Africa, and the Americas to Europe and issued in the development of world civilization. The European impact on the rest of the world was enormous, but these discoveries opened a two-way street. Asian contributions to the development of Europe are traced in detail by Lach's monumental study. In the 16th and 17th centuries no group played a larger role here than the Jesuits. The best recent study of Ricci is Jonathan D. Spence, *The Memory Palace of Matteo Ricci* (New York: Viking Press, 1984). A more popular biography is Vincent Cronin's *The Wise Man from the West* (New York: Dutton, 1955).

Nicholas Trigault, *The Christian Expedition Undertaken*
among the Chinese by the Society of Jesus, from the Commentaries
of Father Matteo Ricci of the Same Society

Book 5, Chapter 2: Father Ricci's Chinese writings[26]
How much esteem for the Christian faith was won at this time by the printing
of the books of Father Matteo Ricci.

As our first book recounted, literary works flourished in this kingdom.
Very few people are found here who do not have some interest in such works.
Indeed, this kingdom is unusual in that the religious sects spread their mes-
sages not through sermons preached to the people but rather through books;
this is a fairly well established fact. Since these people do not like to gather in
crowds of people together, they often spread the word of something new in
this way. This did not deter our Fathers. I doubt that these people, who are
addicted to reading books, would have been persuaded in this matter by the
preaching of our men—who are not always eloquent in a foreign language—
as they have been by what they read in their leisure time. Still, I would not
want you to think that sermons to the converts were omitted on feast days; I
am talking, instead, about the local people who are attracted by books and
tend to debate questions in private conversations. It is not uncommon for
these eager readers to commit to memory the major Christian teachings they
encounter while reading spiritual books at home. They then share these
teachings with their close friends. When they noticed this, our Fathers were
inspired to study [Chinese] writings. Though this was a long and demanding
task, they recognized that with perseverance and talent all that hard work and
trouble was—thanks to the help of God's kindness—worthwhile.

Perhaps most important—and surprising and completely unheard of in
all the rest of the world—is the fact that any book published [in Chinese] is
read and understood in Japan and Korea and even Vietnam, the Leucmans
and other kingdoms just as it is in the fifteen vast provinces of Chinese
kingdom even though their speech is totally different. The reason for this is
that the individual characters in their picture writing signify the same individual thing. If the whole earth agreed upon this way of writing, we could
use these written characters to share our inmost thoughts with those people
from whom we are currently prevented from speaking as a result of the
differences in our spoken language.

---

26. John Patrick Donnelly has translated this selection from Nicholas Trigault's *De
Christiana Expeditione apud Sinas suscepta ab Societatis Iesu, ex P. Matthaei Ricii eius-
dem Societatis Commentariis* (Augustae Vind.: Apud Christoph. Mangium, 1615),
pp. 486–91. For a full translation of Trigault's work, see *China in the Sixteenth Century: The Journals of Matteo Ricci, 1583–1610,* translated by Louis J. Gallagher
(New York: Random House, 1953).

Father Matteo was the first [Westerner] to begin studying Chinese characters at that time. The teachings he spread abroad eventually earned him the admiration of those [Chinese] scholars who had previously failed to learn anything by reading a foreigner's writings. . . . As was said earlier, Father Matteo began with the basics of cosmology and astronomy. Though he did not teach anything unusual, or anything that was not already common knowledge to a European undergraduate student, his teaching seemed wonderful beyond belief to the Chinese, who continued to hold erroneous beliefs handed down to them by their ancestors. Thus many of the Chinese, who had previously been stubborn and haughty in defense of their ignorance, sincerely admitted that their eyes had been opened to important matters; up until that day they had not realized how isolated they were in their intolerable blindness. Aside from his short commentaries on the four elements, on friendship, and on moderating the evil inclinations of the heart (these were treated earlier), [Ricci] wrote more than twenty-five short treatises on moderating the evil inclinations of the mind. The Chinese called these treatises *The Sentences*. Ricci thought he ought to have these short treatises read by some of his [Chinese] friends prior to publication. They were met with great approval; indeed, it seemed unbelievable to his friends that somebody from one of the foreign nations—which up to that day they regarded as barbarous—could have discovered things so erudite and fitting. All of Ricci's friends eagerly made copies of treatises. Indeed, when Fumo Can[27] (who was often mentioned above) received his single copy, he had it printed along with an elegant preface in which he praised the book and compared it to another, similar, treatise entitled *The Forty-two Paragraphs* once published by a sect of idol worshipers. Fumo Can did not just compare the two books; his preference for Ricci's book was such that he encouraged all scholars to read it so that they might compare for themselves the vanity of shadowy virtue colored by superstitions with [Ricci's] truth drawn from Christian fountains. Let the scholars make their own comparison and confirm it by calculation—they will see which of the two small books is better suited for the good of individuals and for the universal good of the nation. Our friend Paul added a second preface to Fumo Can's and ended the little book with an epilogue.[28] Both of these [scholars] added to the great prestige of Ricci's work. These great men added as much

---

27. Fumo Can (1555–1606) was a friend of Ricci and a Chinese scholar and magistrate who converted to Christianity.

28. *Paul* is the baptismal name taken by the Chinese convert and scholar Xu Guanqi (1562–1633), who helped Ricci translate the first six books of Euclid into Chinese from the *Euclidis elementorum Libri XV*, published by the great Jesuit mathematician Christopher Clavius (1537–1612) under whom Ricci had studied in Rome. See the cover of this book for a portrait of Clavius.

authority to the faith of Christians as could rightfully be hoped for. Privately, our friend Paul believed that the practices of the Christian faith deserved to be widely praised; he professed that not only did he approve of these practices but had also embraced them.

At this time a certain considerable trouble arose. The first catechism of Christian doctrine was written while our men were still unskilled [in the Chinese language]; they put too much trust in the interpreters translating it. When the Fathers got better trained, this catechism seemed rather too short. Therefore Father Matteo revised the little book carefully, added to it and after recalling the other catechisms circulated this new edition alone. A more detailed tract on Christian doctrine was written. But before this catechism was printed Father Matteo rearranged and revised it especially for non-Christian readers. It seemed to him that neophytes could receive sufficient instruction in sacred matters from classes on the catechism while they were catechumens[29] and by attending sermons after they had already been gathered to Christ. Thus he based the whole book on arguments drawn from the light of reason rather than on the authority of Holy Scripture. With these arguments he paved the road to those mysteries dependant on faith and the knowledge revealed by God. Moreover the ancient books of the Chinese were full of teachings that supported our case. These testimonies were not merely decorative; they also confirmed the [Christian] faith among those believers who were reading literature on their own. In this book Ricci refuted the teachings of all the Chinese sects save for those teachings that had arisen from the law of nature and were largely proclaimed by Prince Confucius[30] and the sect of scholars. There was little to object to in the teaching of this sect, which was rooted in the ancients. Thus a man who has little to say about things he thinks he does not know well is unlikely to fall into error. Our Fathers therefore tried to win this sect over and talked to them only about those things that occurred after Confucius himself (he had preceded the coming of Christ the Savior to earth by more than five hundred years). It seems to me that Doctor Paul was right in his reply to those audiences that repeatedly asked him about the essence of the Christian faith: he neatly reduced the whole matter to four syllables or sayings—*Cive Fo Pu Giu*. That is, "It gets rid of idols and fills out the faith of scholars."

In Ricci's treatise the following things are nicely explained: First, it is

29. Catechumens were persons studying Christian teachings in preparation for baptism.

30. Confucius (c. 551–479 B.C.) is still considered the greatest Chinese philosopher; the Chinese have used his maxims as a moral guide for daily life for the past twenty-five centuries.

proven that there is one beginning or divinity from whom all things arise and are governed; the human soul is immortal; a punishment is prepared for evil actions, a reward for good ones, and that these are meted out mainly in another life. The Pythagorean transmigration of souls, which was familiar to the Chinese, is refuted [in Ricci's treatise].[31] A very useful treatise on God and on man was added to the end of the book. Finally Ricci invites all the Chinese to this faith. (This subject is touched upon rather than explained—with the expectation that a fuller explanation would be sought from the Jesuits.)

Because we needed this book to spread our message in a short time through that whole kingdom, and because it also touched only in passing many subjects about which people tended to ask our Fathers, several curious things were tossed in, like spices to entice the reader. The book was generally read with pleasure. For this reason too it satisfied the constant requests of people who were hearing something or other about our faith; they usually asked for some book in which these same matters could be read about in a more leisurely way. This little book also compensated for [our Fathers'] short conversations with busy magistrates. Given their deep-seated propensity for reading, such magistrates always made more time for reading than for conversation.

This affair seriously wounded the idol worshipers who lacked weapons to defend their worthless cause. We also saw that we faced no danger from the scholars, since it was shameful for them to refute their own profession. Thus, by divine intervention, our faith had its own defenders among the Chinese. Our Fathers noted from the beginning that the views pleasing to the scholars did not on any point oppose the Christian faith. Had we been forced to refute each of the sects individually, we would have been overwhelmed and condemned to everlasting silence by their prestige and numbers. Ricci's tract was printed four times in different provinces by the pagans themselves. A literary scholar, Fumo Can, wanted to print many copies at his own expense. He then gave these copies to our Jesuits so they might give them to whomever they most wanted. He wrote to our Fathers that he considered the sum of money he devoted to the project to be restitution for the time (I know not when) he

31. The next document printed here is Ricci's refutation of the transmigration of souls, which was taught in China by Buddhists but not by Confucians. Trigault calls the doctrine Pythagorean because one of the first Greeks to teach the transmigration of souls was Pythagoras, who flourished around 530 B.C. Pythagoras left no writings; his disciples popularized his teachings. The Chinese would not have known of Pythagoras; the doctrine of transmigration was spread in China by Buddhist monks from India.

had accepted something from somebody on the basis of his doing a favor for him. It seemed to [Fumo Can] that he could do no other work more useful than making available to as many people as possible this tract about the most holy faith. He did this even when he was still a pagan. One can only guess what he might have done had his life granted him some more years in the Christian religion.

Father Matteo wrote another book he called *The Paradoxes*.[32] This book attracted just as many critics as his earlier work since it contained a great deal of material about moral commandments that was new and previously unknown to the Chinese. Here are some concise summaries of the running commentary this book offered on how to organize a good moral life so as to help as many other people as possible: "This life is a march toward death, in which the reward for our works and the punishment owed to us are not completely carried out but are saved up for another life. Although difficult, silence is useful and so is concise speaking. Individuals need to organize their actions and do penance for their evil deeds." These and similar precepts are commented on at great length and are confirmed by appropriate aphorisms and examples. Direct quotes from the philosophers, and the holy Church Fathers, and the books of the Sacred Scriptures themselves were very popular with readers. [Ricci] enhanced the authority of this book with individual paradoxes. These individual paradoxes were inserted into the discussions involving the leading magistrates—men with whom Father Matteo had held long discussions about these matters.

If all famous men who praised Ricci's book collected their assessments into one volume, it would take longer to read that volume than Ricci's book itself. Not only was the value of reading Ricci's book praised in these assessments, but Europe's genius, its multitude of books, and its Christian faith were also extolled with the highest praise.

So they might make [Ricci's book] widely available, our Fathers distributed as many copies as possible. We fulfilled our customary duty of giving presents at the usual times by distributing this book. Our friends also sent to our house typesetters to print copies for them so they too could spread copies among their acquaintances. Thus was the first printing of this book used up in its first year; in the next year there were two new printings. One of these printings was completed at the royal city of Nanjing, the other at Nanchang, the main city of Kiangsi Province.

---

32. The book was published by Ricci in 1608; its Chinese title, *Jiren shipian*, translates as "Ten Chapters of an Extraordinary Man." It has ten short dialogues between Ricci and Chinese scholars who were his friends. It has many quotations from Greek philosophers, especially the Stoic philosopher Epictetus.

Matteo Ricci (1552–1610).

Matteo Ricci, *The True Meaning of the Lord of Heaven*

[The second Ricci selection is taken from his T'ien-chu Shih-i *(The True Meaning of the Lord of Heaven), originally written in Chinese to refute Buddhist ideas about reincarnation. The edition from which this selection is taken featured Ricci's Chinese text and the English translation on facing pages. (The Chinese text has been omitted here.[33]) This section of the text is a dialogue between a Western scholar and a Chinese scholar. The Western scholar is, of course, Ricci himself, who is defending the Christian belief (shared by Jews and Muslims) in the immortality of the soul and the resurrection of the body, against the Buddhist teaching on reincarnation. Most Buddhists taught that humans are reincarnated after death in one of six ways or directions, depending on their moral behavior in their previous life. The six possible reincarnated forms are: a human person, a hungry ghost, an animal, a malevolent nature spirit, a god, or a person sent to hell. The Chinese scholar makes the case for Buddhist and Taoist beliefs in reincarnation. The Christian position would have been new to the Chinese scholars to whom Ricci addressed his arguments.]*

Chapter 5: Refutation of false teachings concerning reincarnation in the six directions and the taking of life, and an explanation of the true meaning of fasting.

258. *The Chinese scholar says:* There are three views concerning man. The first asserts that prior to a man's being born on earth he does not exist, and

---

33. Matteo Ricci, S.J., *T'ien-chu Shih-i (The True Meaning of the Lord of Heaven)*, edited by Edward Malatesta, S.J., translated with introduction and notes by Douglas Lancashire and Peter Hu Kuo-chen, S.J., (St. Louis: Institute of Jesuit Sources, 1985), bilingual ed., pp. 239–51. Used with the permission of the Institute of Jesuit Sources.

that therefore he is unable to leave anything of himself behind after he dies. The second view is that man has three existences: one prior to his birth, one following his death, and his present existence. Thus, the happiness or misfortune experienced by me in this life both stem from the good or evil deeds performed in my previous existence; and the fortune or misfortune I shall experience in the next life will be determined by the correctness or depravity of my actions in this life.

259. Now your revered religion teaches that a man has only a temporary existence in this life, and that this life determines his final dwelling place in the life to come. It therefore goes on to teach that while we are temporarily resident in this world, we ought to make a special point of cultivating our virtue and doing good so that we may enjoy happiness in the life to come. Man is born into this world to be a pilgrim, and his next life is a return to his native land. This present world is the place in which he establishes his merit, and the next world is the place in which he is rewarded. You are certainly right about the life to come, but what is the source of the theory that there is a former existence?

260. *The Western scholar says:* In ancient times, in our Western region, there was a scholar called Pythagoras[34] who was a man of uncommon, heroic abilities, but who was not always as artless as he might have been. He loathed the unrestrained evil-doings of the inferior men of his own day, and taking advantage, therefore, of his personal fame, he created a strange argument to restrain them, insisting that those who did evil were bound to experience retribution when reborn in a subsequent existence: they might be born into a family engulfed in hardship and poverty or be transformed into an animal; tyrannical men would be changed into tigers and leopards; arrogant men into lions; the licentious into pigs and dogs; the avaricious into oxen and mules; and thieves and robbers into foxes, wolves, eagles, and other birds and beasts. The transformation was bound to correspond to the evil done. Other superior men criticized this teaching saying that, although the intention behind it was excellent, there were faults in the teaching itself. There was a true way which could curb evil, so what purpose was served by abandoning the true and following the distorted?

261. After the death of Pythagoras few of his disciples continued to hold his teaching. But just then the teaching suddenly leaked out and found its way to other countries. This was at the time when Sakyamuni[35] happened

---

34. Pythagoras was a fifth-century B.C. Greek scientist and philosopher who argued for reincarnation, a view that remained fairly popular in the ancient world. The notion of reincarnation can be found in Plato's *Republic* and Virgil's *Aeneid.*

35. This is another name for Gautama Buddha (563?–483? B.C.), the founder of Buddhism. *Sakyamuni* means "The Sage of the Sakka Republic."

to be planning to establish a new religion in India. He accepted this theory of reincarnation and added to it the teaching concerning the Six Directions,[36] together with a hundred other lies, editing it all to form books which he called canonical writings. Many years later some Chinese went to India and transmitted the Buddhist religion to China. There is no genuine record of the history of this religion in which one can put one's faith, or any real principle upon which one can rely. India is a small place, and is not considered to be a nation of the highest standing. It lacks the arts of civilization and has no standards of moral conduct to bequeath to posterity.[37] The histories of many countries are totally ignorant of its existence. Could such a country adequately serve as a model for the whole world?

262. *The Chinese scholar says*: I have seen your "Map of the World and All Nations"[38] and its contents accord precisely with the celestial degrees; there is not the slightest error in it. Moreover, you have personally come a great distance, from Europe to China, so that what you say about what you have seen and heard of the Buddha's country must certainly be reliable. Since India is such a mean and lowly nation, it really is laughable that people should mistakenly study Buddhist books, believe in Buddhism's Pure Land, and even wish to enjoy an early death in order that they might be born again in that Land.[39] We Chinese are not in the habit of traveling great distances to foreign lands, so that we are usually rather ignorant of events outside our nation. Nevertheless, although a place may be small and its people mean and lowly, there is no reason why one should not believe what they say, provided it is reasonable.

263. *The Western scholar says:* There is so much that is unreasonable in the theory of reincarnation that I would not be able to give you an exhaustive account of it. I shall simply refer to four or five major points, and you will see what I mean.

264. First, if a person dies and his soul is transferred to another body, becoming another person, a bird, or an animal when he is reborn into the

36. The Six Directions are the six ways a person could be reincarnated, as was noted in the introduction to this selection.

37. Many of the early Jesuits, including Xavier and Ricci, were more impressed by the Japanese and Chinese and their cultures than by what they saw in India.

38. Perhaps the most valuable piece of Western knowledge that Ricci passed on to the Chinese was the world map he drew that included the then recent discoveries by Western explorers. Much of this information was new to the Chinese. Ricci adapted his map for his audience by putting China at the center of it.

39. Here the Chinese Confucian scholar pours contempt on the hope of Indian Buddhists to achieve life after death in the Pure Land.

world, he is bound to retain his original intelligence and ought to be able to remember his activities from his previous existence. But we absolutely cannot remember these things, and I have never heard of anyone who was able to remember them. It cannot be more obvious, then, that there is no socalled "former existence" prior to a man being born.

265. *The Chinese scholar says:* In the writings of Buddhism and Taoism[40] there are many records of people who were able to remember events from their former existence, so there must be people who are able to remember such things.

266. *The Western scholar says:* The Devil wishes to deceive people so that they will follow him. He therefore attaches himself to the bodies of humans and animals, causing them to say that they are the sons of certain families and to give accounts of events in those families in order to prove his lies. Those mentioned in the records you refer to are bound to be disciples of the Buddha and Lao-Tzu,[41] or the records are bound to be of events subsequent to the transmission of Buddhism to China. In all places hosts of living creatures of every kind have come into existence and then die; why is it, then, that from ancient times until the present, although there have been numerous sages in countries with religions other than the Buddhist whose learning has been both broad and deep and who have been able to commit thousands of books and tens of thousands of words to memory, they have not been able to remember a single event from a former existence? Although people easily forget things, how could they forget their parents and their own names? Is it only the adherents of Buddhism and Taoism, and the animals, who are capable of remembering such things and of telling others about them? Perhaps there are some who will accept unfounded statements made to deceive the ignorant, but among the learned, and in the academies and schools where the existence or not of all principles is debated, very few will find it possible not to ridicule such claims.

267. *The Chinese scholar says:* The Buddhists say that the human soul which attaches itself to an animal's body is, in fact, dependent on its former intelligence, but that because an animal's body does not exactly fit a human soul, the soul is circumscribed and therefore unable to express itself.

268. *The Western scholar says:* But when it was attached to the previous person's body it was in perfect harmony with it; why, then, was it still unable to remember events of a former existence? I have already explained that

---

40. Taoism is a mystical Chinese philosophy going back to the sixth century B.C. It later borrowed elements of Buddhism and became more religious in content.
41. Lao-Tzu (c. 604–531 B.C.), the founder of Taoism and author of the *Tao Te Ching,* stressed good moral behavior over religious rituals.

a man's soul is spirit, and a spirit, by its very nature, is not dependent on a body. This being the case, it should be able to use its natural intelligence even though it may be resident in a bird or an animal. How could it possibly be incapable of expressing itself? If the Lord of Heaven really did devise the transformations of reincarnation it must have been for the purpose of persuading people to do good, or to serve as a warning to evil-doers. If I do not clearly remember the good and evil I did in a former existence, how can I determine whether the good or evil fortune met with in this life really does stem from a former existence? Can this be called persuading people to do good or warning them against evil? What benefit, then, accrues from reincarnation?

269. Secondly, when the Sovereign on High first produced men and beasts, there was no need for men to be changed into animals because of sinning, and he therefore gave to each creature a soul which would accord with its own category. If there are now a number of animals to which human souls have become attached, then the souls of animals today are no longer the same as the souls of animals in ancient times, and animals today ought to be intelligent, whereas those of ancient times would be doltish. Yet, I have never heard that there is any difference; therefore, the souls of animals have remained the same from ancient times until the present.

270. Thirdly, all men of learning assert that there are three classes of souls: the lowest class is called the vegetative soul, and this kind of soul can only support the life and growth of that to which it has been given. This is the soul of grain and trees. The second class of soul is called the sentient soul. This kind of soul can support the life and growth of that to which it is given, but can also enable creatures to hear with their ears, to see with their eyes, to taste with their mouths, to smell with their noses, and to be aware of things with their limbs [through the sense of touch]. This is the soul of birds and animals. The highest soul is called the intelligence-soul. This soul, together with the vegetative soul and sentient soul, can aid the body in its growth, cause it to be aware of things, and enable men to reason things out and to clarify the truth. This is man's soul.

271. If you now cause the animal and human souls to be the same, then there will only be two kinds of soul, and will this not introduce confusion into a universally accepted theory? The natures of most things are not only determined by their appearances, but by their souls. Only when it has its essential soul does a thing have its essential nature, and only when it has its essential nature can its category be determined. Only when the category of a thing has been determined does it develop its appearance and physical form. Therefore, differences or similarities in natures rest on differences or similarities of soul; differences or similarities of category rest on differences

or similarities of nature, and differences or similarities of appearance depend on differences or similarities of category.

272. Since the appearances of birds and beasts are different from those of men, it follows that their categories, natures and souls are also different. There is no other way in which man can investigate things and probe exhaustively into their principles except to employ the external appearances of things as proof of their inner nature, to observe what is evident in things in order to understand their innermost secrets.

273. Thus, if we wish to know what kinds of souls are possessed by grass and trees, we observe the fact that grass and trees are only capable of growth and are devoid of consciousness, and this provides proof that all they have within them is the vegetative soul. If we wish to know the nature of the souls of birds and beasts we observe the fact that they are only possessed of consciousness and are incapable of rational thought, and from this we know that they only possess the sentient soul. If we wish to know the nature of man's soul we notice the fact that man alone is able to understand the principles of all things, and from this we know that only he possesses an intelligence-soul.

274. These truths are so obvious, yet Buddhists perversely assert that the souls of birds and beasts are intelligent just as men's are—an assertion which is too irrational for words. I often hear it said that it is a mistake to follow the Buddha; I have never heard it said that it is a mistake to follow after truth.

275. Fourthly, man's bodily form is particularly handsome and different from those of birds and beasts; it follows, then, that his soul is also different. It is like the artisan who must use wood to manufacture a chair, and iron to manufacture a sharp implement. The objects are different, and consequently the material he uses is also different. Since we know that man's bodily form is different from those of the birds and beasts, how can man's soul be the same as the souls of birds and beasts?

276. From all this we know that the Buddhist teaching that men's souls are entrusted to the care of other persons' bodies, or that they are attached to the bodies of birds and beasts to be born again into the world, is a totally erroneous doctrine. Since a man's soul only harmonizes with his own body how can it be made to harmonize with someone else's body, or, even more, with the body of something in a different category? The sheath of a knife is only suitable for holding knives and a scabbard is only suitable for holding swords. How can one relate a knife to a scabbard?

277. Fifthly, there is, in fact, no evidence for the assertion that human souls are transformed into animals. The belief is simply due to perplexity as to whether a person in a former existence lived the wanton life of some

animal or other and whether, in consequence, the Lord of Heaven is punishing him by causing him to be transformed into a certain kind of beast in his later existence. But this can hardly be termed punishment. Who would say that to be able to satisfy one's desires is punishment?

Roberto de Nobili

The Report on the Customs of the Indian Nation[42]

[Roberto de Nobili, S.J., (1577–1656) was born in Rome of noble parents and attended the Roman College, the premier Jesuit school. He entered the Jesuit Order in Naples in 1596. In 1604, a year after his ordination, he traveled to Lisbon and from there to India where he spent the rest of his life. After learning Tamil, the language of southern India, de Nobili worked among the fishermen along the coast. Earlier missionaries had encouraged converts to dress and behave like the Portuguese, often taking Portuguese names. Conversion to Christianity, then, was not just a change of religion but also of lifestyle. These cultural changes made it far more difficult to persuade Hindus to convert to Christianity. Following the example of Matteo Ricci in China, de Nobili decided that he would be a more effective missionary if he adapted native customs and clothing as long as they were compatible with the Christian faith. He began wearing the saffron robes and eating the vegetarian diet of a Hindu holy man or sannyasi. He also deepened his understanding of the Hindus' mentality by reading their sacred literature in Sanskrit. He was the first European to study those venerable classics. Gradually he began to make converts among the elite.

Jesuit missionaries in India had to confront many questions. Should these converts be forced to abandon traditional garb, which often had some religious symbolism? Should converts abandon distinctive Brahmin hairstyles or colored marks on their foreheads? Through his research de Nobili thought he could distinguish what was social custom—and therefore compatible with the Christian

---

42. *Preaching Wisdom to the Wise: Three Treatises by Roberto de Nobili, S.J., Missionary and Scholar in the 17th Century,* translated by Anand Amaldass, S.J., and Francis X. Clooney, S.J. (St. Louis: Institute of Jesuit Sources, 2000), pp. 195–9, 217–24. The whole treatise, *The Report on Customs of the Indian Nation,* runs from page 53 to page 229 in this translation, which is used with the permission of the Institute of Jesuit Sources. This treatise was written in Latin; the other two treatises in this volume were written in Tamil. The first treatise contained many quotations in Sanskrit, the ancient sacred language of India. Since these Sanskrit quotations are immediately followed by an English translation in quotation marks, the Sanskrit has been deleted here.

*faith—and what was an expression of Hindu faith. In 1613 de Nobili wrote
the treatise on Indian customs, part of which is printed here. In 1623 Gregory
XV issued a papal document that largely approved of de Nobili's approach.*[43]
*Unfortunately, several of de Nobili's Portuguese Jesuit superiors disagreed, and
the Jesuits and other Catholic missionaries abandoned his approach after his
death.]*

Chapter 10: What rule should guide us in admitting and judiciously
deciding about India's social customs?

1. *Careful adaptation in missionary method is necessary*

In furthering the conversion of souls and in the matter of adopting or allowing the customs of the unbelievers, the preacher of Christ should always
comport himself in such a manner as to preclude anything that is in the
least sinful, even were he thereby to secure the conversion of the whole
world. He should weigh with all care and discernment which of these customs are purely social, and which are tainted by superstition. Otherwise, it
may well happen that in eagerly pursuing the good of creatures, he may be-
tray both the grace of the Creator and the salvation of his own soul, and (as
happens not infrequently) ultimately render unstable and altogether unprofitable the very spiritual growth he expected for the neighbor. But as
perfectly true as this principle is, we should beware of that other rule which
some people seem to prescribe in deciding matters of custom prevalent
among the people here. That rule goes to the other extreme and sins by excessive scrupulosity; it is so radical that, to judge by the common talk, its
imposition would entail for these people not only the denial of the very necessities of life, but also the forfeiture of everything. Such an extreme policy
(I should think) would find little favor with [St. Paul] who made himself all
things to all men that he might win them all to Christ [1 Cor. 9:22], and
who, far from condemning offhand the various customs of the peoples he
evangelized, made himself, as it were, a man outside the law for the sake of
those who were outside the law.

2. *Three reasons are alleged for condemning certain customs*

Now then, I understand that there are three headings under which not a
few take exception, on the plea that there is superstition in the matter of the
customs and civil manners of ornamentation in vogue among these nations. Their misgivings, in the first place, bear upon certain insignia, on the
ground that these people use those same decorations in their idol-worship.
Second, others object to other practices because they are told that these

---

43. A popular biography of de Nobili is Vincent Cronin, *A Pearl to India: The Life
of Roberto de Nobili* (New York: Dutton, 1959).

heathen men, when observing them, have recourse to some special ritual and recitation. Finally, some other opponents look upon certain objects with suspicion, on the ground that these people regard them as dedicated to various idols and use them as insignia sacred to the gods.

3. Life would be impossible if we condemn those three categories

Well now, if this three-pronged contention were to be taken just as it stands and without any qualification, it would be absolutely impossible, as I have pointed out, to live in India. Not only Indians, but all of us who live in their midst, would have no chance for salvation. For let it be known that the very attitudes which St. Paul so ardently wished to find among his Christian communities in their relations towards the true God, i.e., that in all they do they should always act in the name of Christ—we find that very attitude practiced to a remarkable degree and with great earnestness and exactness in honor of their idols by the heathens who belong to the idolater sect. Indeed, among them there is no action, be it eating, or drinking, or even inhaling air, in fact anything, even of the most ordinary kind and absolutely necessary for life, that is not in some way tainted by superstition. First I shall proceed to show, one by one, what great inconveniences would arise under those three heads I have indicated above. Then, at the end, I shall propose a line of conduct such as will (unless I be greatly mistaken) easily guide anyone in passing judgment on these matters, without danger of loss to these people and without harm to our souls.

4. First group: things used for the idols[44]

So then, as for the first contention, which intends to forbid the use of anything connected with the sacrifices offered up by the heathen of the idolaters' sect: the answer to this is that if the argument were valid, it would follow that to wash one's feet, to wash one's mouth, to gargle, as well as to wash one's hands before sitting down to table, to move a chair to sit on—all these would be unlawful because all these things are done, or are rather imagined to be done, by the idol during the sacrifices offered to Rudra. For the priests present the water successively for each ceremonial act in conformity with the law of the Shaivas [the *Agama*[45]], which describes this type

---

44. De Nobili argues here that to forbid Christians from using everything connected with the Hindu worship of idols would almost bring life to a stop: one could not wash one's feet, hands, or mouth; wear sandals, shirts, or many other garments; use horses and carriages; dance; or play musical instruments.

45. The *Agamas* are three Hindu documents, roughly similar to the Jewish and Christian Bible. The *Shiva-Agama* referred to here teaches that Lord Shiva is the Ultimate Reality. Like the other *Agamas,* it has four parts. The first part deals with philosophical knowledge, the second with mental discipline, the third with building temples and sculpting figures of the gods, the fourth with religious rites and rituals.

of sacrifice: "Remember to present water for cleaning his feet (of Rudra), for gargling, for washing the hands, and also to move the chair he sits on." . . .

Again, playing with musical instruments and dancing as relaxation for the mind would be subject to the same condemnation, since these too are prescribed during the sacrifice in order to entertain the spirit of the idol while it eats and is being provided with everything: "Provide (the idol) with amusement, by means of choice vocal melodies and by playing the musical instruments, and particularly by choral dances."

Similarly banned, too, would be the use of sandals, upper garments, and other items of clothing, the use of carriages, horses, and other vehicles, because these too are gotten ready and provided for the idol. Nay more, these very things must be venerated by the priests at the time when they are presented to the idol, in accordance with the same ordinances: "See to it that various articles of clothing, a carriage and horse or some other conveyance, a pair of sandals, and every other implement is supplied, after duly venerating the same." . . .

From all this, one can see what great hardships would befall human life if all the things which these heathens use for their sacrifices were to be excluded from their social and civil mode of living. There is hardly anything normally used in their civil mode of living which is not requisitioned for the sacrifices of those idolaters. Nay more, the whole ritual procedure adopted at sacrificial functions has been taken from the court ceremonial of the kings and princes, as we read in the same *Agama* a little after the beginning. . . .

Chapter 11: The necessity of sanctioning the ancestral customs prevalent in India insofar as they are purely social.

1. *Violations of social customs are severely punished*

Great is the urgency of allowing the people of India to live according to the social traditions of their forefathers, particularly regarding the ancestral customs of those Indians who live inland, insofar as these are truly compatible with the Christian religion. Far greater indeed is the urgency here than in other parts of the terrestrial globe.

That bad habit common to all nations, to hold fast to their ancestral tradition, is a habit far more deeply rooted in the Indian nation because, confined as they have always been within their own boundaries without ever going abroad and getting to know the splendid civilizations of other nations, they thoughtlessly hold the view that they far surpass other mortal men by the refinement and excellence of their cultural habits. In addition, there is also this singular trait or characteristic, I might say, of this nation among all the other nations, i.e., that they inflict the severest penalties on those who reject the ancestral customs or mere social conventions, as I have indicated at the end of Chapter One of this report.

P. Robertus de Nobilibus Romanus Soc. Iesu

Roberto de Nobili (1577–1656) in Brahmin dress.

In India, apart from the distinct profession its members exercise, each social class boasts its own distinct insignia, its own manner of dress, its own distinct usages and society manners, which they are bound to observe on pain of losing their social grade.[46] This is well known from common practice, and is moreover enjoined in the *Laws of Manu*,[47] in the verse beginning with the words, *shilpena vivaharena*, and in many other texts.[48] Among Indians the loss of one's social grade is considered as the worst of evils. Many would willingly undergo death to redeem it, and not infrequently they do! For as soon as anyone is degraded from the order of his clan he becomes an outcast, deprived of all honor and hereditary dignity, thrown out from any meeting held by members of his grade, scornfully denied any fellowship with his social equals and kinsfolk, and separated from intercourse and companionship with his own family members.

2. *The higher the caste, the severer are the sanctions*

Although this law is common to all of the grades and social orders listed in the same Chapter One, yet it is applied with far greater severity with

46. The Indian caste system assigned people to certain social grades, each of which carried its own distinctive insignia and clothing so that anybody could instantly distinguish persons belonging to the upper castes (e.g., Brahmins [priest-scholars] and soldiers) and treat them with a deference not given to those belonging to the lower castes (e.g., farmers, servants). Only rarely could one climb from one caste to another.

47. *The Laws of Manu* was a classic of ancient Hindu thought, much of which de Nobili memorized. See *The Laws of Manu*, translated by Georg Bühler (New York: Dover Publications, 1969).

48. De Nobili here refers to *The Laws of Manu*, which state that a high-caste family can lose its caste and status "by (practicing) handicrafts, by pecuniary transactions, by (begetting) children on Sudra females only, by (trading in) cows, horses, and carriages, by (the pursuit of) agriculture and by taking service under a king." Ibid., p. 86.

respect to the three orders deemed to constitute the aristocracy: the Brahmins, the rulers, and the merchants. Hence, with reference to them the same legislator, *Manu,* lays down this particular rule: "In regard of the customs which are transmitted by forefathers, as it were by hand, and which in every region are wont to be retained by the three noble clans called the twice-born, let the kings watch with utmost care lest anything repugnant to them be introduced." In Chapter Eight, in the paragraph which begins with the words, "Indeed, it is clearly indicated," we have seen that under the denomination "twice-born" are included only Brahmins, rulers, and merchants, who form the three noble clans.

Moreover, in the case of Brahmins, the law punishes an offender with yet far greater rigor, and precisely on that account it is impossible in this interior part of India which is governed by heathen kings, short of an unheard of divine miracle, for a Brahmin to embrace the faith, unless he be allowed the use of his caste thread and of other cultural and social observances.[49] As soon as a Brahmin rejects the thread, the tuft of hair,[50] and similar caste distinctions which, as I have said, are purely social manners, he not only ceases to be regarded as a Brahmin, but has to face very severe penalties. He will either have his eyes gouged out, or he will be subjected to some public ignominy which they generally dread even more than the loss of their eyesight, i.e., the delinquent, marked with the stigma of lifelong infamy, is banished from all social intercourse to such a degree of barbarity and cruelty that not even his parents will be allowed to approach him under pain of incurring the same penalty. Nor is there any hope of recovering later on either the dignity of their class or their standing in the community. By the king's order their goods and property will be seized and allocated to the public use, to the extent of not leaving them even so much as a loin cloth to cover themselves.

Hence, even should a pagan Brahmin of inland India summon up fortitude enough to bear for Christ's sake a perpetual exile from his parents and his fellow citizens and perpetual infamy and destitution, and even should he not hesitate to betake himself to the towns occupied by the Portuguese with a view to embrace the faith, even in those towns he would have to be supplied with the necessities of life, meals, and clothing, seeing that most Brahmins are incapable of earning a living by manual labor. Such an alternative does not appear to be practicable.

49. According to *The Laws of Manu* members of the upper classes wore a distinctive thread: "A twice-born man is called *upavtin* when his right arm is raised and the sacrificial string or the dress passed under it rests on his left shoulder." Ibid., p. 41.

50. Male Brahmins, the highest caste, shaved their heads except for a ritual tuft of hair, which served to distinguish them as Brahmins.

3. *Necessity of converting the Brahmins to evangelize the other castes*

However that may be, the necessity of allowing the Brahmins the use of their caste thread and other merely social practices may be gathered from yet another consideration. In these interior parts of India, if you exclude Brahmins, then by doing so all the other classes of citizens are mostly kept out. Several reasons account for this situation. First, in India the Brahmins, because of their highest nobility, exercise supreme authority and set the example for all others, so that all follow their example without any further inquiry. Second, since in India the Brahmins alone represent the intellectuals and the teaching profession, from the earliest times it became an established custom for just about everyone from the inferior orders, before attempting anything, particularly in matters connected with the sciences and the religious sects, to take counsel on the subject from some learned Brahmin. It is from this popular attitude that emerges our greatest and most frequently encountered obstacle in the way of the conversion of these heathen. We feel this in our religious community. Almost all of those to whom we propound the catechetical teaching of Christ immediately go to consult the Brahmins or bring them along to our house, since they themselves are conscious of their ignorance in such matters. They do this so that they may learn what their wise men have to say in rebuttal. Thus, well versed in logic and philosophy as these Brahmins are, at once they lead the minds of the inquirers astray by their complicated and abstruse arguments.

4. *All our difficulty comes from want of adaptation*

Moreover, regarding our striving to win these people over to Christ, it is from this source, i.e., from the changeover of these people from their own distinct usages, that our difficulty, indeed a formidable difficulty, mainly springs. When these heathen see that our Christian neophytes discard the caste thread and many other time-honored practices of their own culture, and adopt the manner of foreigners, they come to think that those who apply to us for spiritual instruction change not so much their religious beliefs and practices as the very tenor of their civil grade. Therefore, they look upon them as degenerates, in reality cut off from their former grade and consequently, as I have said, deprived of every civil advantage. This is so true that many heathen who have noticed our way of acting in other Christian communities in India have often come to complain at our residence, loudly declaring that they could not understand why we made it a strict condition for following the law of Christ that one should lower one's civil status and deny oneself all human dignity and every human benefit.

Doubtless, in places subject to Portuguese dominion, the inconveniences which this change in cultural manners entails may perhaps not be so formidable, since neophytes there may be defended and protected by the

Portuguese governors. But the situation is quite different in these inland regions of India entirely under the sway of heathen kings. Here no one can abandon the established social manners of his particular clan unless he is prepared, as I have said, thereby to forfeit—both for himself and for his children—not only his former high social standing, but absolutely every kind of human support towards the preservation of life.

5. Indians expect foreign high castes to behave here as Indian high castes

Before concluding, I make one more remark under this head, a remark no less indispensable in view of the conversion of these inland Indians. The herald of the Gospel must himself, as far as possible, conform his way of acting to the social customs of these people. Otherwise, he will not be regarded by these people as either a trueborn gentleman or as one worthy to move and live among them, much less as one from whom they may learn the teaching of salvation. Experience goes to prove this sufficiently and more than sufficiently. Often used and abused among these people is the familiar saying that the propriety of social behavior varies with the accepted customs of various regions, and that it is the part of a prudent man to conform his way of acting, within the frame of his genetic group and the civil grade to which he belongs, to the corresponding usages of the region where he takes up his abode. The same rule is found in the *Laws of Manu:* "A man acts prudently and appropriately when, in the region where he lives, he adapts himself to the ancestral manners retained there by the men of his own class, whether they represent the highest order, or the middle class of society." Of the same import is another proverbial saying: "The established social custom of each region is equivalent to the corresponding custom of one's clan of origin."

From this the people here naturally conclude that everyone whosoever should be disposed not only to adopt the manners of the country where he lives, but also to consider these as his very own and thus, so to speak, as hereditary and inborn. Hence, regarding that text quoted above, in which *Manu* bids the king to beware of permitting anything that goes counter to the customs of the nobility, the commentator on *Manu* forthwith observes that this ruling is to be understood in conformity with the customs of the region, so that (as he says) immigrants in foreign lands are not to abide by the usages of their country of origin unless these correspond with those of the inhabitants of that place.

On the strength of this general opinion and of the *Laws of Manu*, these people almost necessarily conclude that a foreigner who does not adopt the manners observed by the members of the nobility in their own society is not of noble birth and of high rank, and that, on that score, he is not entitled to free intercourse with them. They believe that anyone who has held the rank of professor and learned man in his own home country would certainly and without hesitation behave in society here like the learned men of this country, and that anyone who claims descent from a royal family of some other land would likewise follow the style and manner of acting of kings here, and similarly regarding persons belonging to other grades of nobility. Were he to act differently, these people would naturally be inclined to conclude that his family is one of those plebeian families of the West, which they know to differ both in social standing and in social customs one from the other.

6. *We may be despised for Christ but not for violating rules of caste*

Now if this attitude [of disregard] sprang from a dislike for the religion of Christ, or if it were confined within the limits of an adverse opinion, it could no doubt be put up with. To be despised and to be looked down upon as of low birth, for Christ's sake, is for the preacher of the Gospel the highest title of nobility. But this is not the case. For one thing, if we are an object of contempt, it is not by reason of our religion, but solely (as I have said) by reason of the social conventions (which we reject). For another thing, this contemptuous attitude is not limited to mere mental disapproval, but it reaches so great an extreme that the heathen are scared and turn away from the Christian teaching, while our recent converts are subjected to cruel persecution and involved in inextricable difficulties. All this is, as I said, to no purpose nor to any advantage, since it has no relation whatever to the faith. Nor do these people understand how anyone can take lessons in right living from a man of low birth, without by that very fact sinking to the low level of social manners and to the mean social standing belonging to that same teacher.

Which man, then, will be induced at such a price to put on the livery of social degradation and contemptible social status? Conversely, who will deny that it is one's first duty of charity, in view of the salvation of souls, to set aside that tenor of life into which one was born, second nature though it may have become to him, and to assume a different one, if this new way of acting is purely of a social character and entirely free from any moral blame? Indeed, who does not know that such a course of action has a sweet force of attraction and has often been adopted by saintly men in cases of less urgency than ours here? To make oneself all to all [in social matters] has from earliest times been the policy of the apostles of the Christian faith. Christ himself, the guide and master of the apostles, did not deem it below his august dignity to move freely with those he came to save, and even to comport himself in their company with such familiarity that on this score he was adversely criticized by the Pharisees[51] and leaders of the people.

---

51. The Pharisees were opponents of Jesus who criticized him for consorting with sinners and not obeying minor Jewish rituals and patterns of behavior: see Mk. 2:16, 2:25, 7:4; Mt. 9:11.

7. Alexander's example of adaptation

In this matter that interests us from a religious viewpoint, let me be allowed to draw an analogy from a secular precedent. What Alexander [the Great] had to say in connection with the subduing of nations conquered by force of arms is well known. He maintained that what most effectively ensured the control of the nations thus conquered was the willing cooperation of a population won over by means of a mutual interchange of social habits.[52] Indeed, I am convinced that the spiritual conquest which is our objective must be achieved in much the same way as that political conquest (which was the objective of that conqueror). Just as the overlord of city-states must [to ensure his sway] adopt many of the local institutions, so too must the ecclesiastical leaders set over the Christian communities. Just as the proper government of nations depends on a policy of give and take, so too the pastoral care of souls in view of heaven must (to use Alexander's words) comprise two things: we must give them certain advantages, and must also learn certain lessons from them. In other words, we must learn and tolerate their human ways of acting in society, so that in turn we may teach and strengthen in them the ways of God.

8. The general approves our method

Therefore our Rev. Father General [Claudio Acquaviva], on being duly informed of the social structure of this nation, realized clearly the problem that the state of affairs in India presents, a problem by no means easier, but rather much more complicated than that which confronts our companions in the Chinese empire. He has therefore been pleased, both on several occasions in previous years and particularly last year, to praise our way of acting and to direct that we should conform ourselves to the ancestral usages of this nation regarding food and clothing and other social practices, insofar as it is necessary, and insofar as a sincere zeal for religion and Christian perfection allows. This connection is necessary lest these poor people, who are withheld from entering upon the way of salvation by ordinary reasons and, in particular, by reasons based in their own religion which by themselves constitute a very serious deterrent, should in addition be further frightened away by this other reason which is of a social character and injurious to their normal mode of life.

By following this method of adaptation, we certainly seem to bring about the desired result. People of every class approach us and listen without fear to the teaching of the faith. Members of royal families and men

---

52. Alexander the Great (356–23 B.C.) was the king of Macedon who conquered the Persian Empire. He tried to integrate Persians into his army and administration and to win their favor by following some of their customs. He also took a Persian wife.

who hold a high position in the state, and, what is more, Brahmins too, well versed in Law and philosophy, do not hesitate to pay us that reverence which befits our calling. Moreover, not a few persons of whatever social rank they may belong, Brahmins included, come to us not only to discuss religious matters, but also become convinced of the truth of our religion and embrace the faith in Christ.

May the infinite goodness and mercy of God vouchsafe for his greater honor and glory to bless this undertaking with solid and lasting results. Praise be to God and to the Most Blessed Virgin Mary!

Roberto de Nobili

Antonio Ruiz de Montoya

The Spiritual Conquest Accomplished by the Religious of the Society of Jesus in the Provinces of Paraguay, Parana, Uruguay, and Tape[53]

[Montoya, the illegitimate son of a Spanish soldier, was born in Lima, Peru, in 1585. He attended the Jesuit College of San Martín in Peru. Though his youth was distinctly dissolute, he later made the Spiritual Exercises, reformed his life, and entered the Jesuits in 1606. Five years later he was ordained. From 1612 to 1622 he worked as a missionary among the Native Americans of the Jesuit province of Peru. Over the next fourteen years he served as the superior at the mission in Guaíra. In 1636 and 1637 he served as superior of all the Jesuit missions among the Guarani Indians. During these years he acquired an exceptional command of the language of the Guarani. He later wrote a Guarani grammar book and dictionary, published in Spain in 1639 and 1640. He also wrote and published a Guarani catechism (1640).

In 1637 the Jesuit provincial superior of Peru sent Montoya to plead with the Spanish King Philip IV to protect the Jesuit reductions. The reductions, large communities for Christian Indians run by Jesuit priests, were being attacked by bandeirantes, *slave raiders largely from São Paulo in Brazil. Chapters 76 and 77 of Montoya's book give a gruesome account of one of these*

53. Antonio Ruiz de Montoya, S.J., *The Spiritual Conquest Accomplished by the Religious of the Society of Jesus in the Provinces of Paraguay, Paraná, Uruguay and Tape,* translated by C. J. McNaspy, John P. Leonard, and Martin E. Palmer, introduction by C. J. McNaspy (St. Louis: Institute of Jesuit Sources, 2003), pp. 48–9, 52–6, 182–5. The selections are used with the permission of the Institute of Jesuit Sources. For a popular overview of the Jesuit work among South American Indians, see Philip Caraman, *The Lost Paradise: The Jesuit Republic in South America* (New York: Seabury, 1976).

chronic raids. [54] *This book, which was written from memory in 1639 while Montoya was waiting to make his case before Philip IV, was published that same year in Madrid. Undoubtedly Montoya hoped it would encourage support for the missions and opposition to the slave raiders. His petition to the king stressed, among other points, that governors should enforce previous laws against enslaving Indians and that Indian captives should be freed and sent to Buenos Aires, where the Jesuits would arrange their transport back to their homes and families. Most controversial was Montoya's argument that Indians should be allowed to acquire firearms so they could repel the well-armed bandeirantes. Neither Portuguese nor Spanish settlers wanted Indians to have firearms. Montoya returned to Peru in 1640 with royal approval for many of his petitions. But there was little Philip IV could really do to help the missions, since he was facing three severe crises of his own in 1640: Spain was at war with France, the Spanish kingdom of Catalonia was in revolt, and Portugal and Brazil (ruled by the kings of Spain since 1580) were now fighting successfully for independence. Since the* bandeirantes *were invading the Jesuit missions in Paraguay from Brazil, there was little the Spanish king could now do to stop them. Save for a brief period spent with his beloved Indians in Paraguay, Montoya's last years (1640–52) were lived out in Lima.]*

Chapter 10. *Customs of the Guarani Indians.*

The pagans lived, and still live today, in quite small villages (as already mentioned), but not without government. They had their caciques [chiefs], who were universally recognized as possessing noble status inherited from their ancestors, based upon their having had vassals and ruled over people. Many acquire noble status through eloquence of speech, so great is their esteem for their language—rightly so, for it is worthy of praise and of being celebrated among the tongues of renown. By their eloquence they gather followers and vassals, thus ennobling both themselves and their descendants. The common folk serve them; they clear their ground and sow and reap their crops; they build their houses and give them their daughters to the caciques when they crave them. In this matter they behave with pagan freedom: we met some with fifteen, twenty, or thirty wives. A surviving brother sometimes takes his dead brother's wives, but this is not common. In this regard they show the greatest reserve towards their mothers and sisters, and would not even think of having relations with them, considering it a crime against nature. Even after becoming Christians, if they are related

54. Similar raids more than a century later are vividly depicted in the 1986 movie *The Mission.*

to a woman in any degree, even one that is dispensable or licit without dispensation, they will not without dispensation admit her as wife, asserting that she is their own blood. . . . To this day Christian caciques do not marry common women, but those from the prominent families; they are very particular about this, even though common women may be naturally endowed. Many arguments confirm that they never had permanent wives. Being people without contracts of any sort, they never had any thought of the burdensome contract of permanent marriage. Moreover, as lovers of freedom and ease, they considered it disgraceful for a man to be bound to one wife by a tie he could not dissolve at will. Others have found grounds for the opposite opinion; my purpose is not to decide debates. They knew of God's existence, and even in a certain way of his unity. This is gathered from the name they give him, *Tupá*. The first syllable, *tu*, expresses wonder, while the second, *pá*, is an interrogative; thus it corresponds to the Hebrew word *Man-hu*, "What is this?" in the singular. They never had idols, though the devil was already imposing upon them to venerate the bones of certain Indians who had been famous magicians during their lifetimes, as we shall see later. . . .

Chapter 11. *Our method for ending these abuses and preaching the faith.*
At this time a companion joined us. He was Father Martín Urtasun, a native of Pamplona, where he abandoned his inheritance as eldest son, an income of three thousand ducats, for the rumor of rich mines of souls in the poor province of Paraguay. We divided ourselves between two settlements, Loreto and San Ignacio, a pair of us working in each. We set up a school to teach the youth reading and writing, and indicated a period of one hour every morning and evening for the adults to come to catechism classes. Although in these classes and in the sermons we gave each Sunday we treated the mysteries of our holy faith and the commandments of God with all clarity, we kept silence in public on the sixth commandment so as not to wither these tender plants and arouse hatred for the gospel. Those in danger of death, however, we instructed with all clarity. This silence lasted two years, and was quite necessary, as the outcome proved, as we shall see. The devil tried to tempt our purity through the caciques' offering to us some of their women on the complaint that they considered it unnatural for men to engage in domestic work such as cooking, sweeping, and the like.

We gave them a full account of priestly chastity, explaining that this was why our first concern had been to enclose a small area around our house with a stake fence to keep women from entering our house. They marveled at our doing so; however being barbarians, they did not find it admirable since among them it was a matter of honor and prestige to have numerous wives and serving women, a widespread failing among pagans. Besides the town of San Ignacio, Fathers José and Martín had two others as colonies to which they went as needed. Father Simón and I had one at Loreto, three quarters of a league distant. Its cacique was a valiant and respected Indian named Roque Maracaná, who was venerated by the whole territory. We took turns every Sunday going there to catechize these people, all recently settled. As they were very numerous, this gave us a great deal of labor, although it was welcome because of the large numbers being won for baptism. We had adults and sick people with whom we were obliged to handle the topics of marriage and monogamy, and this demanded much effort. This was our regular practice; at daybreak we would visit the sick; then we would celebrate Mass, with a sermon after the gospel, after which the pagans were dismissed, much to their chagrin at seeing themselves ejected from the church like dogs. They envied the Christians who stayed behind, and this spurred them to learn the catechism for baptism as soon as possible and to set aside every obstacle. Taking time out at noon to pray the hours of the divine office, we would return (still fasting so as not to annoy the Indians by asking for anything) to the church where we gave instruction, baptizing up to two, three, or four hundred each day. Night had already fallen when we would return to Loreto exhausted and with our heads bursting, still fasting and with no desire to eat. Our Father Martín Urtasun soon died from this toil, as we shall recount.

We Fathers in San Ignacio had a prominent cacique who, after varied fortunes in different places, where he was baptized and married, finally by his eloquence became as it were lord of the people there. He was a servant of the devil. Attracted to a woman, not for her beauty but her noble status, he repudiated his legitimate wife, banishing her to a farm and putting the girl in her place with the title of legitimate wife. With shameless effrontery he asserted that she was his legal wife, and she had herself waited on as mistress of numerous serving women. The poor wretch went even further with his fraudulence; to gain greater prestige with his followers, he pretended to be a priest. In his private chamber he would put on an alb; robed in a mozetta[55] of brilliant feathers and other adornments, he pretended to say Mass. He would spread a table with cloths and place upon them a manioca cake and a painted cup of maize wine; muttering a number of ritual formulas, he would show the cake and wine as priests do, finally eating and drinking everything. His vassals consequently venerated him as a priest. His life was exceptionally scandalous as he had a large number of concubines, with the full consent and encouragement of his pretended wife. We baptized eight of his infant children—the year's crop—all of them blessed indeed for they died shortly after being baptized. Our own purity and modesty was an offense to him; he disliked our obliging the sick and those who wanted to

55. A mozetta is a short cape with a small ornamented hood.

be truly cleansed through baptism to give up their concubines. His resentment reached such a pitch that he began to incite his vassals' minds against us. In various gatherings he told them: "The devils have brought us these men, for with new teachings they want to take away from us the good old way of life of our ancestors, who had many wives and servant women and were free to choose them at will. Now they want us to tie ourselves to a single woman. It is not right for this to go any further; we should drive them out of our lands, or take their lives."

There were many among them who had love for us and esteemed our virtue, good example, and teaching. These put him off with the suggestion that it would not be good to carry out his design without consulting Roque Maracaná for his opinion, and that, if he agreed, it could be put into effect. Then this cacique, whose name was Miguel Artiguaye, came to visit the Fathers, seemingly friendly and with smiling countenance. After a few words of courtesy, he turned into a wild beast and burst out shouting—"You are no priests sent from God to aid our misery; you are devils from hell, sent by their ruler for our destruction. What teaching have you brought us? What peace and happiness? Our ancestors lived in liberty. They enjoyed all the women they wanted, without hindrance from anyone. Thus they lived and spent their lives in happiness, and you want to destroy their traditions and impose on us this heavy burden of being bound to a single wife." And as he left the room he said: "This shall not be; I am going to do something about it." The Fathers, who had listened like lambs to this wolf's howlings, tried detaining him to reason with his irrationality, but without success. On the contrary, he went on shouting with uncontrollable diabolical fury: "We can no longer tolerate the freedom of these men who want to compel us in our own lands to live in their evil fashion."

Chapter 12. *Departure of this cacique from his town to discuss his evil intention with Roque Maracaná, and what happened to him.*

The following night Miguel conferred on this matter with his people, as did the Fathers with God. The upshot was that at daybreak great racket and din was heard throughout the settlement—preparations for war, drums, flutes, and other instruments. Three hundred warriors assembled in the town square, armed with shields, swords, bows, and great quantities of arrows, all splendid with rich painting and variegated feathering. On their heads they wore gorgeous feathered crowns. The most elaborately decked out was the cacique Miguel. He wore a rich robe all of varicolored feathers very skillfully woven; on his head was a feathered crown. He was armed with a sword and shield; at his sides walked two burly young fellows each bearing a bow and a large quiver of arrows for the cacique. At the head of all these people he set off to embark on the river. They left the landing with a great show of bravery, to the sound of flute and drum.

Let us leave them for the moment on their way downstream and return to Father José and his companions. Apprehensive about this journey, they could only conclude that it was to consult with Roque Maracaná about their deaths and then, with his approval, to kill Father Simón and me at Loreto and then return to kill themselves [spiritually]. This was confirmed by the opinion of some who remained in the settlement. Further, the cacique Miguel had been heard to say: "These Fathers will wake up one morning with their heads gone." The probability of the cacique Roque's going along with him was increased by his own vested interest in the many young women he possessed and by his being a very unrestrained and impetuous young man.

Amid these discussions the Fathers withdrew to hold a spiritual conference on how they should go about preparing to meet death. They decided to make a general confession of their entire lives (although in the general confession of his whole life which Father Martín made a few months later as he died in my arms, I found nothing that was or that I could conjecture to be serious). They made their confession for death, placing themselves in the hands of God, whose protection was their only defense. In this predicament our Lord came to his servants' rescue in the following manner.

Beyond San Ignacio there was another quite large town made up of people whom we had settled there. Their cacique was an excellent Indian named Araraá. Immediately upon hearing of the cacique Miguel's defiance, he dispatched a good boat with a message to the Fathers: "I have learned of that cacique's shamelessness and of his plan to kill you. I would be greatly pleased if you would come to this town of yours for protection against your enemy. You will not lack for anything you need or for people to defend you, for I have vassals who will be able to do it. So that your coming will not be delayed for want of a boat, I am sending you this one and look forward to seeing you here in this town of yours."

Unwilling to show cowardice and trusting in God, the Fathers preferred to await whatever happened. So, replying to his offer with gratitude, they remained in continuous prayer, which is mightier than any weapons, as was proved that very day.

The cacique Roque—along with Father Simón and myself—was quite unaware of all this agitation, when he heard a great hubbub and the beating of drums. He asked his servants what this unexpected occurrence was all about. Once fully informed, he called for a sword and seized a shield, showing himself valiant (as indeed he was) and very well disposed. The cacique Miguel leapt ashore. His soldiers lined up in two rows, with himself as commander in the middle, grasping his shield and girded with his sword. In the style of the ancient nobles, he began striding and shouting aloud: "My brothers and sons, the time is over for bearing the evils and disasters these men we call Fathers have brought on us. They shut us up in a house (he meant church) where they harangue us and tell us the opposite of what our ancestors did and taught us: our ancestors had many wives, and these men take them away from us and demand that we be content with one. We do not agree to this; let us take measures against these evils."

The cacique Roque advanced a few paces from his house, escorted by only twelve or fourteen of his vassals armed with bows and arrows. Miguel paid his compliments. Before letting him go forward, Roque asked: "Are you bringing letters from the Fathers of your town for the Fathers down here?" Miguel replied: "This is no time for letters but for honoring our ancestors' way of life and for doing away with these Fathers and enjoying our women and our freedom." At this, Roque lunged at him; seizing him by the front of his clothes and giving him a couple of hard jerks, he flung him to the ground. Miguel, his shield, and his sword went rolling off in different directions. Turning to his men, Roque said; "No one shoot an arrow. Let them start; I will finish them off if they do, for I am going to punish this fellow's impudence." Poor Miguel, seeing how ill he was received, shouted to his men: "Let's retreat, let's retreat!" They all did so. He had himself taken across the river, about a musket-shot wide. There he leapt ashore, stripped off his fancy clothes along with his crown and feathers, dressed in a shirt or coat he got from an Indian, left behind his sword and shield, and, with a staff in hand like a penitent, set off for his own town alone with a servant.

The Fathers there were anxious to learn if they had already killed us, expecting their own end as well, when they caught sight of Miguel, unrecognized in his garb. He came in the Fathers' doors, fell to his knees, folded his hands, and said: "For the love of Jesus Christ and St. Ignatius, I implore you to forgive my stupid insolence towards you. I was crazy and had lost my judgment, but now I have got it back, because God has punished my pride, and so I beg your forgiveness. You have preached to us how readily God forgives those who offend him; imitate him and forgive me. Furthermore I beg you to shield and defend me, for I have good reason to fear that these people will kill me. I certainly deserve death for my folly, but as true Fathers and servants of God you have to pardon and protect me."

Father Jose took him in his arms. As a father, after all, even to such an evil son and as true and loving shepherd, he raised him from the ground and consoled him, warning him to look out in the future and to choose the true path after experiencing how badly his mad schemes had turned out. Thus was the tempest calmed. Miguel pretended to give up his concubine, the cause of all this trouble, and brought his true wife home. Outwardly pretending to live a good life, he continued to live a bad one, and thus died an evil death, as we shall recount.

Chapter 76. *Invasion of the reduction of San Cristóbal.*

The reduction of San Cristóbal was four leagues from that of Jesús-María. Father Juan Agustín de Contreras was in charge. He had been in the devastated province of Guaíra, and when he saw the brutalities they [the *bandeirantes,* Spanish slave traders] were already starting to perpetrate, he moved all his people to the reduction of Santa Ana, only three leagues away. The Father had hardly left when they invaded, pillaging and laying waste the food supplies. Sixteen hundred of our warriors assembled to hold off the enemy until the reinforcements that had been requested from other towns could arrive. In Jesús-María the Castilians already had a stake fort or corral for assembling their prey, twice the size of the plaza here in Madrid. They set up a church there, where the two chaplains said Mass—whether for rescuing souls from purgatory or for capturing the living I cannot say. The fugitive secular priest, who had been publicly denounced for leaving his curacy without permission, was under excommunication by his bishop. Both said Mass in the wilderness, using the privilege given those who convert Indians and settle them in reductions—deeming there to be no difference between settling them and subjugating them by violence.

Our sixteen hundred Indians were in San Cristóbal, where they celebrated Christmas by hearing Mass with what little joy their deadly enemy allowed them. Under the assumption that the Spanish would remain inactive that day, at least following the example of the brutes—"the ox knows its owner"—and refraining from violence on such a blessed day, the people scattered in search of food. But as St. John rightly said of the Jews, "His own did not know him" [John 1:11]. The raiders from São Paulo thought quite differently: the great festival was a perfect opportunity to catch the people hearing Mass in church, unarmed and intent only on their devotions. They put their plan into effect.

When our men realized this, they mustered and fought defiantly for five hours; it would have lasted longer if night had not taken away the daylight. Even with such unequal weapons—the Indians having no covering and only frail cane arrows while the Spanish [i.e., the *bandeirantes*] were well protected and armed with muskets—they twice forced them into a forest and nearly took their flag. Many died on both sides, until night separated them. The Spanish had seized the area of the church, which they immediately sent up in flames—not the sort of action one would have expected on such a holy day.

Chapter 77. *The reduction of Santa Ana retreats to that of Natividad; cruelties of the enemy.*

News of these events reached me at a considerable distance. Traveling as rapidly as I could, I arrived that same Christmas day at the reduction of

Santa Ana. There I found a terrible panic. We spent the whole night in the consultation that was required to meet these calamities. The conclusion was to move the people from this town and from San Cristóbal to Natividad; it was a fairly strong position because of a river that would hold up the enemy, and lay only four leagues away.

The number of the refugees was huge. The river passage was fortified with a good rampart which afforded a sufficient defense against the enemy's seizing our boats as they ferried across the quantities of people who arrived daily in flight from the enemy. Our soldiers wanted to attack the enemy's fort, but we dissuaded them from this obviously risky project. It would be better to await the enemy in the open, where they had taken control of the cultivated land. Here our men were able to operate more effectively: laying ambushes in the woods at every step, they succeeded in killing many without danger to themselves. Already many of the enemy were afraid to go out and forage, sure they would be killed. This tactic eventually succeeded in forcing the enemy to raise camp and leave us.

Our provincial, Father Diego de Boroa, attempted to parley with the enemy, as though they were capable of reason. Several of us Fathers went with him. We found twenty corpses in San Cristóbal, cruelly hacked and bullet-ridden; we stopped to bury them. We found a little pagan girl, about seven years old, lost in the woods; she had two cruel wounds, a long one on her face and another on the head, both covered with maggots. She told us her calamitous story as follows.

"I was with my parents and your children. The men burst upon our houses and divided us among themselves. My little brother and I were taken by a different master, and to this day I have heard nothing of my parents. Finding ourselves both orphans and slaves, we ran away hoping to find you so that you could protect us as our Fathers. They chased us and in a terrible rage gave these wounds to me and another on the neck to my little brother that left him unable to move his head. Then they left us for dead. I came to my senses and realized that my little brother was still alive. I ran in panic into the woods, carrying my little brother in my arms. I was with him for three days, without food or drink and sustained by the hope that he would recover consciousness and we would be able to go on. But, with him at his end and myself as you found me, I abandoned him still alive, though I was torn with grief. I tried to carry him on my back, but I could not." We treated her body and her soul as well through baptism. At every step we stumbled across corpses—beheaded, pierced with arrows, or hacked to death.

We reached the palisade they had put up in Jesús-María, where the first battle took place. It had been a fragrant flowerbed of pagans who had become Christians, whose promise for the future seemed secure but now that they are in captivity is considered doubtful. We were met by a terrible odor from the dead, the stench so overpowering that we were unable to tally them. We found only one woman alive, but she was unable to speak and a swarm of flies were sucking on her. We prized her teeth open with a knife and gave her a drink of wine; then she could talk and said, "Oh, they have taken away my mother, my brother, and all I possess!" She made her confession and then gave up her soul. She might well have been burned to death along with so many others, but it was her good fortune that her hut lay aside from the rest and was not reached by the fire. No one will ever be able to form an idea what I myself am incapable of writing down. Here we did not find, as elsewhere, bodies of people hacked to death or with their throats cut, women split open by sabers; here we found rational human beings—children, women, men—who had been roasted alive. We saw one woman roasted to death with her twin children, who had been burned as they clung to her.

These murderers have the common practice, when departing with their booty, of burning the sick, the aged, and those unable to travel, for if they remain alive, those who leave will remember them and try to go back. We spent many hours carrying the charred bodies to a trench, into which we threw them one after another. The spectacle was such that four hundred Indians who accompanied us, stricken at the sight, turned on their heels and left us.

We found another woman who had miraculously escaped sword and fire. They had tried to take her prisoner, but she resisted stoutly, saying that she wanted to die as a Christian among the Fathers. They dragged her and beat her, but finding her unyielding they gave her a deadly wound on the head, smashing her face with a rock. To make sure she was dead, they tried to burn her; but the fire showed itself merciful, to the shame of their inhuman fury. We found her nearly gone, but with human support and the divine support of baptism, she preserved her freedom and her life.

Many who have traversed the forests there have assured us that they were strewn with the corpses of people who had fled and been hunted down with sabers, swords, and cutlasses. And if these actions are a disgrace to Christianity and to the gospel itself, which falls into discredit and repels the pagans, what a disgrace to Christianity will it not be that Christians have befouled the very altar where the life-giving sacrifice of the Mass had so long been celebrated! They disfigured the altar and used it for their filthy purposes. It broke our hearts to see this irreverence.

The number of people they took away is not known, but some indication may be given by the tithes they paid the church: they gave five hundred persons to the Religious [Order priest] as his share, just as a cattle herder pays a tithe of his sheep or cows. The secular priest got two hundred.

These events, in sum, constituted my motive for coming to the font of justice and to His Majesty's feet. I consider this a blessed task, confident as I am that the necessary measures will be taken so that those sheep, enjoying the meadows allotted them by nature (that is, their own lands) may exercise that freedom which is common to all, and, expressing their gratitude through whatever tribute their poverty permits, may live protected by the powerful arm with which His Majesty (may God grant him increase) defends his own vassals.[56]

Jean de Brébeuf

"Important Advice to Those Whom It Shall Please God to Call to New France, Especially the Country of the Hurons"

[The French were the first to colonize Canada; they also explored much of the American Midwest. They established towns and fortresses west from Pittsburgh to St. Louis, and south to New Orleans. Jesuit missionaries such as Jacques Marquette (1637–75) were among the first white men to explore much of this vast region.

French Jesuit missionaries attempted to bring Christianity to the Native Americans of Canada and the Midwest. Jean de Brébeuf (1593–1649) was arguably the greatest of these missionaries. Born and raised in Normandy, Brébeuf entered the Jesuits at Rouen after completing his university studies and was ordained in 1622. He volunteered to serve as a missionary in Canada and arrived at Quebec in June 1625. He was soon assigned to work among the Hurons, who lived some eight hundred miles to the west and south of Quebec. The Hurons, who came to the French settlements to trade furs, did not want to take Brébeuf and his Jesuit companion to their lands, but generous gifts persuaded them. Brébeuf was a large and powerful man—his size proved a disadvantage on the month-long canoe trip, except on the portages, where his ability to carry heavy loads impressed the Hurons. Once settled among the Hurons, he had to learn their language and study their beliefs and customs. He wrote a Huron grammar book and translated a catechism. Still, converts were hard to come by. The Huron priests blamed a drought on the Jesuits. France's defeat in a minor war against the English forced Brébeuf to return to France from 1629 to 1633; it was there that he wrote the document printed here. He returned to the Huron mission in 1634.

---

56. This is the end of Montoya's account. He then appends three more chapters containing related documents. One is a letter from the governor of Buenos Aires to Philip IV in which the governor relates that he saw in Rio de Janeiro how the Indians captured by the citizens of São Paulo were being sold as slaves. He calculates that sixty thousand Indians were abducted from the Jesuit reductions.

On March 16, 1649, Brébeuf was captured during an Iroquois attack on the village where he was working. After repeatedly torturing him, the Iroquois cut out his heart and ate it. The Iroquois later destroyed most of the Huron nation, whose remnants drifted to Ontario, Ohio, Michigan, and Wisconsin. Brébeuf and the seven other Jesuit North American martyrs were canonized in 1930.[57]

This excerpt from Brébeuf was written to warn eager young Jesuits about the hardships they would face if they volunteered to work in North America.[58] *According to Brébeuf only the truly courageous should apply. Brébeuf stresses both the physical hardships and the spiritual consolations such young men will experience in bringing help to a people with a frugal lifestyle and dangerous enemies. This document was printed in the* Jesuit Relations *of 1636. (The* Relations *were annual reports that described the work of Jesuit missionaries and encouraged Frenchmen to support the Jesuits' work.)]*

We have learned that the salvation of so many innocent souls, washed and made white in the blood of the Son of God, is stirring very deeply the hearts of many, and is exciting new desires in them to leave old France that they may come to the New France. God be forever blessed that he, as this shows us, has at last opened to these Tribes the bowels of his infinite pity. I wish not to chill the ardor of this generous resolution. Alas! it is those hearts after God's own heart whom we are expecting; but I only wish to give one word of advice.

It is true that "Love is as strong as death" [S. of S. 8:6], the love of God has power to do what death does,—that is to say, to detach us entirely from creatures and from ourselves; nevertheless, these desires that we feel of working for the safety of infidels are not always sure signs of that pure love. There may be sometimes a little self-love and regard for ourselves, if we look only at the blessing and satisfaction of putting souls in heaven without considering fully the pains, the labors, and the difficulties which are inseparable from these evangelical functions.

57. For a detailed biography, see Joseph P. Donnelly, S.J., *Jean de Brébeuf, 1592–1649* (Chicago: Loyola University Press, 1975). For a sample of Brébeuf's writings and those of the other North American martyrs, see *An Autobiography of Martyrdom: Spiritual Writings of the Jesuits in New France,* edited by François Roustang, translated by M. Renelle (St. Louis: Herder Books, 1964).

58. This excerpt is found in Reuben G. Thwaites, *The Jesuit Relations and Allied Documents* (Cleveland: Burrows Bros., 1896–1901), vol. 10, pp. 87–115. Latin quotations scattered through the document have been translated by John Patrick Donnelly.

On this account, in order that no one may be deceived in regard to this, I will show him how much he ought to suffer for the name of Jesus. True, the two who came last, Fathers Mercier and Pijart, had no such trouble in their journey as those of us who came here the year before. They did not paddle; their men were not sick, as ours were; they had not to bear the heavy loads. Yet notwithstanding this, easy as may be a trip with the savages, there is always enough to greatly cast down a heart not well under subjection. The readiness of the savages does not shorten the road, does not smooth down the rocks, does not remove the dangers. Be with whom you like, you must expect to be, at least, three or four weeks on the way, to have as companions persons you have never seen before; to be cramped in a bark canoe in an uncomfortable position, not being free to turn yourself to one side or the other; in danger fifty times a day of being upset or of being dashed upon the rocks. During the day, the sun burns you; during the night, you run the risk of being a prey to mosquitoes. You sometimes ascend five or six rapids in a day; and, in the evening, the only refreshment is a little corn crushed between two stones and cooked in fine clear water; the only bed is the earth, sometimes only the rough, uneven rocks, and usually no roof but the stars; and all this in perpetual silence. If you are accidentally hurt, if you fall sick, do not expect from these barbarians any assistance, for whence could they obtain it? And if the sickness is dangerous, and if you are remote from the villages, which are here very scattered, I would not like to guarantee that they would not abandon you, if you could not push yourself to keep up with them.

When you reach the Hurons, you will indeed find hearts full of charity; we will receive you with open arms as an Angel of Paradise, we shall have all the inclination in the world to do you good; but we are so situated that we can do very little. We shall receive you in a hut, so mean that I have scarcely found in France one wretched enough to compare it with; that is how you will be lodged. Harassed and fatigued as you will be, we shall be able to give you nothing but a poor mat, or at most a skin, to serve you as a bed; and, besides, you will arrive at a season when miserable little insects that we call here Taouhac, and, in good French, fleas, will keep you awake almost all night, for in these countries they are incomparably more troublesome than in France; the dust of the cabin nourishes them, the savages bring them to us, we get them in their houses; and this petty martyrdom, not to speak of mosquitoes, sand flies, and other like vermin, lasts usually not less than three or four months of the summer.

Instead of being a great master and great theologian as in France, you must reckon on being here a humble Scholar, and then, good God! with what masters!—women, little children, and all the savages, and exposed to their laughter. The Huron language will be your Saint Thomas and your

Aristotle;[59] and clever man as you are, and speaking glibly among learned and capable persons, you must make up your mind to be for a long time mute among the barbarians. You will have accomplished much, if, at the end of a considerable time, you begin to stammer a little.

And then how do you think you would pass the Winter with us? After having heard all that must be endured in wintering among the Montagnet savages,[60] I may say that is almost the life we here lead among the Hurons. I say it without exaggeration, the five and six months of winter are spent in almost continual discomforts,—excessive cold, smoke, and the annoyance of the savages; we have a cabin built of simple bark, but so well jointed that we have to send some one outside to learn what kind of weather it is; the smoke is very often so thick, so annoying, and so obstinate that, for five or six days at a time, if you are not entirely proof against it, it is all you can do to make out a few lines in your Breviary. Besides, from morning until evening our fireplace is almost always surrounded by savages, above all, they seldom fail to be there at mealtimes. If you happen to have anything more than usual, let it be ever so little, you must reckon on most of these gentlemen as your guests; if you do not share with them, you will be considered mean. As regards the food, it is not so bad, although we usually content ourselves with a little corn, or a morsel of dry smoked fish, or some fruits, of which I shall speak further on. For the rest, thus far we have had only roses; henceforth, as we have Christians in almost every village, we must count on making rounds through them at all seasons of the year and on remaining there, according to necessity, for two or three whole weeks, amid annoyances that cannot be described. Add to all this, that our lives depend upon a single thread; and if, wherever we are in the world, we are to expect death every hour, and to be prepared for it, this is particularly the case here. For not to mention that your cabin is only, as it were, chaff, and that it might be burned at any moment despite all your care to prevent accidents, the malice of the savages gives especial cause for almost perpetual fear; a malcontent may burn you down, or cleave your head open in some lonely spot. And then you are responsible for the sterility or fecundity of the earth, under penalty of your life; you are the cause of droughts; if you cannot make rain, they speak of nothing less than making away with you. I have only to mention, in addition, the danger there is from our enemies; it is enough to say that, on the thirteenth of this month of June, they killed twelve of our Hurons near the village of Contarrea, which is only a day's journey from us; that a short time before, at four leagues from our village, some Iroquois

59. The theological training of the early Jesuits was based on the writings of St. Thomas Aquinas; their philosophical training was based on Aristotle.

60. The Montagnets were a tribe of Canadian Indians who lived on the north shore of the Gulf of St. Lawrence and spoke an Algonquian dialect.

were discovered in the fields in ambush, only waiting to strike a blow at the expense of the life of some passer-by. This [Huron] nation is very timid, they take no precautions against surprise, they are not careful to prepare arms or to inclose their villages with palisades; their usual recourse, especially when the enemy is powerful, is flight. Amid these alarms, which affect the whole country, I leave you to imagine if we have any grounds for a feeling of safety. After all, if we had here the exterior attractions of piety, as they exist in France, all this might pass. In France the great multitude and the good example of Christians, the solemnity of the feasts, the majesty of the churches so magnificently adorned, preach piety to you; and in the houses of our Order the fervor of our brethren, their modesty, and all the noble virtues which shine forth in all their actions, are so many powerful voices which cry to you without ceasing, "Go and do likewise" [Lk. 10:37]. You have the consolation of celebrating every day the holy Mass; in a word you are almost beyond the danger of falling, at least, the falls are insignificant, and you have help immediately at hand. Here we have nothing, it seems, which incites towards good; we are among peoples who are astonished when you speak to them of God, and who often have only horrible blasphemies in their mouths. Often you are compelled to deprive yourself of the holy sacrifice of the Mass; and, when you have the opportunity to say it, a little corner of your cabin will serve you for a chapel, which the smoke, the snow, or the rain hinders you from ornamenting and embellishing, even if you had the means. I pass over the small chance of seclusion there is among barbarians, who scarcely ever leave you, who hardly know what it is to speak in a low tone. Especially I would not dare to speak of the danger there is of ruining oneself among their impurities, in the case of any one whose heart is not sufficiently full of God to firmly resist this poison. But enough of this; the rest can only be known by experience.

"But is this all?" someone will ask. "Do you think by your arguments to throw water on the fire that consumes me, and lessen ever so little the zeal I have for the conversion of these peoples? I declare that these things have served only to confirm me the more in my vocation; that I feel myself more carried away than ever by my affection for New France, and that I bear a holy jealousy toward those who are already enduring all these sufferings; all these labors seem to me nothing, in comparison with what I am willing to endure for God; if I knew a place under heaven where there was yet more to be suffered, I would go there." Ah, whoever you are to whom God gives these sentiments and this light, come, come, my dear brother, it is workmen such as you that we ask for here; it is to souls like yours that God has appointed the conquest of so many other souls whom the Devil holds yet in his power; apprehend no difficulties,—there will be none for you, since it is your whole consolation to see yourself crucified with the Son of God; silence will be sweet to you, since you have learned to commune with God, and to converse in the heavens with saints and angels; the food would be very insipid if the gall endured by our Lord did not render them sweeter and more savory to you than the most delicious delicacies of the world. What a satisfaction to pass these rapids, and to climb these rocks, to him who has before his eyes that loving Savior, harassed by his tormentors and ascending Calvary laden with his Cross; the discomfort of the canoe is very easy to bear, to him who considers the crucified one. What a consolation! For I must use such terms, as otherwise I could not give you pleasure. What a consolation, then, to see oneself even abandoned on the road by the savages, languishing with sickness, or even dying with hunger in the woods, and of being able to say to God, "My God, it is to do your holy will that I am reduced to the state in which you see me,"—considering above all that God-man who expires upon the Cross and cries to his Father, "My God, my God, why have you forsaken me" [Mt. 27:46]. If God among all these hardships preserve you in health, no doubt you will arrive pleasantly in the Huron country with these holy thoughts. "He sails smoothly who is carried by God's grace."

And now, as regards a place of abode, food, and beds—shall I dare to say to a heart so generous, and that mocks at all that of which I have already spoken, that truly, even though we have hardly more of those necessities than the savages have, still, I know not how, the divine Goodness renders every difficult thing easy; and all and every one of us find everything almost as comfortable as life is in France. The sleep we get lying on our mats seems to us as sweet as if we were in a good bed; the food of the country does not disgust us, although there is scarcely any other seasoning than that which God has put into it; and, notwithstanding the cold of a winter six months long, passed in the shelter of a bark cabin open to the daylight, we have still to experience its evil effects; no one complains of his head or his stomach; we do not know what diarrhoea, colds, or catarrh are. This leads me to say that delicate persons do not know, in France, how to protect themselves from the cold; those rooms so well carpeted, those doors so well fitted, and those windows closed with so much care, serve only to make its effects more keenly felt; it is an enemy from whom one wins almost more by holding out one's hands to him than by waging a cruel war upon him. As to our food, I shall say this further, that God has shown his providence very clearly to our eyes; we have obtained in eight days our provision of corn for a whole year, without making a single step beyond our cabin. They have brought us dried fish in such quantities that we are constrained to refuse some of it, and to say that we have sufficient; you might say that God, seeing we are here only for his service, in order that all our work may be for him, wishes to act himself as our provider. This same Goodness takes care to give us from time to time a change of provisions in the shape of fresh fish. We live on the shore of a great lake, which affords as good fish as I have ever seen or eaten in France; true, as I have said, we do not ordinarily procure them, and still less do we get meat, which is even more rarely seen here. Fruits even, according to the season, provided the year be somewhat favorable, are not lacking to us; strawberries, raspberries, and blackberries are to be found in almost incredible quantities. We gather plenty of grapes, which are fairly good; the squashes last sometimes four and five months, and are so abundant that they are to be had almost for nothing, and so good that, on being cooked in the ashes, they are eaten as apples are in France. Consequently, to tell the truth, as regards provisions, the change from France is not very great; the only grain of the country is a sufficient nourishment, when one is somewhat accustomed to it. The savages prepare it in more than twenty ways and yet employ only fire and water; it is true that the best sauce is that which it carries with it.

As for the dangers of the soul, to speak frankly, there are none for him who brings to the country of the Hurons the fear and love of God; on the contrary, I find unparalleled advantages for acquiring perfection. Is it not a great deal to have, in one's food, clothing, and sleep, no other attraction than bare necessity? Is it not a glorious opportunity to unite oneself with God, when there is no creature whatsoever that gives you reason to spend your affection upon it? when the exercises you practice constrain you without force to inward meditation? Besides your spiritual exercises, you have no other employment than the study of the language and conversation with the savages. Ah, how much pleasure there is for a heart devoted to God to make itself the little scholar of a savage and of a little child, thereby to gain them for God, and to render them disciples of our Lord! How willingly and liberally God communicates himself to a soul which practices from love of him these heroic acts of humility! The words he learns are so many treasures he amasses, so many spoils he carries off from the common enemy of the human race; so that he has reason to say a hundred times a day, "I rejoice at your word like one who finds great spoils" [Ps. 119:162]. Viewed in this light, the visits of the savages, however frequent, cannot be annoying to him. God teaches him the beautiful lesson he taught formerly to Saint Catherine of Siena,[61] to make of his heart a room or temple for him, where he will never fail to find him, as often as he withdraws into it; that, if he encounters savages there, they do not interfere with his prayers, they serve only to make them more fervent; from this he takes occasion to present these poor wretches to this sovereign Goodness, and to entreat him warmly for their conversion.

61. St. Catherine of Siena (1347–80) was a medieval mystic and writer. She persuaded Pope Gregory XI to leave Avignon and return to Rome in 1377.

Certainly we have not here that exterior solemnity which awakens and sustains devotion only for what is essential in our religion is visible, the holy Sacrament of the Altar, to the marvels of which we must open the eyes of our faith without being aided by any sensible mark of its grandeur, any more than the Magi[62] were in the stable. But it seems that God, supplying what we lack,—and as a recompense of grace that he has given us in transporting it, so to speak, beyond so many seas, and in finding a place for it in these poor cabins,—wishes to crown us with the same blessings, in the midst of these infidel peoples, with which he is accustomed to favor persecuted Catholics in the countries of heretics. These good people scarcely ever see either church or altar; but the little they see is worth double what they would see in full liberty. What consolation would there be, in your opinion, in prostrating ourselves at times before a Cross in the midst of this barbarism? Or to turn our eyes toward, and to enter, in the midst of our petty domestic duties, even into the room which the Son of God has been pleased to take in our little dwelling? Is it not to be in paradise day and night, that we are not separated from this Well-Beloved of the Nations except by some bark or the branch of a tree? "Behold, there he stands behind our wall" [S. of S. 2:9]. "I have sat beneath the shadow of him whom I desire" [S. of S. 2:3]. See what we have within. If we go outside our cabin, heaven is open to us; and those great buildings which lift their heads to the clouds, in large cities, do not conceal it from our view; so that we can say our prayers in full liberty before the noble chapel that Saint Francis Xavier loved better than any other. If the question is of the fundamental virtues, I will glory not in myself, but in the share which has fallen to me; or, if I must, acknowledge it humbly beside the Cross which our Lord in his grace gives us to bear after him. Certain it is that this country, or our work here, is much more fitted to feed the soul with the fruits of heaven than with the fruits of earth. I may be deceiving myself, but I imagine that here is a grand means of increasing the soul in faith, in hope, and in charity. Should we scatter the seeds of the faith without ourselves profiting by them? Could we put our confidence anywhere but in God in a region where, as far as man is concerned, everything is lacking to us? Could we wish a nobler opportunity to exercise charity than amid the roughness and discomfort of a new world, where no human art or industry has yet provided any conveniences? Or to live here that we may bring back to God men who are so unlike men that we must live in daily expectation of dying by their hand, should the fancy take them, should a dream suggest it to them, or should we fail to open or close the heavens to them

---

62. The Magi were the three wise men, often called "kings," who came from the East to present gifts to the baby Jesus in Bethlehem: see Mt. 2:1–12.

at discretion, giving them rain or fine weather at command? Do they not make us responsible for the state of the weather?

And if God does not inspire us, or if we cannot work miracles by faith, are we not continually in danger, as they have threatened us, of seeing them fall upon those who have done no wrong? Indeed, if he who is the Truth itself had not declared that there is no greater love than to lay down one's life, verily and once for all, for one's friends, I should conceive it a thing equally noble, or even more so, to do what the Apostle said to the Corinthians, "Every day I die for your glory, my brothers, which I have in Christ Jesus our Lord" [1 Cor. 15:31] than to drag out a life full of misery, amid the frequent and ordinary dangers of an unforeseen death, which those whom you hope to save will procure for you. I call to mind occasionally what Saint Francis Xavier once wrote to Father Simon [Rodrigues],[63] and wish that it may please God to so act that at least the same thing may be said or written one day even of us, although we may not be worthy of it.

Here are the words [of Xavier], "Good news has been brought from the Moluccas [Islands], namely that John Beira and his companions are working with a mighty increase of the Christian religion."[64]

There seems to be one thing here which might give apprehension to a son of the Society, to see himself in the midst of a brutal and sensual people, whose example might tarnish the luster of the most and the least delicate of all the virtues, unless especial care be taken—I mean chastity. In order to obviate this difficulty, I make bold to say that if there is any place in the world where this so precious virtue is safe, for a man among us who wishes to be on his guard, it is here. "Unless the Lord guards the city, he who guards it stands watch in vain" [Ps. 126:1]. "I know that I can only be continent if God grants it. And this of itself is wisdom, to know whose gift it is" [Wis. 8:21]. It is said that the victories which this Daughter of Heaven [i.e., chastity] gains over her enemies are gained by flight; but I believe it is God and no one else who puts to flight this very enemy in the most severe encounters, before those who, fearing nothing so much as his approaches, go with bowed heads, and hearts full of confidence in his Goodness, where his glory calls them. And where should we seek this glory? I should say, where find it more fully purified and disentangled from our own interests than in a place where there is nothing more to be hoped for than the reward of having left all for the love of him of whom Saint Paul said, "I know in whom I have believed" [2 Tim. 1:12]? You remember that plant, named

---

63. Rodrigues was the superior of the Jesuits in Portugal.
64. Juan de Beira (1512–64) started the Jesuit mission in the Moluccas Islands (Indonesia), where he opened a school for children on Ternate. Many Jesuits regarded him as a saint.

"the fear of God," with which it is said our Fathers at the beginning of our Society charmed away the spirit of impurity: it does not grow in the land of the Hurons, but it falls there abundantly from heaven, if one has but a little care to cultivate that which he brings here. Barbarism, ignorance, poverty, and misery, which render the life of these savages more deplorable than death, are a continual reminder to us to mourn Adam's fall, and to submit ourselves entirely to him who still chastises disobedience in his children, in so remarkable a way. Saint Teresa [of Avila] said once that she never found her meditations more profitable than in the mysteries in which she found our Lord apart and alone, as if she had been in the Garden of Olives; and she called this a part of her simplicity.[65] You may reckon this among my follies, if you like; but it seems to me that we have here so much the more leisure to caress, so to speak, and to entertain our Lord with open heart, in the midst of these uninhabited lands, because there are so few people who trouble themselves about him. And, on account of this favor, we can boldly say, "I fear no evil because You are with me" [Ps. 23:4]. In short, I imagine that all the guardian angels of these neglected and abandoned nations are continually endeavoring and laboring to save us from these dangers. They know well that if there were anything in the world that ought to give us wings, to fly back whence we came both by obedience and by our own inclination, it would be this misfortune, if we were not shielded from it by the protection of heaven. This is what excites them to procure for us the means to guard against it, that they may not lose the brightest hope they have ever had, by the grace of God, of the conversion of these peoples. I finish this discourse and this chapter with this sentence: If, at the sight of the difficulties and Crosses that are here prepared for us, someone feels himself so fortified from above that he can say it is too little, or like Saint Francis Xavier, "More, more," then I hope that our Lord will also draw from his lips this other confession, in the midst of the consolations he will give him, that it will be too much for him, that he cannot endure more. "It is enough, Lord, it is enough."

---

65. St. Teresa of Avila (1515–82) was a mystic, gifted writer, and reformer of the Carmelite nuns. She was canonized on the same day in 1622 as Ignatius of Loyola and Francis Xavier. The Garden of Olives was the place outside Jerusalem where Jesus prayed the night before his crucifixion.

CHAPTER 4

JESUIT OPPOSITION
TO PROTESTANTISM

INTRODUCTION

Pedro de Ribadeneira (1526–1611), Loyola's earliest biographer, depicted the founder of the Jesuit Order as the champion of Roman Catholicism against Luther and Protestantism. But Ribadeneira's description is only half right. True, the Jesuits were arguably the most effective Catholic opponents to the spread of Protestantism from 1550 to 1650. They wrote hundreds of books in which they attempted to refute Protestant ideas and ran hundreds of schools that tried, often very successfully, to inculcate Catholic beliefs and practices. Loyola himself toward the end of his student days at Paris added an appendix to *The Spiritual Exercises* entitled "Rules for Thinking with the Church," in which he sharply opposed the Protestant ideas that were spreading among students at the University of Paris. He devoted his life to reforming the Catholic Church and had no sympathy for the distinctive theologies of Luther, Calvin, and their followers.

Yet the original goal of Loyola and his first companions was not to oppose Protestantism but to work for the salvation of souls in Jerusalem. During Loyola's lifetime, the growth of the Jesuits was fastest in Portugal and Sicily, lands hardly touched by the spread of Protestant ideas, and where Islam was considered to be the main threat to the Church. In contrast, growth of the Jesuits was very slow in German-speaking lands. In his more than six thousand letters Loyola never once mentions John Calvin by name; he only mentions Luther once or twice. In the century after the Order was founded in 1540 the Jesuits expended far more effort in educating young men and evangelizing rural Catholic peasants and the native peoples of Asia and the Americas than they did in mounting offensives against the Protestants.

Protestant apologists usually saw the Jesuits as deceptive schemers and disciples of Machiavelli.[1] Jesuit schools were not allowed in Protestant

---

1. Niccolò Machiavelli (1469–1527) was a Florentine politician; his most famous work, *The Prince*, was seen as advocating immoral behavior in politics—e.g., that the end justifies the means.

countries, so Jesuits usually had to work secretly in such places. If caught in England, they faced arrest, imprisonment, and often execution, as will be seen in the selection by Edmund Campion printed in this chapter. In what ways did the Jesuits oppose Protestantism? Reviving Catholic doctrine and practice in Catholic countries was perhaps the most obvious means to block the spread of Protestant ideas. In officially Catholic areas where there was a considerable Protestant minority—for example, in Poland and the Habsburg lands in central Europe—Jesuit schools were often open to Protestant students. Their Jesuit teachers hoped to convert such students or at least to undermine their hostility to Catholicism. Jesuit theologians wrote many controversial works to refute Protestant teaching, the most famous of which is Robert Bellarmine's *Controversies;* this chapter contains a key section from that work.

Jesuits cultivated good relations with Catholic rulers, sometimes serving as royal confessors or simply as trusted but unofficial advisers. Jesuit royal confessors often tried to influence Catholic rulers to unite against Protestant rulers or against the Turks. This chapter prints Loyola's letter urging Peter Canisius to use his warm friendship with Emperor Ferdinand I (1556–64) to have Protestants excluded from positions of authority at the royal court and in universities.

Loyola's Letter to Canisius on How King Ferdinand Should Oppose Protestantism in Austria

[Loyola's most militant statements against Protestantism are found in this letter of August 18, 1554, to the leader of the German Jesuits, St. Peter Canisius (1521–97). In the letter Loyola suggests many ways to block the spread of Protestantism in Vienna and Austria and encourages Canisius to share these suggestions with King Ferdinand. Ferdinand was king of Hungary and Bohemia and ruled Austria in the name of his brother Emperor Charles V. When Charles abdicated in 1556, Ferdinand became emperor; he founded the Austrian Habsburg dynasty, which ruled much of east central Europe until 1918.[2] Although he was a strong Catholic and a supporter of the Jesuits, Ferdinand was slow to implement Loyola's suggestions for fear they would stir up unrest among Ferdinand's subjects. The letter nonetheless gives valuable

2. In 1552 an alliance of the German Lutheran princes with Henry II of France defeated Charles V. This defeat led to Charles' abdication and the Peace of Augsburg (1555), which gave Lutherans equal rights with Catholics and curtailed the power of the Habsburg emperors.

insight into how Loyola thought Catholic rulers should deal with their Protestant subjects.³]

Greetings and lasting love, etc. We understood what you were requesting with devout concern in your letters written on July 7 and 17, namely that we consider what could help his royal majesty [Ferdinand] keep these lands in the Catholic faith, and that we write on how to reestablish that religion in those areas where it has collapsed and shore it up where it is shaky. It seems we must make a greater effort because the heart of this truly Christian prince is regarded as well disposed to listen to our suggestions and carry them out. Otherwise, if we fail to do our utmost to execute our plans, our efforts will be regarded as something to mock rather than as having any worth. It will be up to you to use prudence in deciding which of the things written here should be proposed to his royal majesty. They all seem very useful if the disposition of place, time, and persons affords the opportunity to undertake them. But it may be necessary to dispense with some of them because of the adverse disposition of the regions and the men with whom one often has to work. Hence you and Father Rector [at Vienna, Nicholas Lannoy] have been forewarned about these recommendations. You should note, after making a choice, which of these suggestions will aid our purpose and ignore the rest. I will give you a short account of what several other important theologians of our Society think about this matter; they are men of learning, good judgment, and a strong, loving disposition toward Germany.

Just as when a body is in bad health one should first get rid of those things contributing to sickness and then bring in things contributing to strength and a good disposition, so too in this sickness of minds—which has festered in the king's territories through various heresies—the first thing to consider is how to get rid of the causes of this disease, then how the vigor of healthy Catholic teaching can be restored and strengthened in them.

For the sake of brevity the conclusions I offer here will be as succinct as possible, since anyone with eyes can see what reasons have led us to specific measures.

First of all, if his royal majesty will claim, as he has always done, that he

---

3. This translation is by John Patrick Donnelly from the Latin text printed in *Beati Petri Canisii Societatis Iesu Epistulae et Acta,* edited by Otto Braunsberger (Freiburg im Breisgau: Herder, 1896) vol. 1, pp. 488–94. For the life of Canisius, the founder of the Jesuits in Germany, see James Brodrick, *St. Peter Canisius, S.J., 1521–1597* (New York: Sheed and Ward, 1935).

is not only a Catholic but also the dangerous enemy of heresies, and has declared open and not hidden war against all heretical errors, this will doubtless be the most effective and important of human remedies.

Something else of greatest importance follows from this: if his royal majesty will prevent any heretic from sitting in his royal council, he will be seen as holding those men in low esteem whose advice, both open and hidden, should ultimately be regarded as favoring and supporting the heretical depravity with which they have been stained. Moreover, it will be very useful if he permits no one infected by any heresy to hold a job in governing a province or any area, especially on the highest levels, or in any magistracy or level of dignity.

Lastly, I wish it to be approved and made clear to all that as soon as anybody has been convicted of heretical depravity or has been under grave suspicion, he should not have honors or wealth conferred on him; rather he should be cut off from them instead. This remedy will be more effective if some examples are made known by punishing some people with the expropriation of their life or goods or with exile—in this way it will be understood that religious matters are dealt with seriously.

All public professors and all persons holding administrative positions at the University of Vienna or other universities should be stripped of those positions if they speak negatively about things pertaining to the Catholic religion. We feel the same about rectors, administrators, and teachers at private colleges, lest those who should be guiding young people to godliness corrupt them instead. Hence those who are suspect should not be retained there lest they taint young people. Those who are openly heretical should certainly not be retained. It also seems obvious that those students, if any, who seem incapable of reconsidering, should also be expelled. All schoolmasters and teachers should understand this and be fully aware of the fact that they will hold no position in the king's provinces unless they are, and comport themselves as, Catholics.

All heretical books, as many as have been discovered in a careful previous investigation of libraries and private collections, should be burnt or shipped out of all the provinces of the kingdom. The same should be done to any non-heretical books—such as books on grammar, rhetoric, or logic—written by known heretics; such books should be completely banned out of hatred of their authors' heresy. Since heretics insinuate themselves through such books, the authors should not even be named, especially not to young people who might be attracted to them. Other, more learned books that are free of this serious danger can be found. Also, it would be very helpful if all publishers were forbidden, under severe penalties, to print any heretical books. . . . It should also be illegal under the same penalties for any merchant or other persons to import similar books, printed elsewhere, into areas under royal jurisdiction.

No priests or confessors should be tolerated who have a bad reputation regarding heresy. As soon as they are convicted of heresy they should be stripped of all ecclesiastical revenues. It is better for the flock to have no shepherd at all than to have a wolf for a shepherd. It would also be good to severely punish any pastors who are Catholic in faith but who through their great ignorance, bad example, and public sins corrupt the people. Their bishops should strip them of their stipends and certainly not entrust the care of souls to them. The plague of heresy was brought into Germany through the evil lifestyles and ignorance of such priests.

Preachers of heresy, heretical leaders, and (finally) all those found infecting others with the plague of heresy should be severely punished. A public declaration should be made, in whatever place you think best, that those who recant their heresy within a month of the day of the declaration will be kindly absolved under both church and civil law. After that month has passed, those caught in heresy should perhaps be regarded as shameful and ineligible for any honors; and if it seems appropriate, such heretics could be punished by exile, prison, or even sometimes by death. But I am not suggesting we establish the Inquisition[4] or capital punishment there because such measures seem out of the question in Germany as presently constituted.

Any person who calls the heretics "evangelicals" should be subject to a monetary penalty lest the devil rejoice that the enemies of the Gospel and of the cross of Christ usurp a name contrary to the facts. Heretics should be called by their right name; it would be terrible to even misname such people who cover their deadly poison with the cloak of the saving name.

Perhaps unlearned clergymen and those seduced by others will recant after they are taught the truth by synods of bishops and by declarations of dogmas and the main decrees of the Church issued by [Ecumenical] Councils. By clearly stressing the abominable errors of the heretics good preachers, curates, and confessors will also aid the people, so long as the people profess the Catholic faith and believe in the things necessary for salvation. We may need to close our eyes on some other questions that can be tolerated.

So far [we have addressed the issue] of reversing errors. Now [I will

---

4. The notorious Spanish Inquisition was authorized by the pope in 1478 but remained under the control of the Spanish monarchs; it dealt mainly with Spanish Jews and Muslims who outwardly claimed to have converted to Catholicism but continued to practice their religion in secret. The Papal Inquisition was set up in 1542 to prevent the spread of Protestantism in Italy. Its effective jurisdiction was restricted to central and southern Italy. Both Inquisitions resorted to torture and execution of relapsed heretics. Loyola did not want Jesuits to serve as inquisitors, not because he opposed the Inquisitions, but because that task was largely left to Dominican and Franciscan friars who would resent the Jesuits' invading their turf.

address] those issues pertaining to the cultivation and solid teaching of Catholic truth. First, it will help if the king will, in his council and elsewhere in his court, favor, honor, and promote only Catholics; likewise, he should honor only Catholics with revenues and secular and ecclesiastical honors and titles. If Catholics are to be appointed as governors, magistrates, or to other positions of command and authority over the people, let them first swear that they will always be Catholics.

Careful attention must be paid to the selection of good bishops who will, in word and deed, edify the people in the areas under royal jurisdiction. As many preachers as possible must be sent out along with confessors from the religious orders and members of the diocesan clergy who, in their zeal for God's honor and the salvation of souls, will fervently and steadily propose Catholic teaching to the people and confirm it through the example of their lives. Church dignities and stipends should be granted to these men. By traveling through the towns and countryside, these men can teach the people on feast days those things appropriate for the salvation of their souls and can return afterwards to their churches. Their explanations of the Gospel will be more edifying if offered free of charge. If ignorant [priests] and those suspected of disseminating incorrect doctrine cannot be easily removed from their benefices, they should be ordered to feed, at their own expense, the skilled and good shepherds who will tend to the people in their place by administering the sacraments and announcing the word of God. Such ignorant priests must abstain completely from these duties. Henceforward a benefice with the care of souls should be granted only to somebody who, having been examined, was found to be a Catholic and a good man of sufficient intelligence. All such funding is owed only to those [priests] who do not refuse to take on the care [of souls].

It seems prudent that all administrators, public professors of universities and academies—both rectors of private colleges and also schoolmasters—and indeed all teachers should be found to be Catholics by a preliminary examination or by confidential information and should be recommended by the testimony of Catholics before they are hired. They ought to take an oath that they are Catholics and will remain so in the future. If such persons are later discovered to be heretics, they should be severely punished for perjury. Some men should be given the responsibility of checking those books imported by merchants and those that are to be printed in the areas of royal jurisdiction. Books can be sold only after having been approved by these censors. It would be helpful if teachers everywhere could suggest to their students one or two catechisms or manuals of Christian doctrine; these books should contain a summary of Catholic truth that the boys and unlearned will wear out through repeated reading. It would also be helpful to have some books composed for curates and those pastors who are less

Peter Canisius (1521–97) preaching in Vienna.

learned but of sound minds. Such books would instruct them in the things they should teach in order that their people will correctly embrace or reject the things that should be embraced or rejected. It would also be good to have a summary of scholastic theology of the sort that will not repel the minds of the learned men of today (nor of those who think themselves learned).

Because in the areas under royal jurisdiction there is an extreme shortage of suitable curates, confessors, preachers, and teachers who are at once Catholic, learned and good, his royal majesty on the one hand should take very diligent care to gather such men from other places, even if he must offer high salaries to do so; on the other hand, he should also prepare as many seminaries as possible [to train] such men for use in his lands. If only a few seminaries are available, then let them be as big as possible. Four types of seminaries might be prepared. The first type could be established by members of those religious orders who are used to performing this sort of work. To this end his royal majesty will find it valuable to carefully increase the number of Germans from both the Society of Jesus and from the other [Religious] Orders in the monasteries and colleges. This increase should be accomplished through royal generosity so that those engaged in literary studies will subsequently become energetic preachers, lecturers and confessors both at Vienna and at his other universities. The second type of seminary is the German College at Rome to which his majesty can send many talented young men at his expense; these young men will all return to his regions when they have matured in good letters and morals—unless, that is, he prefers to set up a similar college at Rome for his Austrian, Hungarian, Bohemian, and Transylvanian subjects.[5] The third type of seminary are new colleges similar to the German College at Rome, which he can establish at his own universities under the leadership of learned and devout men. The students at these colleges will later go out and take on the care of souls or will be trained as schoolmasters or preachers. [Financing for] these three types of seminaries could come partly from the income of deserted monasteries, partly from parochial churches lacking their own pastors, and partly from a light tax levied on the people. One source of income can be assumed—that is, income generated by fees imposed on the bishops and other important priests, or from what sources seem appropriate to his royal majesty. The fourth type of seminary would consist of colleges in which nobles and rich lads—men who later would be apt candidates for secular and ecclesiastical positions of importance, even supreme importance—are supported at their own expense. It seems that in this and in the other three kinds of seminary it will be absolutely necessary to have the sort of rectors and teachers from whom the students can imbibe godliness joined to sound and Catholic doctrine.

At Rome, 18 August 1554.

Edmund Campion

"The Brag" or "Challenge"

[*St. Edmund Campion (1540–81) was born in London and educated at Oxford. After gradually turning away from the Anglican Church, he left England and converted to Catholicism at Douai in the Netherlands in 1571. He entered the Jesuits two years later. In 1580 three Jesuits—Campion, Robert Persons (1546–1610), and Ralph Emerson (1551–1604)—entered England in disguise to minister to the underground Catholic Church. At that time, Catholic*

---

5. The German College was a residence hall under Jesuit supervision in Rome where German and Hungarian students lived and studied. Students took their courses at the Roman College, the premier Jesuit school. It was founded in 1552 and still exists.

priests were forbidden to enter England or celebrate Mass and could be executed if caught. Campion expected to be arrested at some point, and so at the request of friends he dashed off the following challenge, popularly known as his "Brag." In it he challenged the English government to hold a disputation between him and Anglican theologians chosen by the government. Disputations were a standard part of the training at Oxford and Cambridge, and Campion himself had participated in a disputation before Elizabeth I (1558–1603) when she visited Oxford in 1566. Since Campion believed that the truth was on his side, he was confident that he could overcome his adversaries in a fair and public debate.

Though he did not expect the "Brag" to be published, he did want English Catholics to have copies in case the government attempted to claim—via a false confession or statement issued in his name—that he had come to England for political reasons. Handwritten copies of his challenge circulated widely; when some fell into government hands, English officials redoubled their efforts to find and arrest Campion. Meanwhile, Campion's much longer Rationes Decem *(Ten Reasons), a defense of Catholicism in Latin, was published by an underground Catholic press. Copies of the* Rationes Decem *were secretly passed around at Oxford University, much to the government's outrage. Campion was captured on July 17, 1581. The government arranged four disputations with Protestant theologians but did not notify Campion of the debates in advance; he was furnished with only a Bible by way of preparation. As in most Reformation debates, government officials made sure that the rules of engagement strongly favored their own representatives. Campion "lost" the debate and was executed for treason on December 1, 1581. He was canonized in 1970.*[6]*]*

Right Honorable,

Whereas I have come out of Germany and Bohemia, being sent by my superiors, and brought myself into this noble realm, my dear country, for

---

6. This document is reprinted from Thomas H. Clancy, S.J., *An Introduction to Jesuit Life* (St. Louis: Institute of Jesuit Sources, 1976), pp. 327–29, with the permission of the Institute of Jesuit Sources. The spelling and some wording have been modernized by John Patrick Donnelly to make the document easier to read. James V. Holleran's *A Jesuit Challenge: Edmund Campion's Debates at the Tower of London in 1581* (New York: Fordham University Press, 1999) discusses Campion's "Brag" (pp. 25–8) and Campion's later debates as a prisoner with Protestant theologians assigned by the government to refute him. Although not the most scholarly, the classic biography of Campion is Evelyn Waugh's *Edmund Campion* (London: Longmans, 1961). For the larger context of Campion's mission, see Thomas Mc-Coog, S.J., "Our Way of Proceeding," in *The Society of Jesus in Ireland, Scotland and England, 1548–1588* (Leiden: Brill, 1996).

the glory of God and the benefit of souls, I thought it likely enough that in this busy, watchful and suspicious world, that I would either sooner or later be intercepted and stopped from my course. Wherefore, providing for all events and uncertain what might happen to me, when God shall haply deliver my body to suffering, I supposed that I needed to make this statement ready in writing since I desire your good Lordships to read it so you may know my cause. In doing this I trust I shall make your work somewhat easier. For that which otherwise you must have sought for by intellectual labor I do now lay in your hands by a plain confession. So that the whole matter may be understood in order and be better understood and remembered, I therefore reduced it to these nine points or articles, thus directly, truly and resolutely laying open my full enterprise and purpose.

1. I confess that I am, although unworthy, a priest of the Catholic Church, and through the great mercy of God have taken vows eight years ago in the religious order of the Society of Jesus. Thereby I have taken on myself a special kind of warfare under the banner of obedience and have moreover resigned all my interest in or chance for wealth, honor, pleasure or worldly happiness.

2. At the voice of our Superior General, which is to me a warrant from heaven and the voice of Christ, I traveled from Prague to Rome (where our said Father General is always resident) and from Rome to England, as I might and would have done joyously to any part of Christendom or any pagan country, had I been assigned there.

3. My assignment is to preach the gospel free of charge, to administer the sacraments, to instruct the unlearned, to reform sinners, to refute errors— in brief to sound a spiritual alarm against the foul vice and proud ignorance wherewith many of my dear countrymen are abused.

4. I never had in mind and am strictly forbidden by our Father [General] who sent me to deal in any respect with matters of state or policy of this realm since these things do not pertain to my vocation, and from them I gladly restrain and withdraw my thoughts.

5. I do ask for the glory of God and with all humility and at your discretion for three kinds of neutral and quiet audiences. The first is one before your Honors where I will discourse about religion insofar as it touches the good of the people and you noblemen. The second (which I value more highly) is before the doctors and masters and chosen men of both [Oxford and Cambridge] Universities; there I will undertake to defend the faith of our Catholic Church by innumerable proofs from Scripture, the Councils, the Fathers [of the Church], and natural and moral reasons. The third is before lawyers of civil and church law where I will justify the said faith by the common wisdom of the laws currently in force and practice.

Edmund Campion (1540–1581). Note the dagger in his chest, symbolizing his martyrdom.

6. I would be reluctant to speak anything that might sound like an insolent brag or challenge, especially since I am now like a man dead to this world and willing to put my head under every man's foot and to kiss the ground they tread upon. Yet I have such courage in defending the majesty of Jesus my King and so much trust in his gracious favor and such assurance in my quarrel and because my evidence is so impregnable and because I know perfectly that no one Protestant nor all the living Protestants nor any sect of our adversaries (however much they face down men in the pulpit and overrule us in their kingdom of grammarians and unlearned ears) can uphold their doctrine in a disputation. I ask most humbly and urgently to dispute with them, one and all, and the best leaders that can be found. I claim that in this trial the better prepared they are, the more welcome they shall be.

7. And because it has pleased God to enrich Queen [Elizabeth], my sovereign lady, with noble gifts of nature, learning and a princely education, I really do trust that—if her Highness would grant her royal person and good attention to such a conference as I have mentioned in the second part of my fifth article, or to a few sermons, which in her or your hearing I am to utter,—such clear and fair light may be cast upon those controversies by good method and plain dealing that possibly her zeal for truth and love of her people shall incline her noble Grace to disfavor some proceedings hurtful to the Realm and procure more fairness for us oppressed [Catholics].

8. Moreover I do not doubt that you, her Highness' Council, being of such wisdom and discretion in very important cases, when you shall have heard these questions of religion opened faithfully, which many times our adversaries have jumbled up and confused, will see on what substantial grounds our Catholic Faith is built, how feeble is that side which by the fluctuation of time prevails against us, and so at last for your own souls and for many thousands souls that depend upon your government, you will reject error when it is disclosed and listen to those who would spend the best blood in their bodies for your salvation. Many innocent hands are lifted up to heaven for you daily by those English students, whose posterity shall never die, who beyond the seas are gathering virtue and sufficient knowledge for the purpose; they are determined never to give up on you but either to win you heaven or to die on your spears. And touching our Society, let it be known to you that we have made a league—all the Jesuits of the world, whose succession and multitude must overreach all the practices of England—cheerfully to carry the cross you shall lay upon us and never to despair of your recovery while we have a man left to enjoy your Tyburn[7] or

7. Tyburn was the usual place for executions on the outskirts of Elizabethan London, now near Hyde Park. Campion was hung, drawn, and quartered there.

to be racked with your torments or consumed with your prisons. The expense is reckoned, the enterprise is begun; it is of God, it cannot be withstood. So the faith was planted, so it must be restored.

9. If these offers of mine are refused and my endeavors cannot take place, and I, having run thousands of miles to do you good, shall be rewarded with rigor, I have no more to say but to recommend your case and mine to almighty God, the searcher of hearts, that he send us his grace and bring us to agreement before the day of payment, to the end that we may at last be friends in heaven, when all injuries shall be forgotten.

Robert Bellarmine

De Controversiis Christianae Fidei
(Selections on Scripture and tradition)

[St. Robert Bellarmine, S.J., (1542–1621) was the leading controversial Catholic theologian[8] *of the Reformation. After his youth and early education in Italy, he studied and taught theology in Belgium at the University of Louvain from 1569 until 1576. He shaped his courses there to answer the objections raised by the Protestant reformers against Catholic teaching. In 1576 he was called to the Roman College to take over the new chair in controversial theology. The lectures he delivered there formed the basis of his* De Controversiis Christianae fide *(On the Controversies of the Christian Faith), which appeared in three volumes: 1586, 1588, and 1593. The* Controversies *went through twenty editions and provided the most comprehensive Catholic response to the Protestant reformers. Bellarmine was named a cardinal in 1599 and devoted most of his last twenty years to administrative duties in Rome.*

The selections from Bellarmine translated here come from the First Controversy, on the word of God. At the heart of the Protestant Reformation movement was the question "How do we know what is true in theology?" And the Protestant answer to that question was that Scripture is the only

---

8. Controversial theological writings aimed to defend the doctrinal teachings of the author's church against the claims of those who denied or attacked those teachings. Never were theological polemics or controversies so popular as in the Reformation. Just as a willingness to fight a duel was a badge of honor for young noblemen in the 16th century, so too skill at defending the teaching of one's church established a theologian's reputation. Catholics fought Protestants; Lutherans attacked Calvinists. To give but one example, more than one hundred books were published during the Reformation in the controversy between Lutherans and Calvinists over the nature of Christ's presence in the Eucharist.

acceptable and sure source of Christian doctrine. That answer had serious theological ramifications: the criteria accepted for religious truth obviously dictated the answers to all other specific questions regarding such important issues as justification, the sacraments, and so forth. Bellarmine divided his treatise on the word of God into four books: the first book largely addresses the question of which books belong in the Bible; the second examines various editions of the Bible; the third is concerned with the interpretation of Scripture; and the fourth considers tradition as a supplement to Scripture. Bellarmine's arguments were based on a wide array of quotations from the Bible and the early Church Fathers as well as references to the Catholic and Protestant theologians of his time. William Whitaker (1548–95), an English Puritan theologian who wrote a book defending the doctrine of Scripture alone against Bellarmine, said that despite Bellarmine's belonging to "the Jesuit swarm of papist locusts," he seemed "an invincible champion, as one with whom none of our men would dare to engage, whom nobody can answer, and whom, if anybody should hope to conquer, they would regard him as an utter madman."[9] Bellarmine's tract employs many citations to Scripture and the Fathers of the early Church; reference to such medieval scholastics as Thomas Aquinas (1224?–74) are conspicuously absent. Bellarmine's Protestant opponents felt that the early Church was generally free from errors; they held that the institutional Catholic Church fell from the true faith during the Middle Ages. Controversialists who supported their case with abundant quotations from the Church Fathers were considered to be arguing from a strong position, whether they were Roman Catholics or Protestants; hence Bellarmine frequently references the Church Fathers. Both Lutherans and Calvinists felt that Roman Catholic teaching on the role of free will and good works in the process of salvation was contrary to the teaching of both St. Paul[10] and St. Augustine.[11] In fact Luther and Calvin cited Augustine more than any other nonbiblical author.

Chapter 5, on Jesuit spirituality, and Chapter 7, on the duties of a Christian king, include very different contributions from Bellarmine. In the first selection he is writing primarily for theologians; in those chapters he is writing for a devout lay audience.]

9. Quoted in Jonathan Wright, *God's Soldiers: Adventure, Politics, Intrigue and Power; A History of the Jesuits* (New York: Doubleday, 2004), p. 40.

10. Theologians of the Reformation attributed fourteen of the twenty-seven books of the New Testament to St. Paul. He was also considered to be the best theologian of the New Testament writers.

11. St. Augustine (354–430), the most influential theologian of the early Church, is best known for his *Confessions*.

Book 3: On the interpretation of the word of God[12]

Chapter 1: *Scripture is not so clear of itself that it suffices for settling controversies about doctrine without explication.*

I thought it good to begin in this third book on the scriptures with this question about the interpretation of the Divine Letters: Are the sacred Scriptures easy and clear by themselves, or do they need interpretation? Martin Luther[13] indeed speaks thus in the preface to his assertion of the articles condemned by Pope Leo [X]:[14] "This sentence ought to be supported by the judgment of Scripture—which it cannot be. Unless we have given Scripture the leading role in all the things which are attributed to the Fathers, namely that it is by itself the most certain, easy and clear interpreter of itself, proving, judging, and illuminating all things in all cases," etc. Here he argues that Scripture is clearer than the commentaries of all the Fathers. He teaches the same thing in his book on the servitude of the will and elsewhere.

But Luther saw that an objection could soon be raised: "Why, then, are there so many controversies if Scripture is so clear?" He thought up two ways of escape. First, that even if Scripture is obscure in some places, it still states the same matter clearly elsewhere. Secondly, that even though Scripture is of itself most clear, it is nonetheless obscure to the proud and unbelievers because of their blindness and depraved disposition. [Johann] Brenz adds a third way of escape in his *Prolegomena* against Pedro de Soto:[15] that scripture is also sometimes obscure because it includes phrases in a foreign language, that is, Hebrew and Greek; still the meaning of scripture is very clear. This contention is obviously false because Scripture itself bears witness to its own difficulty and obscurity. In Psalm 119[:34], "Give me understanding that I

12. This whole discussion covers pp. 14–141 in the first volume of *Roberti Bellarmini Opera omnia* (Naples: Apud Josephum Giuliano, 1836). Only key parts are translated here by John Patrick Donnelly.

13. Martin Luther (1483–1546), greatest of the early Protestant theologians, insisted that the Bible was the only criterion for determining true Christian doctrine and justifying religious practices.

14. Leo X (pope 1513–21) condemned several of Luther's famous Ninety-five Theses of 1517. Bellarmine here cites Luther's reply to that condemnation.

15. Johann Brenz (1499–1570), a leading Lutheran theologian in the decades after Luther's death, wrote extensively against both Catholics and Calvinists. Pedro de Soto (1500–63) was a Spanish Dominican friar who taught at the Catholic University of Dilligen in Germany; he answered Brenz's attack in his *Defensio catholicae confessionis . . . adversus prolegomena Johannis Brentii*, which was published in Antwerp in 1557.

may search your law." In the same place [Ps. 119:18]: "I will open up my eyes and gaze on the marvels of your law." In the same place [Ps. 119:135], "Let your face shine on your servant and teach me your laws." Certainly David knew all the Scripture that existed then, and he knew the idioms of the Hebrew language; he was neither proud nor unbelieving. Dealing with these statements in his epistle to Paulinus, St. Jerome[16] rightly says on this point, "If so great a prophet confesses the darkness of ignorance, how much night of unknowing do you think surrounds us, who are little children, almost nursing on milk?"

Moreover, in the last [chapter] of Luke [24:27] the Lord interpreted the Scriptures for his disciples, who certainly knew Hebrew idioms since they were Hebrews; they were not proud or unbelieving. The eunuch of the queen of Ethiopia in Acts 8[:28–35] was wrestling with the Scriptures and was reading them carefully and was holy, devout and humble, as Jerome teaches in his epistle to Paulinus on the study of Scripture. Still when Philip asked him, " 'Do you think you understand what you are reading?' He answered, 'And how can I, unless somebody shows me?' "

Finally, blessed Peter asserts in the last chapter of his second epistle [3:16] that "the ignorant and unstable twist" certain passages in the epistles of Paul which are hard to understand. It is to be noted there that the Apostle Peter did not say that these things were difficult only for the ignorant and unstable, as the heretics make out, but difficult absolutely. For blessed Augustine, who was certainly not ignorant and unstable, confesses in his book *De fide et operibus* (On faith and works), Chapters 15 and 16, that he found it very difficult to understand this passage from 1 Corinthians 3[:12], "But if somebody builds upon the foundation," etc. He says that this is one of those passages about which blessed Peter warned that they were difficult to understand.

Secondly, aside from the testimony of Scripture, the same thing can be proved from the common consensus of the ancient Fathers. [A long section of this chapter, omitted here, consists of quotations from the following Church Fathers: Irenaeus, Origen, John Chrysostom, Ambrose, Augustine, and Gregory the Great].[17]

---

16. St. Jerome (342–420) was widely regarded as the greatest biblical scholar of the early Church; his translation of the Bible into Latin, known as the *Vulgate,* was the official translation of the medieval and early modern Catholic Church. His view that the Bible was hard to understand cut against Luther's claim that Scripture was self-clarifying.

17. The dates of Irenaeus's birth and death are unknown, but he was bishop of Lyons and the leading theologian of the late second century. His most important work was *Against Heresies.* Origen (185?–254?) taught and wrote at Alexandria and Caesarea. His most famous work is his refutation of the pagan philosopher Celsus'

Aside from these authorities, reason also does not fail to prove the same point. For two things can be considered in the Scriptures: the things spoken about and the way in which they are spoken about. If you were to consider these things, it would be necessary to confess that the Scriptures are very obscure since they deal with the supreme mysteries, about the divine Trinity, about the incarnation of the Word, about the heavenly sacraments, about the nature of angels, about God working in the human mind, about eternal predestination and reprobation,[18] and also about other hidden and supernatural things which are investigated not without great keenness and work and not without grave danger of error. Certainly if the knowledge of metaphysics is more difficult and obscure than all other natural disciplines because it deals with the highest causes, how will sacred Scripture not be most obscure, which deals with things far more lofty? A large part of Scripture contains prophecies about future events and prophecies written in poetry, than which nothing certainly is more difficult and nothing more obscure.

But if we were to examine the way things are said, we would find countless obscure passages. First there are in the Scriptures many passages that at first glance seem contradictory, as that statement of Exodus 20[:5]: "I am a jealous God, visiting the sins of the fathers on the sons in the third and fourth generation." And that of Ezekiel 18[:20], "The son will not bear the iniquity of his father, but the person who sins, he will die." Second, there are ambiguous words and statements, as in John 8[:25] to the Jews who asked, " 'Who are you?' Christ replied, 'The beginning, who am also speaking to you.' " Here all the exegetes torture themselves marvelously, and even now it is not known what "The beginning, who" means. And in the Greek the business is even more obscure where "beginning" is in the accusative case: "ten archen." Third, there are incomplete statements, as in Romans 5[:12], "Just as through one man sin entered into the world and through sin death; and so death has passed over to all men, in whom all have sinned," and what follows. In that whole sentence there is no main verb.

---

attack on Christianity. His writings popularized allegorical interpretation of the Bible. St. John Chrysostom (345?–407), the patriarch of Constantinople, was regarded as the greatest preacher of the early Greek-speaking church. He wrote biblical commentaries and a treatise on the priesthood in six books. St. Ambrose (340?–97) was bishop of Milan; he is known for his sermons on the Bible and his book on the Holy Spirit. St. Gregory the Great (540?–604) was pope from 590 to 604; he organized the papal administration and sent missionaries to England. His theological writings are more practical than speculative.

18. *Eternal predestination* means that God from all eternity has chosen a person for salvation and heaven; *eternal reprobation* means God from all eternity has chosen one for damnation and hell.

Fourth, there are proleptic[19] statements, as in Genesis 10[:31], "These are the sons of Shem, by their families, their tongues, and their lands by their tribes." Immediately the beginning of Chapter 11 follows, "But the earth was of one tongue and of the same speech." Fifth, there are idioms restricted to the Hebrews, as Psalm 89[:30], "His throne is like the days of heaven." Likewise Psalm 119[:109], "My life is ever within my hands" and very many other passages. Sixth, there are many figures of speech, tropes, metaphors, allegories, inverted word orders, uses of irony, and countless other similar figures of speech.

Lastly comes the confessions of our adversaries: whether they like it or not, they are forced to acknowledge this truth. For if the Scripture were as clear as they say, why did Luther and the Lutherans write so many commentaries? Why have they published such different translations of the Scripture? Why do they explain the Scripture so differently? Certainly [Andreas] Osiander, in refuting the writing that Philip [Melanchthon] published against him, witnesses that there are twenty very different views of justification according to the Scriptures being employed just among those who [accept] the *[Augsburg] Confession.* And has not Luther himself in his first book against [Huldreich] Zwingli and [Johann] Oecolampadius left this in writing:[20] "If the world were to stand longer, it would again be necessary, because of the different interpretations now being given Scripture, for us to accept the decrees of the Councils and to take refuge in them, for the sake of preserving the unity of the faith." I ask, whence come so many interpretations of Scripture if Scripture is so easy and clear? Do they not fight among themselves in wondrous wise over this question?

Luther, in the preface of the assertion of his articles, asserts that Scripture is of itself completely open and clear and boasts in his book on the enslaved will that there are no difficulties in the sacred letters and that no passage

---

19. *Proleptic* means "by anticipation, by looking ahead."

20. Andreas Osiander (1496?–1552) was a maverick Lutheran reformer who worked in Nuremberg; he was often at odds with the city government and with other Lutheran theologians on a wide range of questions. Several of his teachings were condemned by later Lutherans. Philip Melanchthon (1497–1560) was Luther's right-hand man at Wittenberg. After Luther's death Melanchthon was the most prominent Lutheran theologian, although his teaching on the Eucharist edged toward that of Calvin. He was the author of the 1530 *Augsburg Confession,* which has long served as the most basic statement of the Lutheran faith. Huldreich Zwingli (1484–1531) and Johann Oecolampadius (1482–1531) were the leading Swiss theologians of the early Reformed tradition, at Zurich and Basel respectively. Their main differences with Luther were over the presence of Christ in the Eucharist and over the use of religious art.

can be brought to him that he cannot easily interpret; nonetheless he himself in his preface on the Psalms says, "I would not want anybody to presume of me what none of the most holy and learned men so far has been able to do, that is, understand and teach the whole Psalter in its legitimate sense. It is enough to have understood some of them, and those only partially. The Spirit keeps much to himself so that he may always have us as disciples. He shows many things only to entice [us], he entrusts many things so that he can influence [us]." Later [he says], "I know that it would be very insolent and rash should some one dare to claim to have understood one book of Scripture in all its parts." On page 12 of his book on the Councils he says, "Twenty years earlier I was forced to spurn the commentaries of the Fathers when lecturing on Scripture in class and to seek its true and genuine meaning with much sweat."

Book 4: On the unwritten word of God

Chapter 4: *The Need for Traditions is Demonstrated.*

Now as we come to the proof, we will try to demonstrate three things. First, that the Scriptures without Traditions were neither absolutely necessary nor sufficient. Second, that apostolic Traditions are found dealing not just with morals but also with of faith. Last, how we can be certain about true Traditions.

I prove the first from the various eras of the Church. Some Church of God existed in the world from Adam right up to Moses, and people worshiped God by faith, hope, and charity and by external rites, as is clear from Genesis where Adam, Abel, Seth, Enoch, Noah, Abraham, Melchizedek,[21] and other just persons are introduced. Also from Augustine's *City of God,* Book 11 and the following, where he traces the City of God from the beginning of the world right down to the end. But there was no divine Scripture before Moses, as is clear, both because by common consensus Moses was the first sacred writer and because in Genesis there is no mention of written doctrine but only doctrine handed down. God says in Genesis 18[:19], "I know that [Abraham] will command his children and his household after him to keep the way of the Lord." Therefore religion was preserved for two thousand years by Tradition alone. Therefore Scripture is not absolutely necessary. For just as that ancient religion could be preserved for

---

21. All of these except Melchizedek were descendants of Adam and predecessors of the Jewish nation as traced in the book of Genesis. Melchizedek was "king of Salem who brought out bread and wine; he was a priest of God Most High" who blessed Abraham (Genesis 14:18–20). He is also referred to in Psalm 110:4. The author of the Letter to the Hebrews (5:6; 6:20; 7:1–19) links the priestly role of Jesus to that of Melchizedek.

two thousand years without Scripture, so too the teaching of Christ could have been preserved for fifteen hundred years without Scripture. Then from Moses up to Christ for another two thousand years the Scriptures did indeed exist, but they were the sole possession of the Jews, but the rest of the nations, in which there were some people with true religion and faith, had the use of only unwritten Tradition.

For besides the Jews many other people belonged to the Church, as is clear from Job and his friends.[22] Likewise from Augustine who constantly asserts this in his *On Original Sin*, Book 2, Chapter 24 and his *On the Predestination of the Saints*, Book 1, Chapter 9, and his *City of God*, Book 18, Chapter 47. Also in the very people of God, even though the Scriptures existed, the Jews used Tradition more than Scripture, as is clear from the [statement] of Exodus, Chapter 13[:8], "You will relate to your son in that day saying, 'This is what the Lord has done,'" etc. [Here Bellarmine adds further quotations from Dt. 32:7, Jb. 8:8, Jgs. 6:13, Ps. 44:1, Ps 78:3–4, and Sir. 8:9.] And yet Ecclesiasticus [the author of the book of Sirach] was from the last writers of the Old Testament.

The reason why the Hebrews used Tradition more than Scripture seems to have been because right up to the times of Ezra[23] the Scriptures were not edited to the form of books so that they could be used easily and comfortably; rather they were dispersed in various annals and notes and meanwhile they were not found because of the negligence of the priests, as is clear from 2 Kings 22[:13] where it is related as a new discovery that in the days of Josiah a volume of the law of the Lord was found in the Temple.[24] But after the captivity[25] Ezra gathered everything together and organized it into one corpus, adding in Deuteronomy the last chapter about the life of Moses and some other things thereafter toward continuing the history. . . . [26]

---

22. Bellarmine here means that Job and his friends are not Jews but believers in the true God (Job 1:1).

23. Ezra was a Jewish priest and scribe who lived in Babylon but returned to Jerusalem where he addressed the people and presided over a two-day reading from the Jewish Bible—so it is clear that much of the Bible was in written form by his day (Neh. 8:3, 13).

24. Josiah was king of Judah (640–609 B.C.). During his reign Hilkiah discovered the book of the law in the temple at Jerusalem and gave it to Josiah, who ordered his secretary to read it to him (2 Kg. 22:8–20).

25. The elite of Jewish society were forced into captivity at Babylon by Nebuchadnezzar in 586 and were encouraged to return to Israel in 539 by Cyrus the Great, founder of the Persian Empire. This period is known as the "Babylonian captivity."

26. Bellarmine credits Ezra with gathering and organizing various manuscripts into what became the first five books of the Bible. Many of these manuscripts were

Indeed, after the coming of Christ the Church was for many years without Scriptures so that even in his time Irenaeus wrote, Book 3, Chapter 4, that there were some Christian nations which lived splendid lives without the Scriptures but only with Traditions. Therefore it its rather clear from this deduction that the Scriptures are not absolutely necessary. But what [John] Chrysostom says in his first homily on Matthew that Scriptures were not necessary for the patriarchs and apostles but are necessary for us because of human corruption—this is to be understood not because of an absolute necessity but for our well being, that is, our utility, because there were generally many sinful persons even in the times of the patriarchs and apostles.

My first proof that the Scriptures do not contain everything so that they themselves suffice without another Tradition is this: because either the whole canon of Scripture taken together is sufficient, or the individual books are sufficient by themselves. Chemnitz[27] cannot say that the individual books are sufficient, for then it would be false what he also says, that the use of Tradition was used in the Church up to the completion of the whole canon of the Scriptures. Moreover we see that the individual evangelists do not contain everything. For John wrote nothing about the annunciation, the nativity, the circumcision, and the epiphany of the Lord and about many other things. The same can be said about the other books. Likewise, if one book sufficiently contains everything, what need was there for so many books?

Finally, [Protestants] themselves say openly that the whole canon is needed for this—that sufficient teaching be available. But not even that can be rightly asserted. For many truly sacred and canonical books have perished; therefore we do not have and have not had for 1,500 years sufficient teaching if everything is located in the Scriptures. In his homily on Matthew 9, regarding the statement that Jesus was called a Nazarene [cf. Mt 2:23], Chrysostom teaches that many books of the Old Testament have perished. He says, "Many of the prophetic documents have perished, which can be proved from the history of Chronicles. Since the Jews were lazy and not only lazy but also evil, they lost some things out of negligence, but others they

brought to Jerusalem by Ezra and other Jews returning from Babylonian captivity. The last chapter of the Book of Deuteronomy describes the death of Moses, so it was not written by Moses. Bellarmine credits Ezra with writing this chapter, but that is a guess.

27. Martin Chemnitz (1522–86) was, in the last two decades of his life, the most influential Lutheran theologian. He wrote a four-volume attack on the Roman Catholic Council of Trent and played a key role in drafting the Formula of Concord, which reunited various Lutheran factions.

both burned and tore up."[28] He teaches the same thing in his seventh homily on First Corinthians. It cannot be alleged that all those things that perished were restored by Ezra, for Chrysostom wants to prove that not all of the predictions of the prophets are extant now, and he proves it because the Jews lost many of them.

Ezra, moreover, did not restore the lost books but repaired and collected those which were extant; the last chapter [29:29] of First Chronicles says, "The acts of David, from first to last, are written in the book of Samuel the seer and in the book of Nathan the prophet and in the volume of Gad the seer." And in 2 Chronicles 9[:29], "The remaining deeds of Solomon are written in the words of Nathan the prophet and in the book of Ahijah the Shilonite; also in the vision of Iddo the seer." And 1 Kings 4[:32] [says], "Solomon spoke three thousand proverbs, and his poems numbered five thousand." Are these all? It is likely that the epistle of Paul to the Laodiceans has perished from the New Testament; he himself in the opinion of some recalls it in the last chapter of Colossians [4:16], and undoubtedly another epistle to the Corinthians [has perished]; there seems to be a reference in 1 Corinthians 5[:9], in those words, "I wrote to you in the epistle." And it can easily have happened that still some other things have perished. So let the heretics try to figure out how they are going to sew back together such a nasty tear.

Second, the same point is proved by the difference that existed between the apostles' preaching and Scripture. For if it had been the purpose of Christ and the apostles to narrow and restrict the word of God to Scripture, Christ would above all have openly commanded something of so much importance, and the apostles would have testified somewhere that they were writing by the Lord's command just as they were teaching by the Lord's command throughout the whole world. But we never read that. Moreover, the apostles did not wait for an opportunity or need to come up for preaching orally; they went forward spontaneously of their own accord, but they did not apply their mind to writing except when pressured by some need.

Eusebius[29] writes in Book 3, Chapter 24 (or Chapter 18 in another edition) of his history that Matthew wrote on the occasion when after having preached to the Hebrews, as he was preparing to go to the Gentiles, he judged it useful to leave some memorial of his teaching and preaching to those from whom he was departing in body. Eusebius also relates in Book

---

28. Obviously Bellarmine shared the anti-Semitic attitudes that were so common in 16th-century Europe.

29. Eusebius (260?–340?) was born in Palestine, served as bishop of Caesarea, and attended the Council of Nicaea. Because of his *Historia ecclesiastica* he is known as the Father of Church History.

2, Chapter 15 of his history that Mark wrote his gospel neither of his own choice nor because of an order from Peter (whose disciple he was) but under pressure from the requests of the Romans. The same Eusebius in Book 3, Chapter 24 of his history notes that Luke wrote only because he saw many other people who were rashly presuming to put into writing things which they did not fully know. [He wrote] so that he could steer us away from the unsure accounts of others.

In the same place Eusebius also writes that John preached the Gospel until extreme old age without any Scripture, and Jerome adds in his book on ecclesiastical writers that the bishops of Asia finally forced him to write his gospel because of the heresy of the Ebionites[30] that was popping up then. Therefore, had the heresy of Ebion not existed, perhaps we would not have John's gospel, just as [we would not have had] the other three if the aforesaid occasions had not come up. Rightly does Eusebius write in the passage noted earlier that only two of the twelve apostles wrote [gospels], and those [two] were driven to it by some need.

From this we obviously gather that the first intention in the minds of the apostles was to preach the Gospel, not to write. Moreover, if they had wished to commit their teaching to writing of set purpose, they certainly would have prepared a catechism or similar book. But either they wrote a history, as did the evangelists, or epistles on some occasion, as [did] Peter, Paul, James, Jude, and John; in them they deal with disputed questions of doctrine only obliquely. Finally, either the individual apostles would have produced a written account of evangelical teaching since each of them had care of some province, or certainly they all would have gotten together before they dispersed to their provinces and written some joint book, just as it is agreed that they composed together the Creed of the Faith, which, however, they did not write out but passed on only orally, as is taught by blessed Irenaeus in Book 3, Chapter 4; by Jerome in his letter to Pammachus against the errors of John of Jerusalem; by blessed Augustine in his book *De fide et operibus;* by blessed Ambrose in Letter 81 to Syricius; by blessed Leo in his Letter 13 to Pulcheria; by Ruffinus; and by Maximus in his exposition of the creed.[31]

---

30. The Ebionites, who get their name from their supposed founder Ebion, were a Jewish Christian sect that began in Palestine, spread to Syria, and continued from roughly 100 to 300. They strongly opposed the teachings of St. Paul.

31. This is a good example of how Bellarmine employs citations from the Church Fathers to support his arguments. We have already noted Irenaeus, Jerome, and Augustine. St. Ambrose (340?–97) was bishop of Milan. His writings included many sermons and scriptural commentaries. He played a key role in the conversion of St. Augustine. St. Leo I (390?–461) was the first pope counted among the Church

A third proof [comes] from many things which cannot be ignored but which are not contained in the Scriptures. First, in the time of the Old Testament, they undoubtedly had some remedy for women no less than for men by which they were cleansed of original sin; still in the opinion of many circumcision was established for men, but about what there was for women, the Scripture has nothing. Moreover, it is completely unbelievable that there was not at that same time some remedy for males that died before the eighth day, on which alone circumcision could take place, but nothing on this point exists in Scripture.

Third, many Gentiles were able to be saved and were saved in the time of the Old Testament and really belonged to the Church, as we showed above; but the Scriptures contain nothing at all about their justification from original sin and other sins.

Fourth, it is necessary to know with certainty that truly divine books exist, which cannot be obtained in any way from the Scriptures. For even if Scripture says that the books of the prophets and apostles are divine, still I certainly would not believe it unless I had previously come to believe that the Scripture which says this was divine. For we read scattered through the Koran of Mohammed that the Koran itself was sent by God from heaven,[32] but still we do not believe it. Therefore this dogma which is so necessary, namely that there is some divine Scripture, cannot be sufficiently based on Scripture alone. Hence, since faith rests upon the word of God, we will have no faith unless we have an unwritten word of God.

Fifth, it is not enough to know that there is divine Scripture but one has to know which it is—something which cannot in any way be obtained from the Scriptures. How can we gather from Scripture that the gospel of Mark and Luke are true and that those of Thomas and Bartholomew are false? For reason would rather say that more belief should be put in a book bearing the name of an apostle than of a nonapostle.

Where am I to get to know that the epistle to the Romans is really by Paul and the epistle to the Laodiceans which is now passed around is not by

---

Fathers. He convened the Council of Chalcedon (451) which condemned the Monophysites, kept Attila the Hun from sacking Rome, and wrote many sermons and letters. Tyrrannius Ruffinus (345?–410) was a monk in Egypt before returning to his hometown of Aquileia in Italy; he is best known for translating writings of Eusebius and Origen from Greek into Latin. St. Maximus the Confessor (580?–662) was a Greek monk and writer; he opposed writers who argued that Christ had only a divine and not a human will.

32. The Koran is the sacred book of Islam. Muslims believe that it is literally the words of God conveyed by the angel Gabriel to Mohammed, who wrote them down.

Paul? Both have the title *by Paul* on the front, and Paul says in the last chapter of his epistle to the Colossians [4:16] that he wrote to the Laodiceans, but he never says he wrote to the Romans.

Sixth, we must not only know which are the sacred books but also specifically that we now hold those books in our hands. It is not enough to believe that the gospel of Mark is true, that the gospel of Thomas is not true; we must also believe that this gospel which is now read under the name of Mark is the true and incorrupt one written by Mark. This can certainly never be gained from the Scriptures. How shall I gather from the Scriptures that this gospel is not a fake substitute, as the Muslims say, or certainly completely corrupted as once the Manichees used to say and the Anabaptists [say] now?[33]

[The rest of this chapter presents and answers various objections against tradition raised by John Calvin, Johann Brenz, and Martin Chemnitz, the leading Protestant theologians in the previous decades. Bellarmine gives several examples of traditions that are not found in Scripture such as infant baptism and Mary's perpetual virginity.]

33. The Manichees were members of a religious system, founded by Mani in the third century A.D., which spread through the late Roman world. Manichaeism taught that there were two divinities—Light, or Goodness, and Darkness, or Evil— locked in perpetual struggle. The Anabaptists who arose in Switzerland and Germany in the 1520s generally rejected infant baptism. Some of them valued the Holy Spirit speaking in their hearts over the written Bible.

CHAPTER 5

JESUIT SPIRITUALITY

INTRODUCTION

All faiths have developed their own rich traditions of spiritual literature, and spiritual texts have always outsold books of theology. The first and most popular book of Jesuit spirituality was Ignatius of Loyola's *Spiritual Exercises*. Since several selections from *The Spiritual Exercises* are printed in Chapter 1, that book is not represented in this chapter. Other early Jesuits wrote hundreds of books on spirituality, many of which became best sellers.[1]

Early Jesuit spiritual writers were strongly influenced by the 15th-century movement called the *devotio moderna*. The most prominent work of this movement was *The Imitation of Christ*, attributed to Thomas à Kempis (1380?–1471); the *Imitation* strongly influenced Loyola's own spiritual development after his conversion and was, for a long time, required reading for Jesuit novices. Book 4 of the *Imitation* encourages Christians to receive the Eucharist frequently, a practice the Jesuits also advocated. Above all, the *Imitation* stressed inwardness—a deep personal union with God. The Jesuits embraced this idea in general but rejected the anti-intellectualism inherent in the *devotio moderna*.

The most influential scholar and spiritual writer in the first two decades of the 16th century was Desiderius Erasmus (1466?–1536), the prince of humanism; though he was deeply indebted to the *devotio*, he too opposed its anti-intellectualism. He also opposed the scholastic philosophy and theology that dominated the universities of his day. For Erasmus, the scholastics were so dry and caught up in their own abstract speculations that they ignored the practical, pastoral dimension of theology. He and many humanists urged a return to teaching of such early

1. The classic work on Jesuit spirituality is Joseph de Guibert's *The Jesuits: Their Spiritual Doctrine and Practice; A Historical Study*, translated by William J. Young (St. Louis: Institute of Jesuit Sources, 1964). De Guibert discusses the four authors in this chapter: Rodriguez (pp. 261–64), Bellarmine (pp. 248–49), Nadal (pp. 204–7), and La Puente (pp. 253–56).

Church Fathers as St. Augustine, whose writings combined scholarship with concern for the needs of his flock. Loyola and the Jesuits tried to embrace both the Church Fathers and the medieval scholastic theologians, especially St. Thomas Aquinas. Above all, they tied scholasticism, humanism, and their own personal spiritual growth to helping others, especially those people in greatest need. They helped prostitutes reform their lives; they visited people in prison; they educated young men in their schools; they evangelized peasants in rural areas; they sent out missionaries to Asia, Africa, and the Americas. Jerome Nadal—whom Loyola sent to explain Jesuit spirituality to communities in Italy, Spain, France, and Germany—put it this way: "The world is our home." To the Jesuits spiritual growth was (and is) not a private matter; they felt it should flow out to others.[2]

During his university studies Loyola found that the delight he took in prayer was distracting him from his academic studies, which were essential for his gaining the knowledge he needed to be an effective apostle to others. He then forced himself to cut back severely on the time he devoted to prayer. Later, he wanted young Jesuits in training to devote no more than an hour each day to formal prayer in addition to the time they spent in attending Mass. He expected them to devote half an hour to a formal meditation similar to those found in *The Spiritual Exercises*. Priests were given more latitude to devote more time to meditation and were required to recite, privately, the prayers of the Divine Office. This took about seventy minutes daily, far less than the amount of time Benedictine monks or such mendicant friars as the Dominicans and Franciscans devoted to the singing, in common, of their Office. Many friars denied that the Jesuits were a true religious order precisely because the Jesuits did not sing or recite the Office in common together.

Why did Loyola and his early companions insist on Jesuits' praying the Office in private? Because private recitation would save about two hours a day that could be devoted to working for souls: teaching, writing, studying, preaching, hearing confessions, visiting hospitals, and other apostolic works. Did this mean that the Jesuits were less spiritual than the monks and friars? Not if they took to heart a key goal of Jesuit spirituality: *finding God in all things*. Jesuits wanted every one of their activities—indeed, the activities of all Christians—to be part of an effort to see God in all they saw and did, not only in formal prayer. They believed they should try to see God in

2. For a fuller discussion of Jesuit innovations in spirituality, see John O'Malley, "Some Distinctive Characteristics of Jesuit Spirituality in the Sixteenth Century," in *Jesuit Spirituality: A Now and Future Resource*, edited by John O'Malley et al. (Chicago: Loyola University Press, 1990), pp. 1–20.

all the beauties of nature, in the face of everybody with whom they came into contact, in their own joys and sorrows. Action and contemplation were not considered to be opposites. Jesuits were invited to be, simultaneously, men of action and men of contemplation. They were to encourage all the women and men with whom they worked to the same goal. As the English Jesuit poet Gerard Manly Hopkins (1844–89) wrote:

> The World is charged with the grandeur of God.
> It will flame out, like shining from shook foil;
> It gathers to a greatness, like the ooze of oil crushed.

This chapter presents selections from the spiritual writings of four early Jesuits. The first selection is by Alfonso Rodriguez. Rodriguez's book on the practice and perfection of Christian virtues was compulsory reading for Jesuits; it was also popular among members of other religious orders from the 17th century until the mid-20th century. The selection by Rodriguez printed here reveals the ways in which the early Jesuits saw their spiritual life as distinctive. The second selection is from Jerome Nadal, Loyola's closest assistant in his last years. Nadal here presents a systematic meditation on the birth of Christ. Loyola stressed that those making the Spiritual Exercises must use their imaginations to mentally re-create the biblical scenes and events on which they were centering their prayers, and Nadal's meditation book included splendid engravings designed to help readers envision the events of Christ's life. The third selection is taken from the meditations of Luis de La Puente (1554–1624). Few books of meditation were as popular or as detailed as La Puente's. In the selection included here he reflects on the devotional meaning of Christ's first parable, that of the sower. The fourth selection, from Robert Bellarmine's *Ascent of the Mind to God*, develops the same theme of the crowning meditation in Loyola's *Spiritual Exercises*, the Contemplation to attain love, in which Loyola teaches Christians to see God in all things. Here Bellarmine directs his readers' spiritual gaze above, to the sun and the stars as reflections of God's greatness and beauty.

Alfonso Rodriguez

Practice of Perfection and Christian Virtues

[Alfonso Rodriguez was born in 1538 at Valladolid and entered the Jesuits at the age of nineteen. For many years he served as rector or spiritual director at

Jesuit communities in southern Spain; he also taught moral theology. The first edition of his Ejercicio de perfección y virtudes cristianas *was published at Seville in 1609. The revised and definitive edition came out in 1616, the year of his death. The modern English edition runs to 1,744 pages in three volumes. Though Rodriguez lived during the golden age of Spanish mysticism, his massive book hardly addresses mystical spirituality. Many contemporary Spanish religious writers of his day offered a more vibrant style and deeper spiritual insight. Rodriguez, on the other hand, provided readers with a somewhat bland but encyclopedic synthesis of Christian spirituality with a bent toward practical applications. He divided his work into twenty-four treatises averaging some twelve chapters each. The first two volumes of his book address the virtues and religious beliefs and practices of all devout Catholics. The third volume is aimed at the special virtues, vows, and practices that members of religious orders were expected to cultivate.*

Within ten years after Rodriguez's death, his book appeared in seven Spanish printings and was translated into six languages. During the 17th century there were six different French translations, one of which went through eighty-three editions. By the mid-20th century some three hundred printings existed in twenty-three languages. In some convents Rodriguez's book was read to the nuns at breakfast every day of the year.

Given the comparative blandness of Rodriguez's style, why did his book achieve such lasting success? For starters, his style was simple, his suggestions prudent—he did not advocate severe penances and austerities. He laced in apt quotations from the Bible, the early Church Fathers, and such medieval saints as Benedict, Bernard, and Francis of Assisi as well as colorful anecdotes to illustrate the points he was making.[3] He avoided controversial topics. Aside from the Eucharist, his treatment of the sacraments was brief. Christians were called, he insisted, to devote themselves to private prayer, the love of God, and the service of their neighbors. Rodriguez did not dwell much on the social application of the Gospel or such deeper mysteries of the Christian faith as the Trinity or the Incarnation. He did, however, set himself against two movements prevalent among the Spanish Jesuits of his day. Some of the Spanish Jesuits wanted to devote much more time to prayer and less time to pastoral work or teaching; for such priests the goal of Jesuit life was a mystical union with God. Other Jesuits wanted to overhaul the highly centralized authority of the Jesuit general in Rome and work toward local autonomy. Rodriguez repeatedly refers his readers to the Jesuit Constitutions; his treatise on prayer is grounded

---

3. Benedict (c. 480–c. 547) was the founder of the Benedictine monks, Bernard (1090–1153) was the founder of the Cistercians, and Francis of Assisi (c.1181–1226), the most beloved saint of the Middle Ages, was the founder of the Franciscans.

on Loyola's Spiritual Exercises.⁴ The excerpts printed here are all from Ro-
driguez's Treatise 17.]

"On the end and institute of the Society of Jesus"⁵

Attend to yourself, and attend also to the teaching and instruction of your neighbor; apply yourself with all diligence to the one and to the other, for in this way you shall save yourself and also them that hear you. In these two things consists the end for which the Society was instituted, as our Constitutions and the apostolic bulls⁶ say: "The end of this Society is not only to attend by the grace of God to the salvation and perfection of our own souls, but by the same to apply ourselves earnestly to the salvation and perfection of our neighbor." And this is to be done not in any "as you like it" fashion, but "earnestly," a word expressive of vigor, efficiency, fervor, and intensity. The Society looks for men who will go about attaining the end of their calling with fervor, vigor, and energy. Here we must take note that, as in our own case, our aim should be not salvation merely, but salvation with perfection, so we are required by our Institute not to be content with helping our neighbors unto salvation, but we should endeavor to get them to make progress and go forward in virtue and perfection, each one according to his state. And so Father General Claudius Acquaviva⁷ in his "Instruction for Confessors" recommends us not to set our eyes on having a great number of penitents, but on those that we have to deal with making good progress. We should take the same interest in the progress and perfection of our neighbor as in our own, using the same care and diligence over the one as over the other.

For this, the Society was founded in these troublous times. Our blessed Father Ignatius saw the Church of God well provided with Religious Orders that attend to their own spiritual progress, keeping up choir and divine service; but at the same time he saw her straitened and afflicted with heresies,

---

4. For an overview of Rodriguez and his book, see John Patrick Donnelly, S.J., "Alfonso Rodríquez's *Ejercicio:* A Neglected Classic," *The Sixteenth Century Journal* 11, no. 2 (1980): pp. 16–24.

5. For the sections printed here, see Alphonsus Rodriguez, *Practice of Perfection and Christian Virtues* (Chicago: Loyola University Press, 1929), vol. 3, pp. 3–6, 12–5, 22–3. Used with the permission of Loyola University Press.

6. The apostolic bulls were formal papal documents authorizing the Jesuits and their work.

7. Acquaviva was superior general of the Jesuits from 1581 to 1615. Chapters 6 and 7 contain Acquaviva's rules for Jesuits working with peasants and serving as royal confessors.

sins, and great losses. Thereupon, inspired and guided by the Holy Ghost, he established this Religious Order, this troop and company of soldiers, to be, as he said, like so many light horse, ever ready to rush to the rescue against the sudden onslaughts of the enemy, and to defend and aid our brethren. And therefore he would have us free and disengaged from choir and other offices and observances which might hinder this end. "The harvest is plentiful, but laborers are few" (Lk. 10:2). How can we have the heart to let our neighbor perish and go to hell when it is in our power to succor him? St. [John] Chrysostom[8] says: "If you saw a blind man likely to fall headlong into a morass, you would lend him a hand; now seeing daily our brethren on the point of falling into the abyss of hell, how can we hold back and fail to stretch out a hand to them?"

Even of those holy Fathers of the Desert, whom God had called to solitude, we read in the Church histories that, when they saw the Church afflicted and persecuted by tyrants and heresies and the faithful in need of teaching and spiritual succor, they quitted the repose of the desert, and went round making excursions into the towns, answering heretics, teaching the Catholics, and encouraging them to martyrdom. So we read that the great Anthony[9] did in the time of Constantine;[10] as also did another holy man named Acepsemas,[11] who had been previously enclosed for sixty years without seeing or speaking to mortal man. And we read the same of many others. One of these, named Aphraates,[12] gave the Emperor Valens[13] a wonderfully good answer in this matter. This holy man, postponing his own peace and quiet to the salvation of the faithful, had quitted the cave in which he dwelt, and set to work to guide and guard the Lord's flock. For the Emperor had given orders to banish the Catholics, not only from their temples and cities, but even from the mountains, where they used to make their processions, singing hymns and praising God. While Aphraates was thus engaged, he passed one day by the house of the Emperor; and someone told Valens: "There goes that Aphraates, of whom all the faithful make so much account." The Emperor had him called, and said: "Where are you going?" He answered: "I am going to offer prayer for your empire." The Emperor said to him: "You would do better to pray at home, as monks generally do." To which the sagacious man replied: "Certainly you say well; that would be

---

8. For more on Chrysostom, see footnote 17 in the previous chapter.

9. St. Anthony (c. 251–356) is frequently called the Founder of the Religious Life; he spent most of his very long life as a hermit in the Egyptian desert.

10. Constantine was a Roman emperor (306–37).

11. Acepsemas was an early fourth-century Egyptian hermit.

12. Aphraates was also a fourth-century Egyptian hermit.

13. Valens was a Roman emperor (364–78).

the better course if you left room for it; and so I did all the time that Christ's sheep had the peaceful enjoyment of their pastures; but now that they are in great danger of being stolen or devoured by wolves, one is obliged to rush in all directions to the rescue. Tell me, Serene Highness, if I were a delicate young girl, and while I sat at my work in my room I saw my father's house on fire, what would be the right thing for me to do? Would it be well for me to sit still, and for my tender years take no heed of the home of my father's being burned, or should I run in search of water to put out the fire? Wherefore, seeing the house of God our Father is now on fire, and that you yourself, sir, have set it on fire, it is to put this fire out that we, who lived before in retirement, now come from all quarters to the rescue."

St. [John] Chrysostom, speaking of the care we ought to have for the salvation of our neighbors, makes use of another very pat comparison. Sailors on the vast ocean, says he, if they catch sight of a wreck a long way off, however good a wind they have to steer on their own course, nevertheless, in disregard of their own advantage, put their ship about, hasten to the spot, take in sail, anchor, and throw out ropes and planks for the drowning mariners to lay hold of and save themselves. So we ought to behave in our navigation of the wide ocean of this world, swept by many storms, pestered by many rocks and sand-banks, and the scene of so many shipwrecks. So, when you see a fellow voyager in danger, in the waves and tempests of this ocean, leave all your business and fly to his succor, for the necessity of a drowning man brooks no delay.

It was to this end, then, that God our Lord raised up the Society in such calamitous times, to succor and meet the particular need which the Church was then experiencing; it was a great stroke of His providence and a singular act of clemency. Writers of ecclesiastical history have noted and observed very reasonably that on the same day on which Pelagius was born in England to pervert and darken the world with his errors, there was born in Africa [St.] Augustine, that great luminary of the Catholic Church, to scatter by his radiant splendor the darkness of a malignant and dangerous heresy.[14] Also the writer[15] of our blessed Father Ignatius's Life observes that in the same year in which that infernal monster, Martin Luther, threw off the mask and began openly to declare war on the Catholic Church by preaching his blas-

14. The year, much less the day, when Pelagius (360?–420) was born is uncertain. His writings stressed the role of human free will in achieving salvation. Augustine devoted many of his most important works to refuting Pelagius and his followers. Both Roman Catholic theologians and the leading Protestant reformers such as Luther and Calvin sided with Augustine against Pelagius.

15. Rodriguez has Pedro de Ribadeneira's pioneering biography of Loyola in mind. It depicted Loyola as the champion of the Catholic Church against Luther and the Protestant Reformation.

phemies and heresies—it was in the year 1521—that same year God our Lord broke the leg of Ignatius at the castle of Pamplona, to heal him and change him from a dissolute and vain soldier into His captain and leader, and the defender of His Church against Luther. Hereby is seen the providence and clemency of the Lord, always careful to send new succors and reinforcements to His Church in the hour of her greatest need. . . .

The lessons we should thence learn for our own spiritual advancement are: first, a great affection for our ministries and devotion to them, as being so exalted, so pleasing to God, and so profitable to our neighbor; secondly, a great sense of shame at God's having called us, being what we are, to a rank so high and lofty; and whereas I am not in a position to give a good account of myself alone, God has over and above entrusted to me and put in my hands the salvation and perfection of others. It is a wonderful good piece of advice which that apostolic man, our Father Francis Xavier,[16] gave like a veteran and experienced soldier in a letter he wrote to the fathers and brothers of Portugal. He says to them: "I advise you, my brothers, never to touch upon the office and ministry that you hold, nor upon the good opinion and esteem that the world has of you, except to turn it to your confusion." . . . The higher the office to which God has called you, the more you ought to humble yourself.

An older father,[17] very distinguished for learning and virtue, used to say that, when he considered the high purpose and end of the Society and looked at himself, he felt so ashamed, seeing how insufficient and unworthy he was, that not only he felt no pride in seeing himself called to so exalted a function, but on the contrary it was an occasion to him of greater shame and humiliation. In this way the high state we are in will do us no harm, nor the opinion of our holiness that the world entertains, nor the honor done us on that account. The third lesson that we have to learn is to apply ourselves in good earnest to our own spiritual advancement, for to deal with our neighbor and make a better man of him, a great foundation of virtue is necessary, as we shall say afterwards. . . .

Since some heart perhaps may be melancholy, thinking that the end of which we have spoken is only for priests, who hear confessions and preach and have such immediate dealings with their neighbor, we will give some explanation here for the consolation of those who serve and help in temporal and exterior offices.[18] This end and enterprise belongs to all who are in the

16. Chapter 3 discusses Xavier's life and includes several of his letters.

17. Rodriguez is referring to Jerome Nadal. The next selection in this chapter is by Nadal.

18. Here Rodriguez has the Jesuit lay brothers in mind. Most were from the lower classes and received no academic training but were bound by the same vows as most other Jesuits. They performed such basic tasks as cooking and cleaning in the Jesuit communities.

Society, and not only to priests and men in their studies. Thus all should know to what end their labors are directed, of whatever sort they be, and the value and merit of them, and thus be better disposed to do them. We all make one body, one Order, one Society; and the end of all this body and Society is what we have said, to attend not only to our own advancement and perfection by the grace of God, but also to attend to the salvation and perfection of our neighbor. For the compassing and attaining of this end proper to our Order, some must be preachers, others confessors, others lecturers, and others coadjutors to aid in outward offices. So in war, for the gaining of victory, it is needful for some to fight and others to guard the baggage. The latter aid the former to fight and gain the victory, and deserve no less reward and remuneration than those who fight. As David said: "Equal shall be the portion of him who goes down to battle and of him who stays with the baggage; and they shall share alike in the division of the spoil" (1 Sam 30:24). Holy Writ says that this is a standing rule in Israel to this day, and with reason, for they are all one army, and for the gaining of the victory the one is as necessary as the other; the one party could not fight if the other did not stay on guard with the baggage. So it is here; we all make one body, one army, one company and troop of soldiers of Christ, for this enterprise of the conversion of souls. This man could not preach, nor that other hear confessions, nor that other lecture or study, if there were not someone to remain in charge of the temporalities. Thus he who minds the latter helps in preaching and in hearing confessions and in saving souls, and has his share in the victory and fruit that is won. St. Augustine says that at the death of St. Stephen, the first martyr, while others were stoning him, Paul was keeping their clothes, and thereby did more than all the rest, since he kept the clothes of them all.[19] If we may say this of an evil deed, much more may we say it of a good deed, since God is more inclined to reward than to punish.

Father Master Avila,[20] in a letter that he wrote to two priests who were on the point of entering the Society, being already missionaries and coming to a Society which makes that its profession, tells them not to fix their minds on rendering spiritual aid to their neighbor, nor be troubled at their not being employed in such ministries, since in the Society all that is done down to the washing of dishes in the kitchen is, he says, for the saving of souls. The saving of souls being the end of this Order, and great profit of souls depending upon its preservation and increase, all that is done to preserve and increase this Society, though it be the discharge of very humble

---

19. The martyrdom of St. Stephen and St. Paul's role in it, are described in Acts of the Apostles 7:54–8:2.

20. St. John of Avila (1500–69) was a good friend of the Spanish Jesuits.

offices, counts for the conversion of souls, and should be done very cheerfully. Members as we are of this body and this Order, every one of us by doing his duty and fulfilling his office helps to the fruit and profit that is made in the body, and so is partaker in the conversions and good works that are wrought throughout the whole Society. Our Father [Ignatius of Loyola] lays this down expressly in the Constitutions, speaking of the temporal coadjutors. So each one should be highly content and comforted in his office, taking it for a great blessing to be a member of this body of the Society, in which God is so well served and so much help is given to souls. Thus in the Society everything is for the conversion of souls, the being cook, the being porter, the being sacristan, because the end of it all is converting souls, and whatever helps the Society helps to that end. . . . Moreover, as we see in the course of nature that a plant, say a lettuce, does not produce seed while it is small, but only when it is grown to maturity—then does it begin to shed its seed, to multiply itself in others—so in the things of the spirit and of grace God requires a man first to be well advanced and grown in virtue into a perfect man before begetting spiritual sons to God and being able to say: "In Christ Jesus through the gospel I have begotten you" (1 Cor. 4: 15). For this reason the first thing the Society takes in hand is to attend to ourselves and to our own spiritual advancement; it would have its subjects well grounded in this first of all. To this end there is such a long probation in the Society; two years of novitiate to begin with, before starting the studies; and when these are over, she puts her men once more into the furnace and the mold, keeping them another whole year in probation, that in case study and speculation have dried up and cooled any of their spirit and devotion, they may refit themselves once more, now that they are on the point of entering upon their ministry to their neighbor, and not treat of matters of the spirit without themselves having the spirit. And even after that it seems that we are never to cease being novices; our profession is put off for so many years[21] that one may say our whole life is spent in novitiate and probation before the Society gives a man his grade as a formed workman in its service. Much is to be entrusted to him, and so he must be much proved and tried first for all he is worth; he is to be put to high things, dealing with others to make them not only good, but perfect, and so it is necessary that he himself be perfect.

Hence it will be seen how great is the mistake of those to whom these probations appear long, and who even fancy that their time is lost in them, and would like to see themselves already preaching and dealing with their

---

21. Jesuits usually made their profession (i.e., took their final vows) only after at least fifteen years in the Society. Members of most other religious orders took solemn vows after several years.

neighbor. The moment they get a little devotion in meditation, or one or two good thoughts, they want to be in the pulpit.

Jerome Nadal

Annotations and Meditations on the Gospels

[Jerome (Gerónimo) Nadal was born in 1507 on the island of Majorca off Spain's Mediterranean coast. He studied at the University of Alcalá and the University of Paris where he encountered Ignatius of Loyola, who encouraged him to join the companions. Nadal declined. After being ordained a priest and earning a doctorate in theology he returned to his native Majorca to work as a priest. But after reading the published letters of Francis Xavier, he was so impressed that he went to Rome and joined the Jesuits in 1545. He so deeply absorbed the new spirit of the Jesuits that he has frequently been called Loyola's Alter Ego and even the Second Founder of the Jesuits. Loyola quickly entrusted major tasks to him. Among other responsibilities, Nadal took on the role of superior at the first Jesuit college for lay students at Messina, promulgated the Jesuit Constitutions in many countries, and worked as a sort of general problem solver for Loyola. After Loyola's death Nadal carried out similar important tasks for later Jesuit generals. He died in Rome in 1580.[22]

Nadal wrote many spiritual works.[23] His largest and most important work was the Annotations and Meditations on the Gospels, *which follows the order of the gospels in the Masses of the liturgical year. Nadal spent his leisure time from 1568 until 1575 writing this massive work, which was not published until 1595. The definitive edition was published in Antwerp in 1604. The delays in its publication arose because of the size of the work (six hundred folio pages) and because Nadal wanted to have it illustrated with 153 engravings. He also wanted Europe's most prestigious publishing house, that of Christopher Plantin in Antwerp, to publish it. Distinguished Flemish artists, the three brothers Hieronymus, Johan, and Antoon Wierix, contributed the engravings.[24]*

The brothers' engravings were not just illustrated afterthoughts. Loyola's

22. For Nadal's life and work, see William Bangert, S.J., and Thomas McCoog, S.J., *Jerome Nadal, S.J., 1507–1580: Tracking the First Generation of Jesuits* (Chicago: Loyola University Press, 1992).

23. Nadal's spiritual writings are discussed by Jean-François Gilmont, S.J., *Les écrits spirituels des premiers Jésuites* (Rome: Institutum historicum Soceitatis Iesu, 1961), pp. 232–49; most of them were written for the use of young Jesuits.

24. A leading expert on early Jesuits and the arts comments, "But by far the most important Jesuit image cycle of the period—and one which was virtually overwhelmed with landscape—was the magnificent set of 153 illustrations to Nadal's *Evangelicae historiae imagines* . . . which were extremely influential not only in

Spiritual Exercises *insisted that those making the meditations should try to re-construct in their imagination the physical scene of the meditations on the gospels—they were to use their imagination much as a modern film director has to visualize and plan out the scenes of a movie.*[25] *Perhaps no Jesuit book of meditations provided so much visual help as did Nadal's. Each engraving has a number of letters inserted at key points of the picture; the subject of each let-ter is spelled out (here A to M) under the engraving. Nadal then provides an annotation or explanation of each subject or miniscene, plus its biblical or pa-tristic sources. The illustrated scenes are to stimulate the imagination and de-votion of those making the meditation no less than the biblical text itself does. The meditation chosen here, Christ's birth in Bethlehem, is the third in Nadal's book. (The two previous meditations are on the Annunciation and the Visitation of Mary to her cousin Elizabeth.)]*

Volume 1: *Infancy Narratives*[26]

The Night of the Lord's Nativity

A. *Bethlehem, David's city.*[27]

B. *The forum where the tax is paid.*

C. *The cave where Christ is born.*

D. *JESUS, newly born, lies in straw on the ground before the manger. The Virgin Mary wraps Him in swaddling clothes.*

E. *Angels adore the newborn Child.*

F. *The ox and the donkey at the manger are roused by the new light.*

Europe but on the missions from China to Paraguay." Gauvin Alexander Bailey, "Jesuit Corporate Culture and the Visual Arts," *The Jesuits: Culture, Sciences and the Arts, 1540–1773,* edited by John O'Malley et al. (Toronto: Toronto University Press, 1999), p. 70.

25. Nadal also produced an edition of *The Spiritual Exercises* with illustrations: *The Illustrated Spiritual Exercises,* edited by Jerome Nadal (Scranton: Scranton Univer-sity Press, 2001).

26. This meditation of Nadal is reprinted from *The Infancy Narratives,* vol. 1, *Anno-tations and Meditations on the Gospels,* edited and translated by Frederick Homann, S.J. (Philadelphia: St. Joseph's University Press, 2003), pp. 127–33. It is printed with the permission of St. Joseph's University Press. The first volume (two more are pro-jected) contains a long and valuable introductory essay, "The Art of Vision in Jerome Nadal's *Adnotationes et meditationes in Evangelia,*" by Walter Melion, pp. 1–96.

27. The letters A through M are all found in the engraving *On the Night of the Lord's Birth* and are explained here.

On the Night of the Lord's Birth: The Nativity of Christ, by Jerome Nadal. Engraving
by Hieronymus Wierix, 1607.

G. *Light from the newborn Christ scatters the darkness of night.*

H. *The Heder (Flock) Tower.*

I. *Shepherds and flocks at the tower.*

K. *An angel appears to the shepherds, and with him the heavenly host.*

L. *An angel that devout belief holds was sent as messenger to the Elders in Limbo.*

M. *The star and the angel sent to the Magi first call them to their journey.*

Gospel reading—Luke 2

Now it came to pass in those days, that there went forth a decree from Caesar Augustus[28] that a census of the whole world should be taken. This first census took place while Quirinius was governor of Syria.[29] And all were going, each to his own town to register.

And Joseph also went from Galilee out of the town of Nazareth into Judea to the town of David, which is called Bethlehem—because he was of the house and family of David—to register, together with Mary his espoused wife, who was with child. And it came to pass while they were there, that the days for her to be delivered were fulfilled. And she brought forth her firstborn son, and wrapped Him in swaddling clothes, and laid Him in a manger, because there was no room for them in the inn.

And there were shepherds in the same district living in the fields and keeping watch over their flock by night. And behold, an angel of the Lord stood by them and the glory of God shone round about them, and they feared exceedingly.

And the angel said to them, "Do not be afraid, for behold, I bring you good news of great joy which shall be to all the people; for there has been born to you today a Savior, who is Christ the Lord. And this shall be a sign to you: you will find an infant wrapped in swaddling clothes and lying in a manger." And suddenly there was with the angel a multitude of the heavenly host praising God and saying, "Glory to God in the highest, and peace on earth among men of good will."

Annotations

A. Bethlehem, or Ephrata, David's city in the tribe of Judah, is set on a little hill six miles south of Jerusalem.

B. The forum at Bethlehem where a tax collector sits at his table. One man pays the tax; others come to do the same.

C. The cave (St. Jerome called it an aperture) where JESUS was born. The manger was hewn from the rock inside. Christ's sepulcher[30] was similar. Here a manger was hewn in the back of the cave, there a sepulcher. Contemplate the lowliness, and at the same time the majesty

28. Octavian Augustus Caesar ruled as the first Roman emperor from 27 B.C. to A.D. 14.

29. P. Sulpicius Quirinius was Roman legate of Syria from A.D. 6 to A.D. 7, but modern scholars doubt that he was governor of Syria at the time of the birth of Jesus.

30. Christ's sepulcher or tomb was also in a cave.

of this most sacred place. Nothing in the sepulcher could be more abject, nothing here more venerable.

D. JESUS, newly born, is set on straw on the ground before the manger in the cave, as He cries and reaches out for His mother. The Virgin Mother, in adoration, exulting in spirit, her soul filled with delight, moves to wrap the shivering Child in the swaddling clothes she made, and nourishes Him. See how in these mysteries Mary keeps her virginal integrity, and how she has a woman to assist her. Her mind is filled with heavenly praise and spiritual exultation at her Son's birth, both eternally from the Father and from herself in time. Most dutifully she cares for her Son. Joseph, rapt in admiration, adores the Infant.

E. Angels sent from heaven to Bethlehem gaze at the manger. Many of them fill sky and earth. They adore the Child born of the Virgin, their King and Lord, singing to Him celestial hymns of praise.

F. The ox and the ass are tied to the manger hewn from the rock. Their heads are raised and turned to the place of birth, as though sensing that the stable saw an unprecedented event.

G. The dark sky suggests night, yet brilliant light from the Infant God Who brought the world celestial light, illumines the cave.

H. Heder (Flock) Tower, where Jacob pitched his tent and pastured his flock, a mile east of Bethlehem [Gen. 35:21; Mic. 4:8].

I. There, shepherds keeping their watch in the fields, marking night vigils, or standing guard over the flock, are terrified at the sight of an angel. Flocks and dogs stare at the new light.

K. An angel from on high approaches the shepherds. The glory of God shines round them. They fear exceedingly, and draw back. They hear from the angel that Christ is born. A multitude of the heavenly host accompanies the angel, praising God and singing *Glory to God in the highest and peace on earth among men of good will.*

L. The angel whom devotion suggests the Infant God sent to the Elders in Limbo to announce His birth as man.[31] (The cavern is not shown however since the artist had to draw the earth open to show a place for the angel and let the viewer look into it.)

M. The new star and its angel mover who was sent by the infant JESUS. At His revelation through the star, the Magi Kings, each in his own

---

31. Nadal here refers to the belief, which had no basis in the Bible, that an angel was sent to Limbo to give the encouraging message to the saints of the Old Testament and others who were going to be saved that their salvation and transfer to heaven was approaching, since the Savior had been born.

realm, were inspired, and began to make ready for the journey. For we know this happened when Christ was born. An angel was sent to the shepherds, another to the Elders in Limbo, a third to the Magi Kings in the East. The newborn Christ was announced to all humankind. God's infinite goodness to us was celebrated on earth, under it, and in the heavens. Can you doubt that every angel in heaven sang divine praises at His birth? that they knew the ruin their peers [i.e., the devils] wrought would be gloriously repaired by the Infant God now born on earth? Not just angels in heaven and humans on and under the earth give thanks for the newborn God-man. The heavens too, the elements, every creature bows to adore the God now born, and to thank Him. They sense how Divinity's presence ennobles them. Heaven, earth, everything rejoices. The hope surges that they can slough off corruption and that no creature will be subject to it any longer.

Meditation

[**Reader:**] Little Child JESUS, today You are born of a humble Virgin in a Bethlehem stable, laid on straw, crying, cold, and poor. Wrapped in swaddling clothes, You lie before a manger because there is no room for You, not even in the inn [Lk. 2]. What shall we admire, herald, and contemplate here first? Some things strike us right away, others more subtly, so that through them we will be even more moved and gracefully refreshed by the first.

What then are these deeper ideas? Are they not Your two nativities, great JESUS? What majestic greatness here! You, immense Word, Who are born as infinite light in eternity, are now born in a stable. Today, I say, You are generated of the Father, God from God, Yourself God, consubstantial with the Father.[32] Because You have been born from eternity, You are always being born, and never cease to be born of the Father. Infinite power, majesty, and divinity, an immense nativity and generation from eternity, are all found in this Your humble birth. Your first nativity has incomparable mystery, and the greatest mystery in keeping with Your generation when, Yourself almighty God, glorious Splendor, and Image of the Father's immense substance, You became man from the substance of a Virgin only, in

---

32. The Nicene Creed asserts that the Second Person of the Trinity is consubstantial with the Father, that is, fully equal and sharing the same substance with the Father. This statement, which was formulated by the First Ecumenical Council, held at Nicaea in 325, condemned the teaching of the Arians, who claimed that the Second Person of the Trinity was a sort of super angel, not true God of true God, not equal to the Father.

her womb, from whom You are now born. [Leo, *Letter* 10.][33] Because each nature's properties were kept when the natures were united in one Person, lowliness was assumed by majesty, weakness by strength, mortality by Your eternity.

Those lofty, infinite mysteries fascinate us. To see Christ born should stir us far more than what we don't see, for we are most deeply moved and delightfully refreshed by what we see. But we aren't, dear JESUS! This, because of our spiritual inertia, our lack of faith and neglect of Your gifts! For who, on using God's gifts a little better, wouldn't first be filled with delightful serenity and celestial light, and then be absorbed with divinity? Knowing God's infinite power, glory, and immense majesty, one would sing praise with divine jubilation through You, Christ JESUS, born of a Virgin's sacrosanct womb, Who are here set in the straw, crying, a cold little pauper wrapped in swaddling clothes. Good Child JESUS, explain these Your wonders to us. This I want to know: What did You work during those nine months in the Virgin's womb? And what marvels will You do when You leave it?

[**Jesus:**]   Why do you ask? You would believe all I could tell you, but only halfheartedly, with no vital, profound assent. Even in My Mother's womb, in a single dynamic spiration with the Father, I eternally *spirated* the Holy Spirit, the Paraclete.[34] With the Father and the Holy Spirit I provided for angels, heaven, and all creation by the divinity's infinite power and wisdom. The angels I gave eternal glory, the demons eternal pain. As Almighty God I reigned in eternity. I filled the Virgin Mother's mind, spirit, and soul with My presence and power. She gave Me bodily substance and food even as I was at work. Each day I made her share more fully in My divine nature. Each day I grew in body from her, she in spirit from Me. I was living by My mother in My mother, she by Me and through Me.

33. This letter of Leo I (pope 440–61) discusses the relationship of the divine and human natures in Christ. His teaching that Christ was one Person possessing both divine and human nature exerted a strong influence one the 4th Ecumenical Council held at Chalcedon in 451. The teaching of the Council on this point remains normative for the Roman Catholic, Eastern Orthodox, and mainstream Protestant churches. J. N. D. Kelly, *The Oxford Dictionary of the Popes* (Oxford: Oxford University Press, 1986), pp. 43–5.

34. The Nicene Creed as used in the Western churches, both Roman Catholic and Protestant, claims that the Holy Spirit "proceeds from the Father and the Son." According to the Catholic Church, this procession has existed from all eternity and continues forever. Traditionally the Father is said to beget the Son; the Father and the Son are said to spirate, or breathe forth, the Holy Spirit.

In her womb, I was generated eternally from the Father, and in time from My Mother. From My Father I had the *Divinity's* infinite fullness, from My Mother growth in human stature and perfection. My bodily senses were not yet active, save for the usual natural functions. My mind worked in a divine mode, above human or angelic faculties and nature. My soul enjoyed celestial paradisiacal delight and unbounded happiness.

[**Reader:**] Great and little JESUS, You were most intimately in the eternal Father's bosom, and ever so humbly and warmly in Your Mother's. You spoke not, You lived in your Mother, and yet with the Father You worked and merited our salvation. Truly You are a hidden God [Is. 41], a Savior from and in the womb of Your Father, and in that of Your Mother. Lord, You have shown me deep mysteries. Through them, blessed Child, now reveal the others.

[**Jesus:**] Indeed as human I had to be shut in my Mother's womb, yet I leaped and exulted as a giant running My course [Ps. 19:5]. I wanted to leave her sweet womb, I longed for birth into your mortal life, to battle Satan, the world, the flesh, death, and Hell, to do battle in My mighty power from heaven, indignant wrath, and zeal, and yet to walk on earth as humble, gentle, and meek, a fragile human.

[**Reader:**] Be born! Come to us, Holy Child! What a transcendent divine blessing! God's profound mystery! The most holy Virgin bore You, God and man! No sorrow there, nothing of the usual needs, no midwife, no solicitous women about. Fruitful herself, the joyful Virgin with the greatest sweetness of spirit bears, adores, and nurses the God-man. Mother and midwife, she wraps Him in swaddling clothes. The angels tend their infant King and their Queen Mother, should they want anything. They get straw for His bedding. Angel hands receive Him at His birth, and reverently place the little One in the straw on the ground. Holy JESUS, I beg You, tell me Your birth in Isaiah's words.

[**Jesus:**] Today I am born a humble child, not for Myself or the angels or God, but for you mortals. Only you need My human birth. My humanity is for you alone [Tit. 3; Is. 9]. I was born for you mortals, and given to you, that is, for you, with this mortal life's endless sorrows, labor, and pains. With truculent thieves I was sentenced to death, to infinite contempt, and to crucifixion. All this for your life and salvation. I, your Lord and God, was given as your brother. I became your friend, aide, and servant, your way, salvation, truth, and life, your wisdom, justice, sanctification, and redemption [Mt. 20; Jn. 13, 14]. Treasures of wisdom, knowledge, and divinity hidden in Me are yours in and through Me [1 Cor. 1; Col. 2]. They are also hidden within you.

I am given to you as food and drink, too. I am your sustenance. Come, My beloved, eat, drink, be filled. Be sated at the breasts of My heavenly, divine wisdom, delight, and grace [S. of S. 5]. All is given to you with Me and through Me. Put to work the infinite power given you with and through Me. It will work in you, if you want it to.

[**Reader:**]   Good, holy JESUS, what incomparable, adorable good will You show us! What immense blessings in and through You the eternal Father told in David's psalm: "I have said you are gods, and all sons of the Most High" [Ps. 81]. So it is, Lord. But what is added terrifies me: "Yet you will die like all men, and fall like any prince," unless I take it as Your Father's warning, and a prophecy about those who are perishing. The warning, the sign, urges us to greater hope in You.

Your Father speaks with intensity because He seeks intensely our salvation. He wants to turn us from our vices to adhere to Him. Gentle JESUS, You were born for us, given to us. What sign do You give of Your power?

[**Jesus:**]   I bear on My shoulders the cross, the preeminent sign of My kingdom. On coming into the world I did that first which I ever did in My Mother's womb, and still do: I offered My death on the cross to the Father for you. That is My kingdom, My reign. With it I will vanquish Satan, Hell, Death, and Sin. With it I will reign for eternity and sit at the Father's right hand, I Who am ever in the bosom of the Father. Through the power of the cross all My Father's elect will reign.[35]

Luis de La Puente

Meditations on the Mysteries of Our Holy Faith

[Luis de La Puente (1554–1624) was born at Valladolid, where he studied theology before entering the Jesuits in 1574. He completed much of his theological training under Francisco Suárez (1548–1617), the greatest Jesuit scholastic theologian. La Puente completed his spiritual training under the guidance of Baltasar Alvarez, S.J., (1535–80), the Jesuit mystic and spiritual writer whose biography La Puente wrote in 1615. La Puente's massive Meditaciones de los misterios de nuestra santa Fe *was first published at Valladolid in 1605. Of all the many meditation books in the 17th century, few could rival his* Meditaciones *for enduring popularity: since its publication more than four hundred editions of the book have been published in many*

---

35. Only roughly half of the whole meditation is printed here.

languages. *The English translation from which this selection is taken runs to six volumes.*[36]

Meditation 44: on the parable of the sower [Mt. 13:3–23]

Point 1

1. "Behold the sower went forth to sow" [Mt. 13:3].

Our Redeemer Himself provided an explanation for this parable; it therefore ought to be meditated on according to His explanation: i. What *seed* this is which he sows. ii. In *what ground.* iii. For what *cause.* iv. *How* he sows it.

i. The seed is *the word of God,* both the outward word, which enters by the ears of the body, and the inward word, which resounds within the soul, which is the divine inspiration, from whence principally spring those fruits which our heart produces, because it gives a feeling of that which is heard, and is as the seminal virtue, which is within the grain that is sown.

ii. The principal sower is *Almighty God.* Three and One, who sometimes sows the seed of His inspiration, by the means of His preachers, in those who hear them; or by means of good books, in those who read them; or by the means of good examples or devout pictures, in those who behold them. Sometimes by Himself alone, He casts the seed of His inspiration on a sudden into our heart.

36. Luis de La Puente, *Meditations on the Mysteries of our Holy Faith,* translated by John Heigham (London: Richardson and Son, 1853), vol. 3, pp. 429–36. Heigham's translation was originally published in 1619 in St. Omer in Belgium. I have modernized his spellings. For discussions of La Puente's life and spiritual writings, see J. Allison Peers, *Studies of the Spanish Mystics* (New York: Macmillan, 1951–60), vol. 2, pp. 241–69 and Joseph de Guibert, S.J., *The Jesuits: Their Spiritual Doctrine and Practice,* translated by William J. Young (Chicago: Loyola University Press, 1964), pp. 253–56. Jesuit meditation books strongly influenced such English poets as John Donne, George Herbert, Richard Crashaw, and Robert Southwell, S.J.: see Louis Martz, *The Poetry of Meditation: A Study in English Religious Literature in the Seventeenth Century* (New Haven: Yale University Press, 1954), pp. 27–50. The first two poets were Protestant clergy, the second two, Catholic priests. Jesuit devotional books, such as Bellarmine's *Ascent of the Mind to God* and his *Art of Dying Well,* were often issued in Protestant adaptations. The most popular English Jesuit devotional work of the Elizabethan age was Robert Persons' *Christian Directory* (Rouen: Fr. Person's Press, 1583). Martz points out that it went through seven editions on the Continent by 1633, but the translation/adaptation by the Protestant clergyman Edmund Bunny enjoyed twenty editions by 1640 (Martz, *The Poetry of Meditation,* p. 7).

iii. The *ground* on which this seed is sown, *is the soul, with her powers and faculties;* in the *memory* are sown holy thoughts and devout imaginations, such are the remembrance of our sins, the pains of hell, the rewards of heaven, the shortness or our life, our death, judgment, the presence of God, and of His benefits. In the *understanding* are sown heavenly illustrations, which suddenly discover the secrets which are enclosed in the mysteries of our faith, and are the seed of meditation and contemplation. He also sows therein good counsels, inspiring it with that counsel which it is to take for itself, or to give to others, sowing likewise, the dictates of *conscience,* which exhort to virtue, and condemn vice. In the *will* are holy desires and. affections, which flash forth like sparks, and produce the fire of perfect love, with the fruit of virtues: such are the effects of the fear of God, of hell, of death, sorrow for sins, love of God, desires to see Him, and to serve Him sincerely.

iv. The r*eason why* He sows this seed in the soul is not His own advantage, which other sowers seek, but *the profit and the utility of the same soul;* forasmuch as this seed has a very special power to alter and improve the ground on which it is sown, even if the ground of itself may be bad, barren, dry, and unprofitable. And this purpose why Almighty God sows it, not for the worthiness of the earth, but only because of His bounty and mercy, because He is good and liberal, and greatly delighted to sow His gifts in us, to amend us with them. Hence it is that He ofttimes sows His seed in all places, times and occasions, especially when it most aids us for our salvation. For which reason Christ our Lord said, "The sower went forth to sow." Giving us to understand that it is His office to sow, and that He evermore fulfils His office in one way or other.

2. From all these considerations, and from every one of them, I am to draw affections of *praise and gratitude* to this divine sower, as also a great esteem of His seed, and very fervent desires, that He sow it within my soul, begging it of Him from my very heart, by colloquies made to all the three divine Persons.

Colloquy. O heavenly Father, who has sent into the world the eternal Word, your Word engendered within yourself, that He might be the seed of all seeds, and of all your words, which are the seeds of our only good; I beg you by this Word your Son to sow in my memory the abundant seed of holy thoughts, that there may spring from thence an abundant harvest of good works. O eternal Word, who came forth from the bosom of your eternal Father, and descended from heaven into our earth to sow the seed of holy doctrine, seed which properly is your own, and not another's, nor begged elsewhere. Come, O Lord, to sow in my understanding abundant seed of divine illuminations, by which I may know you and know myself and I know what I am to believe and do in such way that I may put the same into practice. O most sacred Spirit, who inspires where you will [Jn. 3:8], and will inspire where there is need of your inspiration; touch my will, sow it with the seed of holy affections, and cast into it the sparks of fervent desires, by which there may be enkindled within my heart a vehement fire of divine love, that with your seed may bud forth abundant fruits of the spirit which proceed from this love [Gal. 5:22]. O blessed Trinity, I give you thanks for the liberality with which you sow your seed in a ground so vile and so contemptible. O divine seed, who can esteem you as you deserve! O that I were full of your holy virtue! O my soul, unprofitable ground, do you not desire this heavenly seed? Sigh for it, demand it, solicit it, and you shalt not be denied it.

Point 2   Although this seed be so precious, and efficacious, and that the sower should sow it in very good season, and with a desire that it fructify, yet *three parts of it perish* through the fault and bad qualities of the ground in which it is sown: I will search and examine into myself, what the defects and causes are, and how to remedy them, being sorry to have them, and having compassion on others that have them, and for the loss of so much seed, with so much injury to the sower.

1. *"Some fell by the wayside,"* and was trodden upon by the passers-by, and the fowls of the air came and ate it, so that it did not fructify. The earth by the wayside and without a ditch is a heart hardened, like a way much trodden and trampled upon, which hears the word of Almighty God exteriorly, and receives it superficially, without penetrating or embracing it, giving entrance to all sorts of earthly thoughts, without any guard or circumspection at all; there this seed is tread and trampled upon, and the devils themselves run speedily thither to steal it away out of their heart and memory. In this condition and state will I put myself and say, "Woe is me, who for the hardness of my heart have not desired to receive the word of Almighty God, which, if it has entered in at one ear, has gone out at the other. I am like the wayside or path for travelers, admitting all manner of evil thoughts and desires, which seek to have passage through my heart. I have permitted the infernal fowls, with the beaks of their perverse suggestions, to rob me of the seed of good inspirations, receiving those and rejecting these."

Colloquy. It grieves me, O my God, for the small account which I have made of this sacred seed, and I purpose to till the earth of my heart with the tillage of true mortification and to soften its hardness, that it may receive your holy word and hide and cover it, "that I may not sin against you" [Ps. 119:11]. But as you know my frailty, cause your inspirations to soften me and help me to produce the fruit which you desire for your glory. Amen.

2. *"And some others fell upon stony ground, where they had not much earth,"* as being next to a rock, this seed "sprung up," and grew high, but the sun

with its heat parched it, because it had not deep roots, nor sufficient humidity to nourish it. Such are those who have a certain natural tenderness and facility to hear the word of God with great delight and to read good books, conceiving good desires and resolutions and beginning to put them in execution; but when temptations from the Devil, the flesh, and the persecutions of men arise, immediately that good which they had withered away, and they quite forsake and leave it off, being inconstant and not deeply rooted in humility and confidence in Almighty God, nor have they the humidity and sap of substantial devotion; and as St. Mark says: "They are devout for a little time, which presently passes like the dew that goes away in the morning"[37] or like the flower that withers, and hangs its head with the least heat. Nor is it without mystery that Christ our Lord compares persecutions to the sun, whose property is to shine with its light and to scorch with its heat. By this two sorts of persecutions are represented, one of prosperity, praise, flattery, vainglory, and worldly ambition; the other, of adversity, calumny, dishonor, poverty, fear, and other afflictions, against which we ought to be fortified and deeply rooted, to the end that the fruit does not wither, which the divine inspiration has sowed within us, showing ourselves like the apostles, faithful ministers of God, in "honor and dishonor, by evil report and good report" [2 Cor. 6:8].

Colloquy. O eternal God, since you know my great mutability, fortify me with your holy grace, that I may cast such deep roots in charity, that nothing created may be able to uproot me from it. Amen.

3. *"And others fell among thorns,"* and the thorns grew up and choked them. These are they who hear the word of Almighty God, but do not fructify, because the riches, and cares of the world and pleasures of the flesh, after which they go, choke the spirit. So that there are three things which choke and smother divine inspiration and hinder our spiritual profit, namely riches, pricking cares, and sensual pleasures. All three in the school of Christ are called thorns.

Colloquy. O sovereign master, how different are your judgments from ours; that which the world calls riches and delights, you call thorns and thistles: because, howsoever they delight the body, they prick, hurt, and damage the soul and draw forth a great deal of blood by sins, and pierce it with pains, anguishes and remorse. Deliver me, O Lord, from these thorns and crown me with your own thorns, which, although they prick and pierce the flesh, yet they nourish and comfort the spirit, because there is no greater consolation than to embrace your crown of thorns on earth, with the hope of obtaining the crown of glory in the Kingdom of Heaven.

37. This statement is not found in Mark's Gospel; the idea is found in Hos. 6.4 and 13.3.

Point 3   "And others, (the fourth part), fell upon good ground, and they brought forth fruit." "These are they who are sown upon the good ground," who "in a good and very good heart hear the word and receive it, and yield fruit in patience," "the one thirty, another sixty, and another a hundredfold" [Mk. 4:20].

1. In like manner, therefore, as there are three sorts of wicked who destroy this seed, so are there three sorts of good Christians, who bring forth good from it: some in the state of beginners, with a little profit, others in the state of proficients, with greater profit, and others in the state of the perfect, with great excellence; all laboring with patience and persistence, expecting the reward. And although they are fewer in number than the wicked, yet they compensate by their gain for the loss of the other three parts of the seed.

Colloquy. I rejoice, O sweet and sovereign sower, that there are to be found such grounds in which your seed discovers its virtue and brings forth a hundred for one. O that there were much such ground, that many might glorify and serve you as reason requires. Encourage yourself, O my soul, to serve your God with diligence, and content not yourself with the fruit of thirty, nor even of sixty, but with that of a hundredfold [Mk. 4:20] since proportionate to the fruit of this life will be the recompense of the other. Even in this life God will give you a hundred for one, if you serve Him with fervent affection.

2. Other applications may be made, as the saints say, attributing the fruit of thirty to the *married;* that of sixty to *widows* and *virgins;* and that of a hundred to *martyrs,* or to such Religious[38] as profess a contemplative or mystical life; teaching others the way of perfection, which they themselves tread. Regardless of my own state in life, I ought to aspire after that which is the most perfect, for it may well be that the state be only of thirty, and yet may yield the fruit of a hundredfold, the greatness of the fervor supplying the imperfection of the state.

Robert Bellarmine

The Ascent of the Mind to God

[Chapter 4, "Jesuit Opposition to Protestantism," offers an introduction to the life of St. Robert Bellarmine and his refutation of the Protestant belief that Scripture is the only norm and source of Christian faith. Although Bellarmine is best known as a controversial theologian, his most popular works were his catechisms. His second most popular works were a series of short books written near the end of his life. Each September from 1614 to 1619, Bellarmine took a month off from his administrative work as a cardinal and remade the Spiritual

---

38. Religious are members of religious orders.

Exercises of Ignatius of Loyola at the Jesuit novitiate in Rome; in his spare time during these retreats he wrote five short devotional books. All five of these be-came very popular and enjoyed many editions in several languages. The most popular of these books was the first, The Ascent of the Mind to God *by the Ladder of Created of Things. The influence of Loyola's* The Spiritual Exer-cises—*most notably the Contemplation to Attain Love—on* The Ascent of the Mind *is evident. The theme of physical creation providing a ladder of ascent is one common to all mainstream Christian traditions, to Eastern Orthodox writ-ers and Protestants no less than to Roman Catholics. Several Protestant transla-tions of Bellarmine's* Ascent *have been published over the years.*

The Ascent *belongs to a popular devotional genre called the Ladder of Ascent, which has its roots in pre-Christian tradition. Such Greek writers as Pindar, Plato, and especially Plotinus[39] saw human spiritual development as a series of upward steps toward the Ultimate. The idea of a Ladder of Ascent is found in ancient Chi-nese and Indian religious writings; the theme that life is climbing a ladder to God is also found in the Bible (Gen. 28:12; Ezek. 40:26, 31). Christians such as St. John Climachus (c. 569–c. 649) and St. Bonaventure (1221–74) wrote classic works developing this theme. Bellarmine's ladder has fifteen steps. Each step shows readers how different creatures can lead them to God. Step 3 through Step 6 dwell on the ways the four elements of ancient cosmology (earth, air, water, and fire) re-flect the glory and beauty of God. The seventh step, on the heavens, sun, moon, and stars, has been chosen here as a sample of Bellarmine's longer work. Step 7 is di-vided into six short chapters; Chapters 1, 2, 3 and 6 are printed here.[40]*

The Latin text of The Ascent of the Mind to God *was first published in 1615 by Plantin of Antwerp; it ran through six printings that first year—it was, in its time, a best seller. By 1930 the book had appeared in sixty editions in fifteen different languages.]*

Step 7: The consideration of the heavens, the sun, the moon, and the stars

Chapter 1:   "How the sun is the dwelling place of God, who is high and beautiful."

Here we will not have to work hard to build ourselves a step to God from the consideration of the heavens since we have a predecessor in the

39. Pindar (522?–443 B.C.) was a Theban poet. Plato (427?–347 B.C.) was not only a master of Greek prose but also the most influential philosopher of antiquity. Plotinus (A.D. 205?–70) was the greatest Neoplatonic philosopher.

40. These passages from *The Ascent of the Mind to God* are taken from *Robert Bel-larmine: Spiritual Writings,* edited and translated by John Patrick Donnelly, S.J., and Roland Teske, S.J. (Mahwah, N.J.: Paulist Press, 1989), pp. 119–24, 128–30. They are printed with the permission of Paulist Press.

Royal Prophet [King David] who sings in the psalms, "The heavens show forth the glory of God, and the firmament declares the work of his hands" (Ps. 19:1). There are two times, day and night, by which we ascend from heaven to God on the wings of contemplation. He writes in the psalm about the first, "He has set his tabernacle in the sun, and he, as a bridegroom coming out of his bride chamber, has rejoiced like a giant to run the way. His going out is from the end of heaven, and his circuit over to the end thereof, and there is no one that can hide himself from his heat" (Ps. 19:5–6). In another psalm he writes of the second, "I will behold your heavens, the work of your fingers: the moon and the stars which you have founded" (Ps. 8:4).

Let us begin with the first time. The Holy Spirit by the mouth of David praises in song four features of the sun which we see during the day: the first, that it is the tabernacle of God; the second, that it is very beautiful; the third, that it is always running tirelessly and extremely fast; and the fourth, that it mainly shows its power in illuminating and warming. For all these reasons Ecclesiasticus[41] writes that it is "an admirable instrument, the work of the Most High; great is the Lord that made him" (Sir. 43:2, 5).

First, God the Creator of all things placed his tabernacle in the sun as in the most noble of things; this means that God chose the sun out of all bodily things so that he might dwell in it as in a royal palace or a divine sanctuary. God, of course, fills heaven and earth (Jer. 23:24), and heaven and the heaven of heavens do not contain him (2 Chr. 2:6). Still he is said more appropriately to dwell where he manifests greater signs of his presence in working marvels. Since the Hebrew text says that he placed his tabernacle at the sun in them, that is, the heavens, we gather from this verse of the psalm another excellence of the sun which does not contradict the first one. The sun is large, and for it God made a vast, beautiful, and noble palace. He wished that the sky itself be the palace of the sun in which it might roam freely and do its work and that the sun itself might be the palace of God, the highest prince. Just as we know the greatness and eminence of the sun from the fact that its tabernacle is the sky, so we know the greatness and eminence of God from the fact that his tabernacle is the sun, clearly a marvelous instrument, and nothing more wonderful than it is found among bodily things.

To show from things we know the outstanding beauty of the sun, David compared it to a groom leaving his bridal chamber. Men never dress themselves up more and never desire more to show off their beauty and handsomeness than when they marry. They want beyond measure to please the eyes of the bride whom they love intensely. If we could fix our gaze on the sun and if we were closer to it and if we could see it in all its

---

41. *Ecclesiasticus* was the old title given to the biblical book now known as Sirach.

ROBERTVS·BELLARMINVS·POLITIANVS·S·R·E·CARD·TIT·S·MARIAE·IN·VIA·ARCHIEPISCOPVS
CAPVANVS·ECCLESIAE·CATHOLICAE·ADVERSVS·HAERETICOS·PROPVGNATOR·ACERRIMVS
AETAT·SVAE·ANNI·71

St. Robert Bellarmine (1542–1621) in his
old age.

size and splendor, we would not need the analogy of the bridegroom to grasp its incredible beauty. The whole beauty of colors depends on light, and the whole beauty of colors vanishes if light disappears. Nothing is more beautiful than light, and God himself, who is beauty itself, wanted to be called light. Saint John says, "God is light, and in him is no darkness" (1 Jn. 1:5). Furthermore, there is no bodily object more luminous than the sun and, therefore, nothing is more beautiful than the sun. Besides that, the beauty of lower creatures and especially human beauty fade quickly, but the sun's beauty is never extinguished, never lessened, and always gives joy to all things with equal splendor. Do we not feel that somehow everything seems to rejoice at sunrise? Not only are men happy, but gentle breezes whisper, flowers open, the grain crops up, and the little birds sweeten the air with their song. When the angel said to the blind old man, Tobit, "May joy be to you always," he answered, "What manner of joy shall be to me, who sit in darkness and see not the light of heaven?" (Tb. 5:11–12).

Come, my soul, and think over within you, if the created sun makes all things so happy at its rising, what will the uncreated sun do, which is incomparably brighter and more beautiful, when it rises in pure hearts to be seen and contemplated, not for a short time but forever? How unhappy and sad will that hour be, when condemned men are turned over for burial in everlasting darkness where the rays of neither the uncreated nor the created sun ever penetrate? What will be the joy of the soul to whom the Father of lights says, "Enter into the joy of your master" (Mt. 25:21)?

Chapter 2: "The sun's course shows God's greatness."

Later the same prophet celebrates the truly marvelous course of the sun: "He has rejoiced as a giant to run the way" (Ps. 19:5). He is certainly a powerful giant, if he stretches his stride to match the size of his body and runs with a speed to match the strength of his forces, for he covers an absolutely immense space in a short time. The Prophet, since he had compared the sun to a bridegroom to explain as well as he could the beauty of the sun, later compared it to a giant man so that he could explain as well as possible the sun's speedy course by using the same analogy. Even if he had compared the sun to flying birds, arrows, winds, and lightning bolts instead of to men, however large and strong, he would still have fallen far short of the truth. If what we see with our eyes is true, the sun runs the whole circumference of the earth, and if the circumference of the earth measures about twenty thousand miles—and all this is absolutely true—it undoubtedly follows that the sun completes a run of many thousands of miles every hour.[42] What am I saying, every hour? Rather every quarter hour and almost every minute. Anybody who wants to observe the rising or the setting of the sun, especially above a clear horizon as is found on the sea or a flat plain, will realize that the sun's whole body rises above the horizon in a shorter span of time than an eighth of an hour, and yet the diameter of the sun's body is much greater than the diameter of the earth, which measures seven thousand miles.

Once I myself out of curiosity wanted to find out how much time it would take for the whole sun to set into the sea. At the beginning of its setting I started to read the psalm "Have mercy on me, O God" (Ps. 51:1). I had barely read it through twice when the sun had already entirely set. Hence, the sun in that short time in which the psalm "Have mercy" is read twice had to traverse in its course a distance much greater than seven thousand miles. Who would believe that, unless it had been demonstrated by certain argument? Should some person now add that the body which moves so fast has a mass much greater than the whole earth and that the movement of such a large body at such speeds goes on without any pause or weariness and, if God were to command it, could last for eternal time, certainly that person could not help admiring the infinite power of the Creator unless he was a dunce or a blockhead. Ecclesiasticus wrote accurately that this was a wonderful instrument, the work of the Most High, and the Lord who made it was great indeed (Sir. 43:2).

Chapter 3: "Sun gives light and heat, but God gives true wisdom and charity."

There remains the efficacy of light and heat to consider. David says about it, "There is no one that can hide himself from his heat" (Ps. 19:6). This one luminous body stationed in the middle of the universe illuminates all the stars, all the air, all the seas, and all the earth. Everywhere on

---

42. Bellarmine, like most of his contemporaries, thought that the sun circled the earth each day.

earth it makes all the buds, all the plants, and all the trees become green and leafy by its life-giving warmth, and it makes all the crops ripen. It even spreads its power beneath the earth and produces every kind of metal. This is why Saint James at the beginning of his Letter compared God with the sun: "Every good gift and every perfect gift is from above, coming down from the Father of lights, with whom there is no change, nor shadow of alteration" (Jas. 1: 17). The sun is the father of bodily lights, while God is the Father of spiritual lights, but God differs greatly from the sun in three ways. First, the sun must be constantly changing in order to fill the whole earth with light and heat, but God who is totally present everywhere needs no change. For this reason Saint James says, "In him there is no change." Second, because the sun is always changing its place, it brings day in turn to place after place, leaving some in night, shining on others, bringing shadows elsewhere. But God never moves and is always present to every place. Hence Saint James adds, "In him there is no shadow of alteration." Finally, the greatest boon of all from the sun as father of bodily lights is all the gifts and benefits which are born from the earth. But these good things are not supreme or perfect but rather poor, temporary, failing, and they do not make man good and can be misused by those who so wish, and many turn them to their damnation. But "every good gift and every perfect gift" comes down from the Father of spiritual lights, and these make their possessor very good and perfect. Nobody can misuse them, and they lead him who perseveres in them to the state of true happiness, a state made perfect by the accumulation of every good.

Investigate, my soul, what are these best gifts and perfect boons which are from above, coming down from the Father of lights so that when you discover them, you will be on the alert for them and will strive to obtain them with all your strength. It is not that you have to go far away—the nature of the sun will show you that well enough. The sun achieves all its effects by heat and light, and these are the gifts and boons of the father of bodily lights, light and heat. So too the best gifts and the perfect boons which are from above and come down from God, the true Father of lights, are the light of wisdom and well-ordered love. The light of wisdom, which makes a person truly wise, which no one can misuse, and which leads to the fountain of wisdom which lies in our heavenly fatherland, is the light which teaches us to scorn temporal things and esteem eternal things. It teaches us "not to trust in the uncertainty of riches, but in the living God" (1 Tim. 6:17); it teaches us not to make this exile our fatherland and to endure rather than love this pilgrimage; lastly it teaches us to bear patiently this present life, which is full of dangers and temptations, and see death as desirable, for "blessed are the dead who die in the Lord" (Rev. 14:13).

What is well-ordered love except to love God, who is the end of all desires, without end or limit, and to love other things, which are means to the end, within limits and only to the degree to which they are necessary for the end, that is, for attaining happiness? Nobody among the sons of men would turn things upside down in taking care of his body so that he would love health within limits and love a bitter medicine without limit since he knows that one is the end and the other the means. How comes it then, that so many who want to pass for wise can set no limit in heaping up riches, in seeking the pleasures of the flesh, and in acquiring titles of honor, as if these goods were the end for the human heart? But in loving God and seeking eternal happiness they are content with narrow limits, as if these were means to an end and not the end of all means. This above all is the reason why they have the wisdom of this world and not the wisdom which is from above coming down from the Father of lights and why they do not have a well-ordered love and, therefore, do not have true love, which cannot exist without being well-ordered. Rather they are full of covetousness, which does not come from the Father but from the world. While you are a pilgrim, my soul, away from your fatherland and sojourning among enemies who plot against true wisdom and true love and substitute guile for wisdom and covetousness for love, sigh with your whole heart for the Father of lights that he make the best gifts and perfect boons, namely, the light of wisdom and the passion of well-ordered love, come down to your heart so that filled with them you may run with a sure foot the path of the commandments and reach the fatherland where one drinks from the very fountain of wisdom and lives on the pure milk of love. . . .

Chapter 6: "The order and harmony of the stars mirror the hierarchy of heaven."

Among the ornaments of the heavens there are also the stars. Ecclesiasticus says of them, "The glory of the stars is the beauty of heaven," and immediately adds, "The Lord enlightens the world on high" (Sir. 43:10). Just as with the sun and the moon, whatever beauty the stars have comes totally from the Father of lights. The sun does not illumine the world by day nor the moon and the stars by night; rather it is the Lord who dwells above and illumines the world by the sun, the moon, and the stars. As the Prophet Baruch says, it is he who "sends forth light and it goes; he has called it and it obeys him with trembling; and the stars have given light to their watches and rejoiced. They were called and they said, 'Here we are' and shined forth with cheerfulness to him who made them" (Bar. 3:33, 34). These words signify God's infinite power which instantaneously produced, beautified, and set to work the vast and beautiful bodies with incredible ease. What for us is the word *to call* is for God the word *to create*. "He calls things that are not" (Rom. 4:17) and by his calling makes them exist. When the stars say "Here we are" this means nothing other than their existing and working instantly at his word of command. "With cheerfulness they shined forth to him that made them" suggests that their prompt and ready obedience to their maker brought them great happiness and joy in obeying.

What is utterly wonderful in the stars is how, even though they move with extreme speed and never stop from their rapid course, some moving in slower and others in faster orbits, still they always keep their measure and proportion with the others so that they give rise to a sweet and melodious harmony. God speaks of this harmony in the Book of Job when he says, "Who can declare the order of the heavens, or who can put the harmony of heaven to sleep?" (Job 38:37). This is not the harmony of voices and sounds which our bodily ears hear but the harmony of the proportions in the stars' movements which the ear of the heart recognizes. For the stars of the firmament all race together through the whole circle of the sky at the same speed during twenty-four hours; for those seven stars which are called planets or wandering stars are hurled with differing movements, some faster, some slower, so that the stars of the firmament seem to represent the bass notes (to use the common expression) and the planets play a sort of eternal and sweet counterpoint. But they are above us and that harmony is hearable only to those who live in heaven and grasp the order of their movement. Since the stars keep their proper distances and never tire in turning in their orbit, they seem to behave like a joyous chorus of noble virgins who are ever dancing skillfully through the sky.

Do you, my soul, climb a bit higher if you can and reflect on the utter brilliance of the sun, the beauty of the moon, the great number and variety of the other lights, the marvelous harmony of the heavens and the happy chorus of the stars. What will it be to see God above the heavens, the sun "who dwells in light inaccessible" (1 Tim. 6:16); to gaze on the Virgin, the Queen of heaven, who is "beautiful as the moon" (S. of S. 6:9), who gives joy to the whole city of God; to watch the choirs and ranks of many thousands of angels who, more numerous and brighter than all the stars, add beauty to the heaven of heavens; to see the souls of holy men mingling with the choirs of angels as planets mixed among the stars of the firmament? What will it be to hear the songs of praise and sing sweetly that eternal alleluia with harmonious voices in the streets of that glorious city? May it come about that even the beauty of the sky may not seem great to you and the things beneath the sky be accounted utterly puny and almost nothing and hence contemptible and despicable.

CHAPTER 6

SPECIAL PASTORAL MINISTRIES

INTRODUCTION

This chapter concentrates on Jesuit ministries to people usually held in contempt by the upper levels of early modern society: men engaged in vendettas, prostitutes, peasants, and women accused of witchcraft. These ministries, especially those among peasants, were almost as important to the early Jesuits as were their efforts as educators and missionaries (examined in Chapters 2 and 3, respectively).

The first set of documents in this chapter examines how a Jesuit preacher healed a bitter vendetta in Italy; the second set examines early Jesuit efforts to rehabilitate prostitutes in Italian cities. These documents are taken from Juan Polanco's *Chronicon*.

The third section includes directives for Jesuits who were preaching among peasants. The Jesuits are often seen, and rightly so, as an urban order; Loyola himself left his family's country estate and spent the key parts of his life in Paris, Venice, and Rome. But in the 16th and 17th centuries, the vast majority of Europeans still lived on country farms. The success or failure of both the Protestant and Catholic Reformations pivoted on making real Christians out of the still semipagan rural folk, and the Jesuits and Capuchins (a strict branch of the Franciscans founded in the early 16th century) reached millions through their preaching during missions to the countryside.

The fourth document illustrates how a famous Jesuit attacked the judicial procedures, including torture, employed against those accused of witchcraft—most of whom were poor women. The final set of documents shows how early Jesuits attacked the pastimes of bullfighting and carnivals.

Juan Polanco

Selections from *Chronicon,* on healing vendettas and caring for reformed prostitutes[1]

[We have read selections from Polanco's chronicle of the Jesuits (1540–56) in Chapter 2 and will read still others in Chapter 8. In the excerpt offered here, Polanco relates how the preaching of Father Silvestro Landini put an end to a bloody and long-standing vendetta in an Italian city. Such vendettas were widespread in early modern Europe, particularly in Italy. Landini stood out among the early Jesuits for his skill as a peacemaker. Several other passages from Polanco's Chronicon *printed here illustrate how the Jesuits tried to rescue young women from lives of prostitution.]*

The Year 1549: *Section 407. Silvestro Landini stops vendettas in Correggio.*

. . . [Landini] then came to a large town called Correggio where he was so badly received at first that when he was preaching some people left the church and by throwing stones against the door disturbed his audience. But he preached for eight straight days, sometimes twice the same day. Not only did they stop throwing stones, but right at dawn they came to his sermons with great devotion. The vendettas in that place were so many that forty-five people, three of them priests, had been killed; armed men came right up to the altar. These factions had two opposing leaders who came to Father Silvestro for Confession, something they had avoided for many years, and they indicated that they were ready to enter a peace and to do whatever he ordered. They were very terrifying to other people, but in listening to the daily sermons they bore themselves with great humility. Before vespers a herald proclaimed in public that early in the morning everybody should come to hear God's word, under a certain penalty [for absence]. . . . Previously Communion was seen there scarcely once a year; now it was seen daily. On Sundays they came armed and heard barely half the mass armed; now they came unarmed not to just one [mass], but to as many as were being said in the church. . . . The leaders of the opposing factions finally turned over their controversies to Father Silvestro, and he was hoping that

---

1. *Year by Year with the Early Jesuits, 1537–1556: Selections from the* Chronicon *of Juan de Polanco, S.J.,* edited and translated by John Patrick Donnelly, S.J. (St. Louis: Institute of Jesuit Sources, 2004). These excerpts are used with the permission of the Institute of Jesuit Sources. The section on vendettas printed here is from pp. 97–8. For other examples of Jesuits and vendetta, see Polanco, *Year by Year,* pp. 36, 69, 100, 152, 220, 303, 325, 369, 398, 417.

an edifying peace would ensue and spread very widely. And so peace was forged, and it was the more welcome because the opposing factions had been fighting among each other for thirty years with bitter hatred and great cruelty. They did not go to Confession or Communion, and [the vendetta] also caused enormous losses in temporal goods.

Here is the approach he used: after the word of God had softened the hearts of faction leaders when he preached before a packed audience, he called out by name one of the two leaders—his name was Giovanni Corso. He answered [Landini], "My Father, what do you want me to do?" Silvestro said from the pulpit, "That you should forgive all your enemies, and beyond this, you should ask for pardon from all those you have offended, and that out of love of God you grant them all peace." He immediately threw his weapons on the ground, prostrated himself and began to call in a loud voice, "Peace, peace." The rest of the men from both factions begin to say, "Peace, peace." Then Silvestro came down from the pulpit and said, "May you also do what I am going to do." He began to embrace the men and give them the kiss of peace. They then also embraced their enemies and began kissing them with great signs of love, and indeed with so many tears mixed with joy that they thoroughly drenched one another amidst the kisses of peace. Old and young, men and women, made the whole church resound with "Peace" along with their tears. Those hearts, which a few days before thirsted like lions for nothing except vengeance and murder, were like lambs touched by a gentle and mutual love, and from then on they began to compete with one another in the duties of charity. . . .

[In his Chronicon *Polanco frequently notes that the preaching of Jesuits and their encouragement of frequent confession and Communion found stronger support among women than men. Prostitutes were unusually receptive to Jesuit preaching. Most European cities of the 16th century had legalized prostitution. Some of the prostitutes were wives trying to escape abusive husbands or unhappy marriages, but many poor girls whose parents could not afford a dowry also ended up as prostitutes. There were few other job opportunities for young women. The* Chronicon *relates the story of how Loyola set up the halfway house of St. Martha for women who wished to escape the shame and sin of prostitution. Loyola also helped establish a confraternity of noblemen whose contributions covered the halfway house's expenses. Converted prostitutes could live at St. Martha's until they decided what to do with the rest of their lives. Basically they had three choices: married prostitutes could return to their husbands; converted prostitutes could become nuns in special convents; other prostitutes could receive a small dowry that would enable*

them to marry. Jesuits soon set up halfway houses and confraternities in other cities similar to those in Rome.²]

The Year 1544: *Section 68. Loyola establishes the house of Saint Martha at Rome for women fleeing prostitution.*

Already as 1544 was beginning, through the charity of Ignatius a different pious work was begun at Rome called [the House] of Saint Martha. It was set up for erring young women who wished to recover from a shameful lifestyle but could not be accepted among the nuns converted [from prostitution], either because they were married or because they were not so gifted in spirit that they wished to be cloistered and remain forever in a convent. The House of Saint Martha accepted these women, kept them away from sins and their wicked habits, and trained them in what would contribute to their salvation until they were restored to their husbands (after being reconciled with them), or else had dedicated themselves to the religious life through perpetual vows, or had contracted a respectable marriage. Because our house was laboring under conditions of dire poverty [and so could not be of financial assistance to Saint Martha's], Ignatius first offered one hundred gold scudi (obtained from selling certain jewels) to assist the house in its early stages; for he knew that those who had already refused to be the first to contribute to this work had to be persuaded to do so by the example of someone else. Other people then began to offer their financial support, and a wonderful and helpful work was begun that in a short time achieved great growth.³

The Year 1549: *Section 365. Converting prostitutes at Messina in Sicily.*

Because the Viceroy [of Sicily, Juan de Vega] had commanded women who were public sinners to attend sermons on the day when the Gospel about [Mary] Magdalene⁴ is read and because they were also present for what followed, many of them were converted to the Lord. This was certainly the case for sixteen of them. Lady Eleonora, the Viceroy's wife, received them graciously into her home with her usual charity. She took care of arranging that some of them contracted marriages (after dowries had

2. The selections on converting prostitutes in Italy are also taken from Polanco, *Year by Year,* pp. 27, 93, 272, 284, 331.

3. By 1552 some three hundred women had passed through St. Martha's on their way to living more respectable lives.

4. Mary Magdalene was a woman from whom Jesus expelled seven demons (Lk. 8:2); she was popularly identified (probably incorrectly) with the sinful woman (Lk. 7:37–48) who washed the feet of Jesus with her tears and dried them with her hair.

been provided) and that some entered convents for the converted [prostitutes]; some of them she kept in her household.

The Year 1553: *Section 483. Rehabilitating converted prostitutes at Messina.*

Father Provincial [Doménech], besides being in charge of the Jesuit college, was constantly engaged in works of piety at Messina. Among other things, he prevailed upon the city to establish a house for those women who had led a shameful life but who could not be admitted to the convent of the converted prostitutes, either because the fallen women did not want to become nuns or because the building could not accommodate so many. Immediately some of these women began to enter this new house so that they could prepare themselves there either for marriage or for the religious life, depending on the grace God gave them.

Section 504. Finding support for a convent of converted prostitutes at Messina.

So that the house for converted [prostitutes] might have more stable sources of funds, the provincial arranged that a confraternity of noblemen which had charge of an older monastery would also take charge of this house too. Thus through mutual support they might better foster those pious activities carried on in the same neighborhood. By a special gift of God, Father Giovanni Filippo, who was acquainted with the House of Saint Martha at Rome, seemed suited to help these women.

The Year 1553: *Section 223. Saving a famous prostitute at Venice.*

Some of those who partook of the sacraments [at the Jesuit church in Venice] entered the religious life, both men and women. Some among them were prostitutes who were received into the convent of the converted and began to live chaste and holy lives there. One of them belonged to a well-known family; when she was only sixteen years old and ravishing in appearance, she seemed destined to cause the downfall of many men in that city, as her early plunge into a disgraceful lifestyle clearly and quickly demonstrated. When this girl had been snatched from the devil's jaws and wanted to confess in our church, she had to contend with her angry lovers lying in wait for her. When she finished her confession, she tricked the men waiting for her: she was taken down to a gondola by a different door and then was borne off to a convent of the converted [prostitutes] by a hidden waterway. There she applied herself with great zeal to punishing her body and advancing in the spirit. Two hundred and fifty women lived in that convent; among them her zeal was outstanding, as those who had charge [of the convent] testified.

The Year 1554: *Section 463. Helping former prostitutes in Palermo.*

Here too, just as at Messina, our [Jesuits] worked at setting up a house of probation to which women might repair to recover from a shameful way of living. These were women, whose hearts God had touched, even though they had not yet made so much progress that they wanted to enter a convent for the converted. So it was for such that, in addition to the ordinary house of the converted, a new sort of house was set up in which they might live temporarily until they made a firm decision about the sort of respectable life they should undertake. After that, those who were inclined to the religious life would be accepted at a convent for the converted. For those who preferred to marry, a marriage would be arranged.

Right at the beginning [the convents] had only a slender income, no more than a hundred ducats; but our Jesuits raised so much in alms for helping the women that not only was the house supplied with operating funds, but during the first four or five months of this year, forty of its women were provided with a modest dowry and given in marriage to reputable men. A good number of these women were motivated to embrace a better way of life, to some extent by the sermons preached in our church, which they had to listen to, and to some extent by the Viceroy's edict forbidding concubinage, as I mentioned a little earlier.

Claudio Acquaviva

"Instruction for Those Going Out on Missions to Evangelize Peasants"[5]

[Acquaviva (1543–1615) served as superior general of the Jesuits from 1581 to 1615, longer than any other general during the first two centuries of Jesuit history. Intelligent, energetic, and autocratic, he oversaw the growth of the Jesuits from a small religious order to an international organization that at the time of his death was maintaining 372 colleges in Catholic Europe and major missions in Asia, Africa, and the Americas. Acquaviva's directives organized Jesuit practices for more than a century. The most important of Acquaviva's directives was the Ratio Studiorum (Plan of studies) of 1599; in it, committees of Jesuit professors formulated the rules for Jesuit colleges that largely remained in effect for some three hundred years.[6] Also in 1599 Acquaviva issued a directory for priests giving the Spiritual Exercises; his directions were far more detailed than Loyola's.

Acquaviva's rules for preaching on rural missions were approved in 1593 by the Fifth General Congregation, the highest governing body of the Jesuit Order. The early Jesuits often referred to rural areas as "the other Indies" because most

5. This document is printed in *Institutum Societatis Iesu* (Florence: Typographia a SS. Conceptione, 1893), vol. 3, pp. 365–8. The translation is by John Patrick Donnelly.
6. The text is now available in English—see *The Ratio Studiorum: The Official Plan of Jesuit Education,* translated and annotated by Claude Pavur (St. Louis: Institute of Jesuit Sources, 2005).

European peasants were as ignorant of Christian teaching as were the native people of newly discovered lands in Asia and the Americas. Most diocesan priests knew little theology and had never attended a seminary or university. They seldom preached to their parishioners. In the later Middle Ages, teams of Dominicans and Franciscans preached their way across Europe, trying to educate peasants in their faith and urging them to live more Christian lives. The Capuchins and the Jesuits took up and perfected this work in the 16th century. Two Jesuits famous for this work were St. Jean François Regis (1597–1640) and Paolo Segneri (1624–94).[7]

Acquaviva tried to organize this ministry. In 1590 he ordered every Jesuit province to devote six to twelve Jesuits to travel to country towns where they would preach, hear confessions, and teach catechism. Acquaviva's directives to guide their work are included here.]

1. We have decided that it is necessary to write this Instruction for the direction and practice of the rules of men who are going out on missions. Then Provincial Superiors can add to this Instruction the things that seem appropriate for specific areas and missions.

2. The purpose of these missions is to help the many souls who live in the state of sin and the danger of eternal damnation because they are ignorant of the things needed for their salvation. Hence every effort should be made to ensure that [these Jesuit preachers] have a true and continual union among one another as well as a desire for suffering, since these are the necessary foundations for a solid building of peace among them all and for the achievement of the end proposed. Let the preachers remember that this is the calling in which our first Fathers labored. For the same reason, let them never allow themselves to omit their morning prayers or their evening examination [of conscience], so far as is possible. In these prayers and in other things let them work toward an intimate union with God on whom depends the right arrangement and effectiveness of all our actions.

3. Let the preachers walk carefully through the places they have described in their catalogues, staying in each place as long as shall seem proper, given the number and attitudes of the people. When the preachers first come to a town or village, let them go to the main church before doing

---

7. A fine introduction to rural missions is Adriano Prosperi's "The Missionary," in Rosario Villari, editor, *Baroque Personae* (Chicago: University of Chicago Press, 1995); more detailed is Louis Châtellier's *The Religion of the Poor: Rural Missions in Europe and the Formation of Modern Catholicism, c. 1500–1800,* translated by Brian Pearce (Cambridge: Cambridge University Press, 1997).

anything else, and, after a short prayer (taking into consideration the time and their own convenience), let them talk with the pastor or the other clergyman in charge, showing him signs of their goodwill. Let the preachers take care not to give rise to the suspicion, even in the slightest way, that they come to him on an [official] visitation.[8] Rather, after they have presented their letters of credentials and so forth, let them state that they have this one purpose: to teach catechism, hear confessions, and procure reconciliations and so forth. Let them strive especially to win the approval and satisfaction of the clergy in all things. Let the preachers also point out that they have been ordered by their own superiors not to burden anybody with supplying their food and that they will care for themselves since they have what they need to sustain their life. The preachers should say that all they want is a little room, free of contact with women, in which there is a little bed to sleep in. If there is a small but clean room available in the hospital, let them not seek rooms elsewhere. If this same pastor agrees, let him designate who should buy for the preachers the foods they need. These foods should be sufficient to sustain them but always simple enough to cause edification.

4. Let the preachers question the same pastor about the most common sins among the people—including usury, concubinage, feuds, abuses, superstitions, and so forth—so they can direct their sermons and work with more light and usefulness for the people. It will be especially helpful if the preachers can become friends with a layperson of good reputation on whose assistance they can rely in arranging for the other people to frequently attend the divine sacraments and likewise in linking them to some upright priest. It will help to visit the schools, if it is possible to do so without causing resentment. By getting into the good graces of the teachers the preachers can introduce some pious devotional practice among the students. When they have some free time, the preachers should engage in fruitful private conversations with various people.

5. On the day they arrive at the location in which they are going to stay, the preachers should procure, as soon as possible, a convenient site at which the people can gather. Let the people be called together in the morning and the evening. Let one sermon be delivered that first discusses the need for teaching catechism and the evils that accompany mortal sin so that thereby the people may recognize the need for confession. Then the preachers should explain the cause and purpose for their arrival with the good graces and permission of the

8. Bishops, either by themselves or with a delegated visitor, were required to visit and check up on how well the priest and his parishioners were carrying their duties. Jesuits suspected of being official visitors could meet hostility and expect little cooperation.

Claudio Acquaviva, superior general of the Jesuits, 1581–1615.

bishop; next they should proclaim the jubilee[9] granted by His Holiness [the pope] and their power to absolve from sins and so forth. The preachers should also say that our Society is doing all these things because our Order's purpose is to teach catechism, hear confessions, and so forth. It should be stated that no money or remuneration is being sought and that the preachers are even carrying some little gifts of pious objects for the people. It should also be stated that the preachers will not be a burden on anybody since their superiors have already provided them with all they need. Moreover, the preachers should indicate that in the morning hours they will be hearing the confessions of those people who wish to ease their consciences, and that in the afternoons they will teach catechism to women, boys, and girls. In the evenings, after the Angelus,[10] they will explain catechism to the men. Thus should the preachers encourage the people to come and to send along their servants and other family members.

6. If the town is of some importance, and if there is no other preacher, a short sermon lasting a half hour should be delivered around noon every day, especially during Lent; sermons should be about the Gospel but delivered in a style adapted to the listeners' capacity so that the people are led to the necessary teaching on such matters. As occasion arises, the preachers should make frequent use of examples and should earnestly encourage the people to observe divine worship and treat the clergy with honor and respect.

7. The training of the clergy should include a short consideration of the Trinity and the Incarnation of our Lord, the matter and form of the sacraments, and their uses and practice (especially on the way to hear confes-

9. In certain years, often on special occasions, the pope granted special indulgences to people who went to confession or performed other pious acts.

10. The Angelus was a series of prayers centering on the words of the angel Gabriel to Mary; church bells were usually rung to encourage people to devote a few minutes to these prayers.

sions and to teach the people). The clergy should be encouraged to practice diligence and cleanliness when it comes to divine worship. A catechism should be given to those members of the clergy if they do not have one, also the directory of Father Polanco and of Friar Medina.[11] These things should be done in the morning when the preachers have time free for hearing confessions. But if they are prevented from doing those things at that time, care should be taken to complete these tasks late in the evening.

8. Let the preachers always hear women's confessions in a well-lit part of the church. Likewise the confessions of young people. Let the preachers strive to move along, as quickly as possible, those persons whose presence could give rise to suspicion.

9. The afternoon hours should be devoted to teaching catechism to women and children. Women and children should be encouraged to join outdoor processions, especially on feast days. In such processions, the boys and girls should appear in varied clothing carrying decorated banners and marching at the front. A careful effort should be made to ensure that people learn doctrine accurately. The people should be encouraged to sing hymns instead of mindless songs while they are working in the fields.

10. At around nine o'clock in the evening, after the Angelus, a meeting should be convened at the church with the assistance of the pastor and the other clergy. This meeting should be as large as possible and the governor should be invited, along with the other leading men so that their presence will attract other people. Women, however, should not be allowed to attend this meeting. There Christian doctrine should be explained; the mystery of the Trinity, the Apostles' Creed, and so forth should be reviewed. Every sermon should end with a statement on the evils that abide in mortal sin. Reviewing this material should take about an hour. If one preacher can conduct the meeting on his own, the other one should meantime be engaged in helping individuals by hearing confessions or by bringing feuds to a peaceful end.

11. If it sometimes happens that some monetary alms must be given to somebody who has fallen on very hard times, let the alms be given cautiously and in secret lest the donation become publicly known and result in a throng of poor people complaining that they have been denied alms.

12. When [the Jesuits] meet members of any other religious order, let them strive to give every sign of goodwill toward them and try to win them over so far as is possible. The preachers should take every opportunity to administer the Spiritual Exercises to the members of any other religious order and also to any clergyman.

---

11. Juan Polanco and Bartolomé de Medina, O.P. (1527–80), wrote popular books instructing penitents and confessors how to make a good confession.

13. The preachers will observe and immediately write down those things that seem worth passing on to the bishop so that later, after their return to the city, they may report this information to him face to face. This also applies to major things worth including in the annual letters.[12]

14. When the opportunity arises, the preachers will devote effort to starting and promoting a confraternity, either of the Most Holy Sacrament, or of the Name of God, or of the Rosary, or of Christian Doctrine.[13] Later they will notify Rome that this has been done so that [the confraternity] may be established in accord with Rule 22 of the missions.

15. The first [Jesuit] named in the letter of credentials will be the superior of the mission. The other will be his adviser. Lastly, they should all know that the exact observance of the Rules for Missions has been entrusted to them.

Friedrich Spee

Cautio Criminalis

[Though Friedrich Spee von Langenfeld, S.J., (1591–1635) is now best known as a poet and hymn writer, he gained recognition in his own time for his influential book attacking the persecution of witches. The "golden age" of witch persecution was roughly 1550 to 1650. About eighty thousand people were executed for witchcraft in early modern Europe—far more than were executed for the crime of heresy—and women made up some 80 percent of those executed. The geographical pattern of persecution was uneven: very few witches were executed in Italy, Portugal, or Spain, countries where the Inquisition was strongest, probably because the Inquisitors (mainly Dominican friars) were less subject to the mass hysteria over witchcraft that swept other countries. Nowhere was the persecution of witches more severe than in the German prince bishoprics of the Rhine valley. Spee was stationed at Jesuit colleges in several of these bishoprics and ministered personally to the accused.

12. From Loyola's time onward, a long letter or report relating all the edifying activities of Jesuits for the year was compiled and circulated annually to Jesuit communities. During Acquaviva's term as general the letters were printed as books.

13. The great problem facing these traveling missionaries was that the revivalist fervor they stirred up would quickly wane after they left. So that the effects would be more lasting, the Jesuits set up thousands of confraternities of laypeople—some for men, some for women, some for the nobility—to stabilize their work, especially through the frequent reception of the sacraments of Communion and confession. This effort is studied in Lance Lazar's *Working in the Vineyard of the Lord: Jesuit Confraternities in Early Modern Italy* (Toronto: University of Toronto Press, 2004).

His Cautio Criminalis, *which is divided into fifty-one questions and an appendix, grew out of this work.* [14] *He also taught philosophy at Paderborn where the wave of witch persecution peaked in 1629 through 1631. He used to visit the local prison to lend support to women accused of witchcraft and to hear their confessions.*

Many Jesuits—including the distinguished moral theologian Martin Delrio (1551–1606)—accepted the dominant German view that witchcraft was widespread. Other Jesuits agreed with Spee, who borrowed some of his arguments from the Jesuit theologian Adam Tanner (1572–1632). Despite the fact that he argues against the persecution of those accused of witchcraft, Spee does not claim that there are no witches or that such witches have no connection with Satan. Instead he attacks the prevalent judicial procedures and the use of torture, practices that made it virtually impossible for the accused to clear themselves and that also forced many of them to level accusations against other innocent people. Spee was moved from Paderborn to Cologne and then to the Jesuit college at Trier, where he died while ministering to those stricken by plague.]

Question 20: *What should we think about tortures or questioning? Do they frequently lead innocent people into moral danger?*

Here is my answer: in most cases, the nature of torture is such that—having seen it for myself and having read and heard about it far and wide—I can find nothing in my memory to which I can compare it. As far as I can see, it accomplishes nothing other than to lead innocent people into frequent moral danger and to fill our Germany with witches and unheard-of crimes. And this happens not just in Germany, but also in any other nation that has the same experience.

My reasons for thinking thus are as follows.

Reason 1: By their very nature the most common and widespread methods of torture are terrible and cause suffering of measureless intensity. But such is the nature of these enormous sufferings that when we are allowed to

14. *Cautio Criminalis seu de processibus contra sagas: Liber ad magistatus Germaniae hoc tempore necessarius* (Rinteln: Petrus Lucius, 1631; photo reprint Frankfurt/ Main: Minerva Gmb. H, 1971). The selected passages printed here are translated by John Patrick Donnelly from that photo reprint of the first edition, pp. 111, 130–37, 146–48, 351, 358–61. Marcus Hellyer has translated the whole book with a fine introduction to Spee's life and work: *Cautio Criminalis, or Book on the Witch Trials* (Charlottesville and London: University of Virginia Press, 2003). The whole book is divided into fifty-one questions; the selections here contain parts of Questions 20, 22, and 49.

escape them, we fear nothing, not even death itself. Hence there is danger that in order to escape the rack many women will confess to crimes they did not commit or that they will falsely accuse themselves of whatever crimes their interrogators suggest to them or which they themselves have previously thought about confessing. . . .

Reason 14. The danger also increases if one woman who is truly innocent confesses just once and, overcome by the force of her tortures, claims that she is guilty of the crimes [suggested to her by her interrogators] and deserving of the flames; if this happens, countless other innocent women must immediately be charged with the same crimes and dragged to the same flames. I show this by an example: The innocent woman Gaia[15] lied in saying she was a witch, so she will soon be pressed to point out her companions. She is not believed when she denies having such companions and is hauled off for questioning. If she was not able to save herself earlier, she is not going to save others now. . . . So she will accuse women she does not know, especially those she remembers as having had bad reputations. I have seen this happen more than once; one accusation, coupled with a bad reputation, condemns a woman to prison and torture. And then the women under torture also will begin naming their accomplices. Who cannot see that in a very short time the number of those accusing and those being accused will become endless? The problem worsens when the judge is harsh and follows the opinion of those authors who want to maintain, in exceptional crimes [such as witchcraft], that one or several denunciations of accomplices without any other accompanying evidence is enough to justify torture and even convicting [the accused].

More than once I have trembled, when examining this problem, at Germany's remarkable blindness. Let readers also reflect on this problem. Some readers wonder what to believe in this whole question of witches; some may wonder even whether they should believe anything at all. People under torture are forced to say incredible things about themselves and many lies about others. In the end, what pleases the torturer is the truth. Those being tortured agree to everything, and since they dare not take anything back after the torture has ended, the whole business is ended only when they are dead. I know what I am talking about, and I appeal to that court before which both the living and the dead will appear. In that court many surprising things now wrapped in darkness will be made clear. . . .

Reason 15. The danger likewise increases if a woman submits so fully to the pain that she wishes to plead guilty; she then will have closed every possible door to safety. Once the crime has been confessed to, there is no hope left of escaping. A perilous situation!

---

15. *Gaia* is a name Spee uses repeatedly for any accused woman; it was used much like *John Doe* is today.

For if, after her torture, she corrects herself and claims that it was the intense pain, and not the power of the truth, that loosened her tongue, she is interrogated again. If she could not hold her tongue a short time earlier, she will not hold it now, when she is anticipating the pain to come from a repetition of her suffering. And if after this second torture session she again recants, she will experience that suffering a third time. . . .

Reason 16. On the other hand, the danger also increases if a woman agrees to confess under the pain of torture. She can neither free herself nor cleanse herself of the bitter crime of which she is accused. She will be recalled to the tortures again and again until she breaks and her repeated sufferings force her to talk. Before, it was an accomplishment if, after escaping one storm of interrogation, she was allowed to safely establish her salvation. Now, the repetition and frequent use of the rack, clubs, torches, and the like (which are used everywhere) destroy all hope of ever getting free. Perhaps the devout men who share my opinion on this matter and I are completely crazy. But I am quite unable to see how innocent people can be effectively protected from this danger. Instead, countless people have already perished—and will go on perishing in the future. Recently a very upright and very talented member of a certain religious order made an excellent presentation of this argument before some judges. Toward the end of his presentation he asked the judges to answer the question he posed to them: by what means could a truly innocent man finally gain his freedom once he had been thrown into chains? After considerable time the judges could not satisfy him on the question. But he continued to press them until they finally answered that they would think it over that night. And note well that these judges, who had already burned so many innocent people at the stake did not come the next day to propose an effective way for a truly innocent person to free herself from their clutches. I propose the same question to the rulers of Germany. If somebody thinks he has discovered such a way, the very fact that he thinks so shows he is ignorant of what is going on. And if he doesn't have a solution to the problem, it is a danger to his salvation since he ought to have one. Let such a man read, point by point, what we have already said. It would not be wise for us to say, right now, everything that must be said on this point; the times are such that people will not stand for it. Why should we be surprised if the whole world is full of witches? We should marvel, instead, at the absolute blindness of Germany and her stupid experts. Because these men are accustomed to quiet and leisure, and are used to conversations around their fireplaces, they are clueless about the suffering they cause; it never crosses their minds. They are used to speaking and talking about the torments of the accused—and to freely decide on these torments—the same way a blind man talks about colors, about whose appearance he knows nothing. . . .

So in conclusion, I agree completely with my friend, a certain distinguished gentleman, who jovially and rightly often spoke thus: "Why do we go searching so avidly for witches?" He says, "Hey there, Judges, I'll show you where they are. Get up and grab the Capuchins, the Jesuits, and all those men in religious orders and torture them. They'll confess. If any refuse, torture them three or four times and they'll confess. If they are still obstinate, exorcize and shave them because they are using magic. The devil is helping them resist. Keep it up and they'll surrender in the end. If you then want more witches, grab the Church's bishops, canons, and professors. They will confess. How will those poor, delicate fellows hold out? If you still want more witches, I will torture you. Then you can torture me. I won't deny what you claim. Then we are all sorcerers. We assuredly are strong and stalwart men who can hold our tongues when enduring repeated tortures so many times." That's what he said.

Question 22: *Why are many judges currently reluctant to release accused persons, even those who have cleared themselves during torture?*

I answer that so far I have rarely seen, even though I often could have seen it in many places, a woman clearing herself by claiming innocence during her first torture session. Those thrown into prison are only rarely released, and even then only reluctantly. This could be considered an indication of a zeal for justice and an eagerness for virtue. Far be it, however, that virtue should have such an immoderate dimension; it should exercise its power only within the limits set by the law and reason.

Reason 1: By fair means or foul, [judges] want women they can burn, as I have already stated in a preceding question. I do not know the cause of this blind fury, nor do I know whether it is the fault of the judges or the officials.

Reason 2: Another factor is that the judges imagine that they will be shamed if they are inclined to dismiss a case, as if they had been overzealous in arresting and torturing a woman who is then found innocent. I relate what I saw two years ago. I was in a place where the interrogation of witches had begun. Gaia was tried first because she had a bad reputation in her village. She was taken prisoner and tortured on the basis of this sole charge. Under torture she pointed to Tatia as her colleague; this one accusation carried so much weight that Tatia was then arrested and subjected to the rack. Tatia overcame the torture and steadfastly denied any guilt. Meanwhile, Gaia was brought out to the stake. There she was extremely penitent. Her confessor judged that she was well prepared for death. Gaia then withdrew her false accusation against Tatia, claiming that it was extracted under the power of her torture. Gaia said that she had done evil in betraying an innocent woman and that now she was prepared to testify with her own death that she knew Tatia had committed no evil. With these words Gaia strode into the flames. Now there was no reason to prevent Tatia's release. She should not have been arrested to begin with. Still, she was not released because of what I have said—the judicial staff murmured among themselves that they would acquire a reputation for carelessness if Tatia should thus recover her freedom. Shame! How unworthy was this affair, how unchristian, how contrary to all fairness!

Reason 3: The torturer earns shame, and is considered inept at his craft and unskilled in torture, when he fails to get a confession from a weak woman.

Reason 4: The love of money comes into play if salary—something judges don't want to see decreased—is based on how many heads are chopped off. We're not all saints, nor are we so equally given to self-restraint that our eyes are not then tricked by the glitter of gold and silver. More than once have I heard (and deplored) that judges will seek any means by which they can make an accused woman out to be what they want her to be. They tighten up her chains; they weaken her in a squalid prison; they break her with cold and heat. They hand her over to priests of the sort I described earlier—impetuous or untrained fellows—or to onetime beggars who are now servants of the interrogation. They submit her to ever newer tortures, and finally torment and afflict her until the suffering breaks her and she finally makes a confession, regardless of whether it is true or false. There is no lack of pretty and clever ways to repeat the interrogations and to blot out for the moment the light of one's conscience, even if no new evidence is found, as I will now discuss. . . .

Question 49: *What arguments might be made by those who want to believe that denunciations of witches are trustworthy and who say such denunciations are sufficient for submitting to torture those who have been denounced?*

The many arguments that can be brought forward are easily refuted. We will propose and refute them one by one. . . .

Argument 8: *In their denunciations, many witches target the same person. Therefore this is a sign they are not lying. Therefore they should be trusted.*

I answer that it is not surprising that many of them point to the same person; this can happen for many reasons, as I will show. But if these witches are not otherwise individually credible, they should not be trusted when taken together. The accusers may have been real witches, or perhaps they were innocent women overcome by the force of their tortures to the point that they named other women in order to escape their suffering. Neither of these is surprising, for if they were true witches, they could have [done the following]:

1. Many of them could have maliciously conspired to accuse one woman. Then, if they happened to fall into the hands of the authorities, they would also drag her down to destruction. They could have agreed to refer to the same circumstances before making their accusation; such agreements have been recorded in no few cases, which I will omit for the sake of brevity.

2. As we said above, the devil could have disguised himself as the innocent woman in those [witches'] Sabbaths where she could have been seen and denounced on specific evidence—time, place, and the rest—by many people who have confessed to being present.

3. Those who accuse the same woman and pile on the incriminating evidence could have been motivated to do so by suggestions or orders from the devil.

If such women turn out not to be real witches, it should come as no surprise because:

1. When many women are tortured and questioned it is most likely that several will, by chance, point to the same woman, especially if there are few women left in the village who have not already been denounced and burned.

2. When they don't know other women, most of the accused usually name women about whom there is already a widespread rumor—either women who have already been imprisoned once on that charge or have been burned.

3. It is becoming increasingly apparent, as [Adam] Tanner has noted well, that court officials do not keep secrets. The identities of the accused are broadcast to the common folk; this enables those women who are later tortured to free themselves from torments by accusing those same women previously accused. Here the officials can in no way be excused in their consciences because they have not amended this practice. Where I live almost the whole town already knows about a good number of women who have been recently accused. As the rumor spreads, the accused are talked about; this rumor will produce another trial next year. What awful times! Such is our zeal in Germany!

4. As I have noted above, some malevolent fellows ask about specific people by name during torture sessions. It should come as no big surprise then, that the tortured then accuse those whose names have been put into their mouths.

Argument 9: *The criminal trials have made it clear that almost all those women accused by other people were, in fact, real witches; these witches later confessed as much under torture. So, it follows that the accusers were telling the truth. Therefore we should not hesitate to trust such accusations.*

I answer that their own confessions are not enough to prove that most of the accused are real witches, for it is very clear how little trust can safely be placed in confessions made under torture. This is manifest from the arguments we brought forward above. As I said, it is stupid for any woman accused not to confess her guilt. She will be forced to do so by many torments so that she finally gives in; and if she does not give in, she will be burned alive as an obstinate [witch]. Check again what has been said in various places above. None of those fellows who are accustomed to writing down their speculations in their quiet and leisurely hours really knows how powerful these tortures are. Their hard hearts have never experienced such pain. Not from any hostility, but from good and Christian affection I pray that for their greater good, and for a more sensitive conscience, they themselves should experience seven minutes—just a taste [of the rack]—before going forth to handle these hateful matters with it.

Juan Polanco

Selections from *Chronicon,* on the Jesuit opposition to bullfighting and carnival celebrations[16]

[The Jesuits were not opposed to celebrations and entertainment; they were, after all, pioneers in college dramatic presentations, as we saw in Chapter 2. But when celebrations of what had previously been religious holidays resulted in excesses, some Jesuits reacted in ways that revealed their puritanical tendencies. One such Jesuit was the Spanish preacher Juan Bautista de Barma (1524–60). He was the driving force behind the successful Jesuit opposition to bullfights and wild carnival celebrations in southeastern Spain.]

The Year 1552: *547. The Jesuits oppose bullfighting at Valencia.*

I will not overlook mentioning that when this jubilee occurred close to the feast of Saint James the Greater [July 25], the patron saint of Spain, bullfights were held in accord with the ancient tradition of that country. It was decided that horsemen would also fight one another in a joust with wooden rods. Our Jesuits took exception to this event because the previous day almost everybody had prepared to obtain the jubilee [indulgence] by confessing and receiving Communion. At this time the rector at Valencia

16. Polanco, *Year by Year,* pp. 239–40, 298–99, 303.

was Father Bautista [de Barma]; but eight of our Jesuits, four of whom were priests, made every effort to stop those games, regarding it as inappropriate to hold [such a spectacle] in honor of God and Saint James.

With the permission of the pro-rector, four of the men just mentioned went to the bullring, the first and last with heads uncovered and feet bare, as had been done earlier at Valencia, with ropes tied around their necks. The first of them carried a large picture of the crucified [Christ], the last carried a dead man's scull. The two in between had their backs and arms naked and were scourging themselves with whips. They then reached the bullring just as the first bull had been driven in and penned up. This is why our men were able to enter the bullring safely. All the spectators, both natives and outsiders, were deeply moved by the display and shouted for mercy with groans at the top of their voices. Climbing some steps, one of the four began to preach to the people.

Meanwhile the second group of four [Jesuits], dressed and bearing the same sort of penitential objects, left the college, marched down the main street, and at the top of their voices shouted pleas for mercy. The heart of a certain Ethiopian was moved, and he began shouting the same thing and asked for confession. But when they came to the bullring, the shouts and weeping began again. . . . They approached the area where the duke and duchess were, along with big crowds of horsemen and clerics. There one of the brethren began preaching with great fervor while loud cries for the Lord's mercy went up repeatedly from the whole crowd. The wife of the duke was weeping, as were the women attending her.

The people, however, left the stands and uttering the cries mentioned earlier accompanied our men who were returning home. Some hastened to bring out whatever was needed to heal the welts caused by the whip lashes. The Lord used this occasion to stir the hearts of many people to sorrow for their sins and [the desire] to go to confession, so that people whom the jubilee did not motivate were moved by this public display to receive the holy sacraments. All the bulls were immediately driven away, and the jousting was called off, even though all the horsemen had dressed up for it at considerable expense.

The Year 1553: *757. Countering Carnival at Pamplona.*

In the days before Lent, many people, following their custom, ran about the city in masks, and on every hand many frivolities and unbecoming antics could be seen. Our Jesuits arranged to have some boys stage a procession with some of them in the lead carrying a crucifix; they marched through all the public streets of that city, visiting the churches on their way. In each of them they would kneel and loudly beg for God's mercy. So great was a flock of people following them wherever they went that not only did some boys discard their masks and silly trappings and join the procession, but people of advanced age did the same. Many let it be known that they had intended to leave their homes [wearing] masks and carrying on in bizarre ways, but they gave up their plans after they saw and heard the procession.

830. *Putting a check on the carnival at Onteniente.*

. . . . When [Father Bautista de Barma] preached on the Sunday before Lent at Onteniente,[17] he so moved the citizens that they wholly abandoned some of the foolishness that was everywhere a deeply entrenched custom. By public decree people were forbidden to go about in disguise or to dance to the tune of flute players, drummers, and those singing lascivious songs.[18] They were not to follow their custom of dumping water from their windows and dousing passers-by, nor were they to play games during the entire season of Lent. Those who flouted this ban would be punished with a fine or imprisonment. When six or seven teenagers did something in contravention of the decree, they were thrown into the prison until Father Bautista pleaded for their release. Everything was silent the night [of Mardi Gras] before the first day of Lent, and it almost defied belief that so many people could have passed the night so quietly.

17. Lent, which is a forty-day period of fasting and penance before Easter, begins on Ash Wednesday. In Polanco's day, people were supposed to abstain from eating meat during Lent; hence the term *carnival*—from the Latin *carni vale*—meaning "good-bye to meat." Carnival celebrations usually peaked the Monday and Tuesday before Lent began. These days presented the last chance to celebrate and gorge oneself before the penitential forty days began. *Mardi Gras* is the French term for the "fat Tuesday" preceding Lent. Onteniente is a small city near Valencia in southeastern Spain.

18. These celebrations that the Jesuits were attacking in the 1550s were mild compared to the wild carnival celebrations today in Rio de Janeiro and New Orleans. The Catholic Church has since drastically reduced Lenten fasting.

CHAPTER 7

JESUITS AND POLITICS

INTRODUCTION

During the 16th century and the first half of the 17th century, church and state were closely tied. All European states had an official religion; none officially encouraged religious diversity or pluralism, although some did practice de facto religious tolerance on pragmatic grounds, mainly to head off civil war. The most tolerant countries were the Dutch Netherlands, Poland, and France (after 1598). Gaining the favor of the rulers was especially important for new religious orders such as the Society of Jesus. Jesuit schools, for instance, were largely reliant on rulers and city governments to subsidize their tuition-free educational programs. We have already seen in Chapter 2 how the Spanish viceroy in Sicily, Juan de Vega, played a crucial role in gaining financial support from the city government for the flagship Jesuit college at Messina. The survival of the Jesuit schools depended on the Order's ability to cultivate political leaders.

Those Jesuits who had access to a king's ear—for example, by serving as a Catholic king's confessor, his court preacher, or the tutor of a crown prince—were unusually well positioned to champion the Jesuit cause. Jesuits filled all three of these roles at royal courts in Paris and Lisbon and at Vienna's imperial court. Two documents in this chapter, those by the Jesuit General Claudio Acquaviva and by Cardinal Robert Bellarmine, discuss a royal confessor's responsibilities—and the dangers inherent in holding such a position. One of Loyola's first companions, Simon Rodrigues (1510–79), served as the tutor for the future King Sebastian of Portugal.

Juan Mariana's book *On a King and the Education of a King*, written for his student, the future Philip III of Spain, aroused intense opposition to the Jesuits because it seemed to justify the assassination of tyrannical monarchs. The second selection offered below is taken from the most controversial section of Mariana's book. The Jesuits wrote many books on the duties of a king; in addition to the selection from Mariana's book, this chapter prints three sections from Bellarmine's book written for Ladislaus, the crown prince of Poland; these selections describe the duties of a king toward his confessor, toward his soldiers and court officials, and toward other kings.

The Jesuit superiors general in Rome were acutely aware of the dangers facing those priests who became involved in politics, especially at royal courts. Such priests could easily become swollen with pride and ignore the humility and the vows of poverty and obedience that should characterize members of religious orders. Confessors could come to identify themselves with king and country instead of religious values. Since confessors had access to the king and his family, court officials could try to enlist the Jesuits in support of their own political agendas. Unpopular royal policies were sometimes blamed on the royal confessor or court preacher—and, by extension, on Jesuits in general.

The first document in this chapter prints two decrees of the Fifth General Congregation, the supreme legislative body of the Jesuits, ordering Jesuits to avoid involvement in politics. In practice, however, it was difficult to draw the line between involvement in politics and the legitimate fulfillment of the duties of confessors, preachers, and fund-raisers. (Three earlier documents in this volume deal with Jesuit involvement in touchy political issues: Loyola's suggestions for Charles V on how to fight the Turks appear in Chapter 1; his letter to Peter Canisius urging Ferdinand of Austria to remove Protestants from all teaching and government posts is included in Chapter 4; and Chapter 3 offers a selection from the book Antonio Ruiz de Montoya wrote to win Philip IV's protection for the Guarani Indians.)

The Fifth General Congregation of the Jesuit Order, Canons 12 and 13[1]

[Traditionally, Jesuit General Congregations met (as they still do) to elect a new superior general, who then serves for life. The only general congregation in the first century of the Jesuits that did not meet to elect a superior general but instead to deal with a wide range of ongoing problems was the Fifth General Congregation convoked by Claudio Acquaviva in Rome from November, 5 1593, until January 18, 1594. Among the decrees issued by this congregation were Canons 12 and 13 prohibiting Jesuit involvement in court politics. Jesuits who broke these rules were to be deprived of any office as a superior that they might hold and were to lose their right to vote in, or be elected by, a provincial or general congregations of the Order.]

Canon 12. So that, as far as possible every appearance of evil may be avoided, and so that complaints arising from false suspicions may be

---

1. *Institutum Societatis Iesu* (Florence: Typographia a SS. Conceptione, 1893), vol. 2, pp. 547–48. This excerpt has been translated by John Patrick Donnelly.

refuted, all our men are commanded to avoid involvement for any reason in any public or secular activities of princes which (as is said) pertain to matters of state. This is commanded in virtue of holy obedience [i.e., under the vow of obedience taken by Jesuits] and under the penalty of their being ineligible for any office or dignity or ecclesiastical position. They will also lose the right to vote or be elected. Moreover, one should not dare or presume to attend to the handling these sorts of political matters, regardless of who requests or asks him to do so. Hence superiors are strongly urged not to permit our men to get involved in these matters in any way, and, if they notice men who are inclined to these things, they should as fast as possible have them transferred elsewhere if there is an opportunity or danger anywhere of their getting themselves entangled in such matters.

Canon 13. We must take the greatest care lest our men insinuate themselves into the entourage of princes to the detriment of their spiritual good and religious discipline. Neither should they be occupied in other secular affairs, even if these particular affairs pertain to their blood relatives, friends, or anybody else (unless, perhaps, charity should sometimes urge a different course in the judgment of superiors). In this way, by abstaining from such matters as things alien to us, we try to help our neighbors within the limits of our [Jesuit] way of life. Hence this Congregation rightly recommends that Reverend Father General [Acquaviva] employ, in accord with his prudence, those remedies that will help our men deal with princes according to the principles of our [Jesuit] way of life. He should correct those of our men who are going astray, especially if they are superiors, but also those who work at obtaining something from superiors through the requests or interventions of non-Jesuits. He should correct those who are going astray by punishments that he will have judged appropriate in the Lord, punishments that will also serve as an example for others.

Juan Mariana

On a King and the Education of a King[2]

[No pages written by a Jesuit have caused the Order as much trouble as the sixth chapter of On a King and the Education of a King *(1599) written by*

---

2. Juan Mariana, S.J., *De Rege et Institutione Regis Libri III ad Phillipum III Hispaniae Regem Catholicum* (Madrid: Typis Welchelianis, apud heredes Ioannis Aubrii, 1611), vol. 1, pp. 51–63. Translation by John Patrick Donnelly. In the Latin original the whole chapter is one very long paragraph; here some sections have been dropped and paragraphing inserted. For useful discussions of Mariana's tract, see G. B. Lewy, *The Political Philosophy of Juan de Mariana, S.J.* (Geneva: Droz, 1960), and Ronald W. Truman, *Spanish Treatises on Government, Society and Religion in the*

*Juan Mariana (1536–1624) at the request of Philip II of Spain.*³ *Mariana was the tutor of the future Philip III, and the book was written to teach the young prince his future duties. The sixth chapter weighs arguments, pro and con, on whether it is right to kill not only tyrants but also any legitimate kings who have become tyrannical. Although Mariana claims impartiality, his arguments are usually interpreted as advocating tyrannicide. In fact, they were probably intended to deter the young prince from tyrannical behavior once he assumed power. The book attracted little attention until 1610 when François Ravaillac (1578–1610), a demented former student of a Jesuit college, assassinated Henry IV of France in Paris.*⁴ *Though the assassin had never even heard of Mariana, the Jesuits' many enemies held Mariana—and therefore all Jesuits—responsible for the assassination.*⁵ *Mariana's book was burned by order of the Parlement of Paris, and Jesuits were forbidden to teach thereafter in France even though the Jesuit General Claudio Acquaviva condemned Mariana's book and forbade any Jesuit to advocate tyrannicide.*⁶]

Time of Philip II (Leiden: Brill, 1999), pp. 315–84; Truman also devotes chapters to two other contemporary Spanish Jesuits who wrote on political theory (pp. 277–360), thereby putting Mariana's work in a larger context. Robert Bireley, S.J., *The Counter-Reformation Prince: Anti-Machiavellianism or Catholic Statecraft in Early Modern Europe* (Chapel Hill: University of North Carolina Press, 1990) deals briefly with Mariana's comments on tyrannicide but develops the political thought of three other Jesuits—Pedro de Ribadeneira, Adam Contzen, and Carlo Scribani—at greater length (on pp. 111–87). None of them agreed with Mariana on tyrannicide.

3. Mariana was a haughty but brilliant maverick. He wrote a lively, uncritical history of Spain in twenty volumes. In 1609 he published a book on currency and inflation that accused government officials of fraud. The Spanish government had him locked up in a Franciscan convent for a year. He also urged that the government of the Jesuits be overhauled so that it would become more democratic and less centralized.

4. In 1594 Jean Chastel attempted unsuccessfully to kill Henry IV. The room of Jean Guéret, the Jesuit who had taught Chastel philosophy, was searched and found to contain books treating tyrannicide. Guéret was burned at the stake, and the Parlement expelled the Jesuits from Paris. They were allowed to return to Paris eight years later.

5. Roland Mousnier, *The Assassination of Henry IV: The Tyrannicide Problem and the Consolidation of French Absolute Monarchy in the Early Seventeenth Century* (New York: Scribners, 1973). Mousnier devotes his last chapter to whether the Jesuits bore responsibility for the assassination. He exonerates them.

6. The most recent and erudite study of early Jesuit political thought is Harro Höpfl's *Jesuit Political Thought: The Society of Jesus and the State, c. 1540–1630*

Chapter 6: Is it right to overthrow a king?

The character and behavior of a tyrant is such that it is equally hateful to heaven and to humans. Even though he may seem extremely fortunate, his crimes are turned into punishment so that his evil heart and conscience are wounded by cruelty, lust, and fear, just as bodies are wounded by whips. The vengeance of heaven pushes those it pursues to their ruin and strips them of their reason and wisdom. There are many recent and ancient examples at hand to show how the hostility of the people has been the end of a ruler, however great the strength of the prince, once the hatred of the mob is stirred up. A sad but striking example of this recently took place among the nobility in France; this example shows how important it is to keep the hearts of the common folk—which are not ruled the same way as their bodies—quiet. Henry III, King of France, lay slain by a poisoned dagger, stabbed in the belly by the hand of a friar. This hateful memorable spectacle served to teach princes that their evil deeds do not go unpunished. Princes, no matter how powerful, are helpless once they have lost the respect of their subjects' hearts. Because he had no children, [Henry III] was preparing to bequeath his kingdom to his brother-in-law Henry of Vendôme [later Henry IV, 1589–1610], even though Vendôme had been infected from his tender years by corrupt religious ideas and had at the same time been severely condemned by the Roman pontiffs and stripped of his right of succession. Now that he has been converted, he is the much to be praised Most Christian King of France. When the plan [of Henry III] became known, and other princes both inside and outside France had been informed of the matter, a great number of the nobility took up arms for the salvation of their country and their religion and sought help everywhere. The hope and fortunes of France rested on the courage and family of Duke [Henry] of Guise during this troubled time.[7]

(Cambridge: Cambridge University Press, 2004). He devotes a chapter to tyrannicide and the assassination of Henry IV (pp. 314–38). For his treatment of Mariana, see pp. 318–21. Regarding Mariana he writes, "All Jesuit theologians and writers, including Mariana, taught that it was never justifiable for a private person to kill his own lawful prince on his own authority" (p. 316). For Acquaviva's condemnation of Mariana, see pp. 318–19.

7. The War of the Three Henrys (1585–89) pitted supporters of the strongly Catholic Guise family, led by the Henry Duke of Guise, against moderate Catholics and King Henry III, who also enjoyed the support of Henry of Bourbon [later Henry IV] and the Calvinist minority. Henry III had Henry of Guise assassinated, but Henry III was assassinated in turn by Jacques Clement, who brought the Calvinist Henry IV to the throne. The fighting ended only when Henry IV converted to Catholicism in 1593. Henry IV was assassinated in 1610. Enemies of the Jesuits blamed the assassination of both kings on the Jesuits.

The kings, undeterred, continued to put their proposed plans into effect. Henry [III], who was preparing to take revenge for the efforts of the leading men and was determined to kill Guise, summoned him to Paris. When the anger of the people and their rising up in arms prevented Henry [III] from carrying out his plan, he quickly left Paris after a short delay; he pretended to have been swayed by better plans and claimed that he wanted to hold public deliberations on the common good. He summoned a meeting of all classes at Blois, a city on the Loire River. There, in his palace, he killed Guise and his brother the cardinal, who trusted in the good faith of the meeting.[8] After these assassinations, charges of treason were cooked up against the [Guises] so that the murders might seem to have been committed rightfully. Nobody defended them, and it was decreed that they had been punished under the law of treason. [Henry III] took other people prisoner, among them the Cardinal of Bourbon, whose bloodline placed him in the rightful line of succession regardless of his old age. This business stirred up the hearts of many Frenchmen. Many cities renounced Henry and openly rebelled for the common good. Paris, which had no equal in Europe for wealth, size, and scholarship, took the lead. The uprising of the people was like a river in flood—it swelled only for a short while. When the popular uprising settled down, Henry stationed his military camp about four thousand paces outside Paris; he hoped to take his revenge on the city. The city was close to despair when the daring of one young man quickly and effectively raised its confidence. His name was Jacques Clement, born in Burgundy in the country town of Serbon. He was studying theology at the college of his Dominican order. After learning from theologians with whom he consulted that a tyrant could rightfully be killed, he obtained letters from men in the city whom he had discovered to be open or secret supporters of Henry. Concealing his own plans, Clement determined to kill the king and left for the military camp on July 31, 1589. He was immediately admitted so he could inform the king about the secrets of the people whose letters he was carrying. He was ordered to hand the letters over the next day. On August 1, the sacred feast day of St. Peter in Chains,[9] after celebrating Mass, he was summoned by the king, who was still waking up and not yet fully clothed. After some brief conversation, Clement came close to the king on the pretext of handing over the letters. Then, in a memorable act of outstanding self-confidence, Clement stabbed the king with the

8. For a vivid account of these events, see Garrett Mattingly's *The Armada* (Boston: Houghton-Mifflin, 1962), pp. 376–86.

9. The feast of St. Peter in Chains commemorates the imprisonment of St. Peter by the high priest and Sadducees in Jerusalem and his escape with the help of an angel (Acts 5:17–25).

dagger he held in his hand, inflicting a deep wound above the king's bladder. [The dagger] had been treated with poisonous plants. Driven by pain, the king struck his murderer in the eye and chest with the same dagger, shouting that Clement was a king-killer.

The courtiers rushed in, alerted by the unusual stir. In their ferocious savagery they inflicted many wounds on the prostrated and unconscious [Clement]. Though he said nothing, his countenance indicated that he felt rather joyful because he was escaping the other tortures that he rightly feared, given the deed he had perpetrated. Simultaneously, he greatly rejoiced, amid his blows and wounds, that his blood had won back the liberty of his people and their common fatherland. By killing the king, he had gained a great name for himself. A murder had been expiated by murder: by his hands the [king's] betrayal of the Duke of Guise was paid for in royal blood. Thus did the twenty-four year old Clement—a simple young fellow of no robust physique, but possessing great power that strengthened his heart—die.

The next night, at two hours past midnight, the king, who died without the last sacraments because of the high hopes for his health, muttered with his last breath those words of David, "Behold, I was conceived in iniquities, and in sins did my mother conceive me" [Ps. 51:5]. Had he conformed his last acts to his earlier ones, he would have been happy and would have shown himself to be a prince, such as he was thought to be when he was in command of the troops and the war against traitors under his brother Charles [IX]. Henry [III] held the title of King of Poland by the vote of the leading men of that nation. But his earlier deeds gave way to his later ones, and the disgraceful morality of his mature years wiped away his youthful good deeds. Although Henry [III] was recalled to his homeland and was proclaimed King of France when his brother died, he made such a mess of everything that it seems that he was only raised to the peak of affairs in order that he might rush into a great disaster. Thus does fortune, or greater power, mock our human endeavors.

There is no consensus about the deed of the friar [who assassinated Henry III]. Many praised him and judged him worthy of immortality; other men of prudence and praiseworthy erudition condemned him and denied the right of anybody on his own private authority to kill a king proclaimed by the peoples' consent and anointed as customary with sacred oil, even if that king had degenerated into a tyrant with shameful morals. They supported this opinion with many arguments and examples. How great was the depravity of King Saul of the Jews in ancient times, how profligate were the conditions of his life and morality![10] Evil schemes stirred up his heart—

10. For the sins of Saul, see 1 Sam. 19:1–24 and 1 Sam. 22:11–19.

it tottered through intervals of doing penance for his crimes. On God's initiative, Saul was stripped of his kingship and the right to rule was transferred to David with a mystical anointing. Although Saul was ruling illegally and had slipped into madness and crimes, his rival David did not dare injure him. When [Saul] was returned to power time and again, David could have legally killed him, either to vindicate his own claim to power or to protect his own life. David did not do this, even though [Saul], who had not been provoked by any injuries, was plotting to kill David in all sorts of ways. Meanwhile, Saul was busy tracking down everywhere the footsteps of [David], an innocent man [1 Sam: 18–27]. . . .

You could add that a tyrant is like a ferocious and monstrous animal that strikes out in all directions, destroys, rips apart, and burns everything, causing horrible slaughters with claws, teeth, and horns. Do you think this should be concealed? Should there not be praise for anyone who risks his own life to restore the safety of the people? Would you not judge that all people should take up weapons against anyone who looms over the earth like a cruel monster, forever untamable? If you saw your dear mother and wife being attacked in your presence and failed to come to their aid when you were able to do so, you would be called cruel and incur shame for your cowardice and impiety. Are we to allow a tyrant to harass and ravage our country, to which we are more indebted than to our parents, for his own pleasure? Away with such iniquity and depravity! Even if our lives, reputations, and wealth are endangered, we will save our country from danger and destruction!

These are the arguments employed to defend the two positions. The side to take becomes clear when you have weighed the two arguments carefully. Indeed, I see that both philosophers and theologians agree on this: the prince who takes over a country by force of arms, with no other claim, can be killed, be deprived of his life, and be crowned by anyone without the consent of the citizens. Since he is a public enemy who oppresses the country with all of his evil ways, such a prince clothes himself correctly with the name and character of a tyrant. He may be removed for any of these reasons and driven from power with the same violence he used to gain it. Rightly, then, did Ehud insinuate himself by gifts into favor with Eglon, King of the Moabites; Ehud then killed Eglon by thrusting a sword into his stomach.[11] Ehud freed his people from the harsh slavery to which they had been subjected for the previous eighteen years.

If a prince holds power by the consent of the people or hereditary right, his vices and lusts must be endured until he ignores the laws of honesty and decency that bind him. Princes should not be changed too easily lest greater

11. Jg. 3:15–26.

evils occur and serious upheavals come about (as was noted at the start of this discussion). But if such princes are ruining the country, preying upon private and public funds and holding public laws and our holy religion in contempt; if they make a virtue of pride, arrogance, and contempt for the heavenly powers, these things should not be ignored. Still, we have to pay attention to the reason for forcing that prince to abdicate lest we pile evil on evil and punish crime with a crime.

If there is an opportunity for a public meeting, that is a quick and safe way to deliberate and reach a consensus on what to do. The decision should be fixed and ratified by a common agreement. This process should go forward by these steps. First, the prince will be warned and called upon to return to a healthy outlook. If he behaves, satisfies the commonwealth, and corrects the sins of his past life, I think the process should halt there. If he rejects the medicine, . . . it is right to declare the prince a public enemy and to kill him by the sword. Let any private person exercise this right who will be willing to step up in this effort to help the commonwealth and has given up hope of avoiding punishment and risks his own safety. . . .

If princes oppress the commonwealth and are intolerable because of their vices and foulness, it is a good idea to remind them that they can be killed not only lawfully but also with praise and glory, if they continue to live in this evil way. Perhaps fear might deter kings from allowing themselves to become completely corrupted by vices and flattery. It will certainly curtail their madness.

The main point is this: the prince has to be persuaded that the authority of the whole commonwealth is greater than one person's. He should not believe evil men who in their quest to please him assert the opposite. . . .

Claudio Acquaviva

Rules for the Confessors of Princes[12]

[Jesuit confessors at royal courts were clearly in a better position to effect government decisions than were Jesuits teaching in schools or preaching to peasants. But they all shared the same purpose: to improve society by helping people live devout and moral lives. During their first century Jesuits served frequently

---

12. This letter of Acquaviva was written in 1602. The Latin text, which is printed in *Institutum Societatis Iesu* (Florence: Typographia a SS. Conceptione, 1893), vol. 3, pp. 281–84, is translated here by John Patrick Donnelly. The best study of the role of Jesuit royal confessors in early modern Europe is Robert Bireley's *The Jesuits and the Thirty Years War: Kings, Courts and Confessors* (Cambridge: Cambridge University Press, 2003).

as confessors to the Holy Roman Emperors, the kings of France and of Portugal, and to the dukes of Bavaria. Perhaps surprisingly, the Spanish kings did not employ them as confessors. But the lack of Jesuit confessors at the Spanish royal court did not discourage the enemies of the Jesuits from perceiving Jesuit confessors as secret agents of the Spanish crown.

The role of royal confessors was challenging; confessors were often required to attend royal councils and to give advice on the morality of different policies. For instance, was a planned military operation just in the eyes of God? Persuading monarchs to dismiss their mistresses was often a frustrating task, as was encouraging rulers to protect slaves and the native peoples in their colonies. A royal confessor had to be a man of great intelligence, charm, and integrity. He had to be constantly on guard against courtiers who tried to line up his support for their own projects. When the policies pursued by a king failed or were unpopular, the blame did not stop with him; the confessor, and the Jesuits generally, often shared the blame.

Acquaviva insisted that royal confessors should restrict their advice to the moral and religious dimensions of government policy. For Acquaviva, prudence was the virtue royal confessors needed most. But they also needed humility since their post could easily make them proud, arrogant, and unwilling to live within the poverty and obedience of the religious life.]

1. It is established at the outset that whenever the Society cannot escape such duties (because for various circumstances the greater glory of our Lord God seems to demand this) the basis for choosing the person and his way of carrying out his duty should be such that the prince is thereby helped, the people are edified, and the Society does not suffer harm. It often occurs that in addition to its other troubles, the Society suffers serious harm in many places for the sake of one place. Wherefore we have decided in the Lord— after commending this matter to the Divine Majesty in many Masses and prayers and after timely consultation with the Fathers Assistant—that the following regulations be decreed. If perchance some of the princes should sometimes disapprove of these regulations, they should be told, with all modesty and humility, that according to our laws Jesuits can accept this burden [of confessor] under these and no other conditions. But we hope that [the prince] will see that the interest and conservation of our religious order is closely linked with his own interests and the best interests of his subjects.

2. First, this confessor should always live in our own house or college and should conduct himself like a member [of the Order] and observe the common discipline like all the rest [of the Jesuits] as he was accustomed to do prior [to his appointment]. He should receive no exemption or privilege

King Sebastian I of Portugal being advised by Luís Gonçalves da Câmara, S.J., the royal confessor.

because he is a confessor. Still, because various matters related to the prince may arise and rightly require secrecy, confessors should be allowed to write and receive letters and memos both to and from the prince himself, his secretary, and other persons retained for this duty by the prince. But let not confessors think that thereby they have a general permission to write secretly to Jesuits or non-Jesuit officials or other people on this occasion. They should observe the rule exactly. If the Provincial [Superior] should ever discover an abuse [of this privilege], he should also impose the command and order that the rule be kept to the letter. Still less are confessors allowed to accept, retain, dispense, or give away monies or accept gifts since by these and similar actions—such as going out of the house without permission and going off anywhere at his own discretion—confessors will destroy our whole Order and its spirit in all individuals and contribute nothing to the service of the prince and the right performance of this office.

3. A confessor will not to live in, or spend the night at, court in places where the Society has a house. Even when the prince asks the confessor to remain with him during a journey or a change in dwellings, the confessor should obtain permission to do so from the Provincial Superior or the person in charge. It will be more edifying if the confessor arranges to stay outside the court in some convent of friars or with some respectable priest. At the same time, the confessor should take care that he always has a [Jesuit] companion to console him and act as a witness to his actions.

4. A confessor should take care not to get involved in external matters or politics and should be mindful of the things that the Fifth General Congregation very severely prescribed in its Canons 12 and 13. Instead, he should devote himself solely to those things that pertain to the prince's conscience or things related to it or to certain other pious works. He should carefully avoid spending too much time at the court; he should not go there when he is not summoned, unless he is compelled to go there by some pious necessity or a grave matter that seems to demand handling. It is very important

that the prince himself prevent his confessor from conducting other business. This way the confessor will perform his office with greater freedom and integrity, and his penitent will be free and delivered from the many troubles that are usually created by those who want to use the work of confessors for their own private advantage.

5. Under no conditions should a confessor become involved in so-called contracts by securing favors or offices or by seeking or obtaining [the prince's] goodwill or justice for anybody. When undertaken by a confessor, especially a member of a religious order, such actions usually result in scandal, even in legitimate cases.

6. The confessor should be aware that the more he enjoys the prince's favor, the more he is able to exercise some authority through him. Therefore a confessor should never undertake in word, and certainly never in writing, any of the prince's business or negotiations that should be entrusted to the royal ministers. But when the confessor's Superior judges that the confessor must become involved in some religious matter, the confessor should take care that the prince himself writes and gives orders about the matter. The confessor must be especially careful not to be used as a middleman to admonish or criticize, in the prince's name, the royal ministers and courtiers. The confessor should explicitly decline such a role if the prince should sometimes want to impose it upon him.

7. Again and again the confessor should strive to ensure that people do not come to think that he is very influential or that the prince is ruled by his judgment. Besides being hateful and unwelcome to everybody—and not at all respectful for the prince himself—such perceptions also bring incredible harm to the Society. Our sorry human condition continually gives rise to accusations, both just and unjust, and experience has taught us that hatred is always turned against the confessor. Although we cannot always control what happens in the world, the confessor should still do what he can to avoid such a reputation and should moderate the use of the power discussed just above.

8. The prince ought to listen calmly and patiently to whatever the confessor, following the bidding of his conscience, decides to suggest to him each day according to circumstances. Since [a confessor] will inevitably meet with the prince, a public person, when dealing with a particular matter, the Father is allowed to put forward, with religious liberty, the course of action he judges in the Lord to be for the greater service of God and of the prince himself. A confessor should make suggestions regarding not only those matters he knows about from his penitent but also regarding those other matters about which there is much gossip. Such matters require a remedy in order to hinder the oppressions and minimize the scandals often

brought about by the prince's ministers without his knowledge or consent. The prince himself must conscientiously consider the harm wrought by such matters and must use his foresight to prevent them from happening.

9. If it sometimes happens, as it can easily, that some difficulty should arise concerning the confessor's opinion, the prince should consult with two or three other theologians on the matter. In such a case the confessor should acquiesce and lay his own conviction aside if the theologians decide against his understanding. Likewise, the prince would be equally wrong if he does not agree, for his part, to do what the theologians have decided he should do.

10. In the [Jesuit] house a confessor should be mindful of religious modesty, obedience toward superiors, and his equality with the other [Jesuits] regarding his room, clothing, and all other matters of discipline. Because they are sometimes able to secure royal favors and other benefits for the Society, confessors are often inclined to treat people abruptly, to act in a haughty manner, and to present themselves as somehow better than other men. If such treatment greatly upsets a well-ordered religious community, it is unbelievable how much hostility it also creates in other people.

11. To sum everything up, a confessor should remember that he is just that—only a confessor. He should remember: everything that is alien to this office should be equally alien to himself. Thus the Society should not permit him to become involved in such things, nor should the confessor be upset if his superiors restrict him to this work. On the contrary, he should thank God that in this way he is made more available for attending to the one spiritual task entrusted to him. He should ask God constantly to grant him the light to give good advice. He should consult with his superiors in doubtful cases so that the direction of the Lord's Spirit, and not human prudence, will usefully illuminate his own judgment.

12. Let the confessor always insist that the prince direct his goodwill and inclination toward the Society and not toward his own person, for to do otherwise would be harmful to both the confessor and [our] religious order. Let the confessor keep his penitent's heart so directed that whenever our Order will judge it advantageous for God's service that [the confessor himself] be changed or that his work be used elsewhere, the prince may find easy to accept this change. It has happened in the past that some confessors have failed in this (either willingly or perhaps thoughtlessly) and have handled matters in such a way that they have made themselves enemies of religion and failed to lead to Christ the laymen with whom they are dealing.

13. The confessor should be extremely careful lest his role in the business of the court make him spiritually lax. Through prayer, the Spiritual Exercises, and frequent examinations of his own conscience a confessor should become an instrument so joined to our Lord God that by relying on His

grace and help he does not neglect his own spiritual dimension but is illuminated and directed in his activities by the Spirit. It will also be worthwhile for a confessor to engage in ministries toward his neighbors in the same way as other priests.

14. So that everything may progress peacefully and without any offense to princes we have judged it necessary that when a prince asks [a Jesuit] to serve as an official and stable confessor (it is not right for this to happen time and again, but it often does) he should tell the prince that though he is prepared to serve in this capacity, our laws prevent Jesuits from undertaking such a task without first consulting and receiving the agreement of the Provincial Superior. A potential confessor must ask his Superior for permission. But before granting that power the Provincial Superior (if he judges this good in the Lord, either through himself or though somebody else, or if it would seem wise, through that Father himself) should first show to those asking [the confessor's services] this Instruction of ours [i.e., Acquaviva's 1602 Instruction printed here], provided that the Provincial thinks the confessor is suited to this task and possesses the gifts and virtue that are needed for performing it well. This way, princes will clearly understand what the Society is asking of the priest whom they are choosing as their confessor. Then, let the confessor modestly—but clearly and openly—signify to the prince that from our heart we permit him to use as he wishes this Father's work for his spiritual consolation. But let the prince also understand that the Father's superiors may freely reassign him at such time as seems appropriate, just as they may reassign all other [Jesuits].

Robert Bellarmine

The Office of a Christian Prince[13]

[St. Robert Bellarmine (1542–1621) was the most important Jesuit theologian during the first century of the Jesuits; he was also a very popular spiritual writer. (Chapter 4 contains his arguments against Luther's teaching that scripture was the only criterion for Christian belief and practice, and Chapter 5 reprints a selection from Bellarmine's Ascent of the Mind to God.*)*
Though The Office of a Christian Prince, *written in 1618 and first published the next year in Rome, was one of the six books Bellarmine wrote late in his life while making his annual retreat, it was very different from the other five, which were primarily spiritual works. (See page 180 for more in-*

13. The three chapters printed here were translated by John Patrick Donnelly from *Roberti Cardinalis Bellarmini Opera Omnia* (Naples: Apud Josephum Giuliano, 1862), vol. 6, pp. 530–33, 542–43.

formation on his popular spiritual writings.) He yielded to the request of the Polish Jesuits that he write a book instructing Ladislaus (1595–1648), the young crown prince of Poland, on how to be a good king. King Ladislaus IV ruled the Polish-Lithuanian Commonwealth from 1632 to 1648 and fought a successful war against the Russians (1632–34). He also concluded favorable treaties with the Turks (1634) and Sweden (1635). Whether Bellarmine's book influenced Ladislaus' policies is unclear.

Books on how to be a good prince or ruler were extremely popular during the Renaissance; even the leading humanist, Desiderius Erasmus, wrote a book on the education of a Christian prince for the future emperor Charles V. The most famous (and infamous) of all such books was The Prince *by Niccolò Machiavelli (1469–1527). Written in 1513,* The Prince *purported to teach a Medici ruler how to hold and expand his power in Florence by means both fair and foul. Many Jesuits besides Mariana and Bellarmine wrote books of advice for rulers; several of these books were directed against Machiavelli.*[14]

Bellarmine's writings were always well organized. His work on the duties of a Christian prince is divided into three books. The selections printed here are all taken from Book 1, which has twenty-two chapters. Chapters 1 through 6 and 17 through 22 deal with the prince's duties toward God and toward the different groups of people with which rulers often had to deal. Chapters 7 through 16 explore the different virtues the prince should exercise toward his own subjects: charity, prudence, justice, courage, temperance, wisdom, generosity, clemency, and mercy. Book 2 presents such Old Testament Jewish leaders as Moses and David as role models for kings. Book 3 does the same with Catholic kings who were saints, such as Louis IX of France and Stephan I of Hungary. Book 1, Chapter 6, which is printed here, is concerned with the prince's duty toward his royal confessor. It makes an interesting contrast with Acquaviva's rules for royal confessors; while Acquaviva was laying down rules for a confessor only, Bellarmine was exploring both the prince's duties toward the confessor and the confessor's duties toward his royal penitent. In Chapter 20, Bellarmine alerts princes to their duty to restrain abuses that were rampant among soldiers and court officials. Chapter 21 explores the prince's relations with other monarchs, especially the traditional rules for waging a just war.]

Book 1, Chapter 6. *On the Duty of a Christian Prince toward his Confessor.*

Not without reason do we place the priest-confessor of the prince among those people whom the prince should consider as his superiors. For the

---

14. For Jesuit attacks on Machiavelli, see Bireley, *The Counter-Reformation Prince*.

priest, in hearing the confessions of the powerful (regardless of whether they are princes or private persons), acts as a judge in the place of God and has the power of binding or loosening in the sphere of conscience. There is an obvious sign of the confessor's power: the fact that in passing judgment he sits with his head covered while the penitent (even if he is a king or emperor), on bended knee with head uncovered and with a contrite and humbled heart, seeks absolution as one guilty of having injured His Divine Majesty. Indeed, the prince's eternal salvation depends, to a remarkable degree, on his confessor. One reads of many horrifying examples of confessors who, along with their princes, are condemned and carried off to the punishments of hell. The great task of princes is above all to rule according to their conscience. The prince needs a confessor who is very experienced, very prudent, and very brave. Most important, a royal confessor must desire nothing, have no ambitions, and want absolutely nothing except the eternal salvation of his prince and the prince's people.

We need to discuss different aspects of this office. The confessor plays two roles, that of judge and that of doctor, and the prince has two other roles, a private one and a public one. In acting as judge in the place of God, the confessor cannot, and ought not to, absolve from sins unless he sees that his penitent is truly repentant. For if, perchance, the prince does not want to rid himself of that which is keeping him in the filth of sin, then he is pretending to repent but not doing so when he confesses his sin. But if the confessor does not dare to refuse absolution to such an important man, let him hear the Holy Spirit crying out, "Do not seek to become a judge lest you be unable to remove iniquity, lest you be partial to a powerful man" [Sir. 7:6]. This same thing will come into play with many other sins. Thus the confessor is not able to absolve a penitent unless he makes a full confession. But a prince does not make a full confession if he confesses only the sins that relate to him as a private person (such as sins of gluttony, dissipation, envy, and similar sins) but skips over the sins he has committed as prince. For though there is no lack of princes who are very pious and just as regards their private person, they often know nothing about the sins of their most important ministers who administer the country by oppressing the poor, perverting the judicial system, and scandalizing the common people. The ignorance of a prince does not excuse him before God unless, perchance, it is invincible ignorance. For he should give serious thought to whom he employs as administrators and investigate how they are behaving and how they administer the country.

Therefore, the confessor who acts as judge in God's place ought not be satisfied by the confession that a prince makes as a private person, especially if he knows from public opinion or from another source how badly his administrators are behaving in administrating the country. But if the confessor himself is afraid of offending those administrators, let him listen to the Holy Spirit, who says, "Do not seek to become a judge lest you be unable to remove iniquity, lest you be partial to a powerful man."

Lastly, the confessor cannot absolve his penitent, however powerful, unless the prince is really prepared to make satisfaction—not only satisfaction to God through imposed fasting, alms, prayers, and the other works of penitence, but also in satisfying those to whom he might owe something, in protecting them from hunger, in repairing injuries, in paying his debts, in paying salaries on time. For a prince often owes many things to his subjects that they dare not demand from him lest they incur the prince's wrath. Here the justice of the judge who takes the place of God ought to put the confessor on guard lest perhaps he hears when he exits this life: "Why did you wish to be a judge when you were too weak to stop iniquity and you were timid in the face of a powerful person?" So much for the confessor in so far as he is a judge.

Let us add something as regards the same confessor as doctor. Nobody should be a doctor of souls unless he himself enjoys excellent health, lest maybe somebody say to him, "Doctor, heal yourself" [Lk. 4:23]. Therefore those who go about seeking to hear the confessions of princes deserve, by that very fact, to be rejected like people who are afflicted with a grave sickness. Worse still, they themselves do not recognize their own sickness. Therefore the wise prince, one who is concerned about his own eternal salvation, looks first of all for a priest who has never sought the office of confessor. Then [the prince seeks a confessor] who, by his public reputation and in private information, is said to be truly godly—that is, one who is really free from the sicknesses of vices. Besides, he should be skilled in spiritual medicine. Not only will the confessor have read what the theologians write about the sacrament of penance and what they call cases of conscience, but he will also know the practice and use of this knowledge. In addition, so that he is not often at the royal court, he will not become involved in the business of the courtiers lest from being a doctor of souls he himself becomes a courtier and court official. Lastly, he should employ a restrained freedom, joined to humility and holiness, when he has to admonish the prince. He should not fear being fired from his office as confessor—rather, if this happens he should rejoice over his being freed from a very dangerous burden. If it happens that he sees he is wasting his time on a certain prince because the prince will not go along with his rightful warnings, then he should humbly request permission to depart. Even if this request is not granted, he should leave on his own: suffering the wrath of a mortal prince is less painful than suffering the wrath of God.

So that the confessor can do his job, it is proper for the prince to grant his confessor access and freedom in order that he may faithfully warn and, given his office, command what is necessary for [the prince's] salvation. The confessor should not be restrained by fear or respect. It also seems necessary that the prince should warn the confessor that the confessor is not permitted to become involved in governmental matters or negotiations about jobs or discussions on how to run the royal household unless the prince himself asks for his advice. Far less should the confessor request government jobs or magistracies for anybody. This way he will be far less hateful to other people and less proud. He will please everybody and cause nobody trouble. Lastly, if the confessor belongs to a religious order, the prince should guard against undermining his obedience to bishops or his observance of the rules of his order. He should not offer his confessor any opportunity to dominate his fellow Religious or to seek the position of a bishop. This is not good for either the prince, or for the religious order, or for the confessor. Rather it harms everybody and especially the prince, who greatly needs a very good and devout confessor.

Book 1, Chapter 20. *The Duty of a Prince toward his Soldiers and his Court Officials.*

There remain the soldiers who are counted among the prince's subjects. They serve as soldiers in wartime or guard fortresses or [city] gates or the person of the prince in peacetime. St.John the Baptist[15] spoke so much about these men that there is scarcely anything that we have to add. I will echo, and explain where it seems necessary, the statement of that most wise Precursor. St. John the Baptist had only recently come out of the desert where he had taken refuge for many years. Crowds from everywhere rushed together to see and hear him as if he were a new kind of human being. From his infancy he had not had dealings with people for many years and had not studied writing from any teacher; still, he had been taught by the Holy Spirit and drew upon the testimony of the Scriptures. He passed down various passages to individual groups of people for their instruction. Thus "the soldiers also came to him asking, 'What must we also do?' And he said to them, 'Rob no one by violence or by false accusation, and be content with your wages'" [Lk. 3:14]. This is his succinct yet full teaching about what was proper for a person who was eager to carry out his life so that "he could not defile his life even by a little greed," as the Church sings in praise of him. St. John did not warn the soldiers to fight hard in battle or

---

15. John the Baptist was the precursor of the Christ and, after Mary, the most prominent saint throughout the Middle Ages and up to Bellarmine's time. Christ at the Last Judgment was a popular subject among medieval and Renaissance painters: in such paintings Mary usually appeared to the right of Christ, and John the Baptist to his left.

show themselves obedient to their general or anything of that sort. Partly the love of praise and partly the fear of punishment were enough to motivate them to these things. Indeed, in a military camp the punishment for stubborn disobedience was death. Therefore he dealt only with those actions that by an abuse of military obedience either were not punished or were very lightly punished. But before God they were very grave sins.

Therefore in the first place John the Baptist attacks violent robbery. He says, "Rob no one by violence." For it used to be common among soldiers to employ force on those they were dealing with or their neighbors, even though these were friends and not enemies, or to make them carry burdens or hand over the food they had prepared for themselves or to provide the soldiers with beds or bedrooms that each citizen had for his own use, or to force the people to wait on them as if they were servants. These things and much more are included in the words "Rob no one by violence"—that is, do not force anybody to do things or put up with things that nobody is legally held to do or endure. These injuries are very common among soldiers, as I myself could bear witness. For once, when I was passing through a region where war was being waged, I asked both peasants and also city folk which side they were on. They answered, "On neither. They are all our enemies. Those who are called our friends are often a greater danger to us than those who are called our enemies."

Next, St. John condemns false accusations made by soldiers saying, "Do not make false accusations." This is another vice that soldiers generally fall into. It often happens that they level false accusations against anybody they encounter—they are spies, or enemies, or deserters. And without any basis in justice, the soldiers robbed or wounded such people or took them captive. Unhappy are those who have nobody to testify to their innocence; they are forced to either buy their way out of trouble by a large sum of money or to endure cruel sufferings. Would that such things were not commonplace in Christian military camps! Good princes ought to devote their full strength to driving these things from our midst. In the end, the blessed Precursor of our Lord teaches all soldiers to be content with their wages and not pillage the property of others. We do not know whether the soldiers who heard what St. John said carried it out. We do know this: that in our times not only is this salutary teaching observed rarely, and by few [soldiers], but also no small trouble is inflicted on the citizens of the cities where the soldiers need to have winter quarters or stay for a time. But perhaps city folk are forced to provide the things the soldiers lack because the soldiers are not paid their salaries on time.

This can happen because the soldiers do not receive their salaries on time, but in the interval justice is disregarded. God, who sees and weighs everything on an accurately balanced scale, will severely punish those who do evil. Princes therefore ought to work so that the salaries owed the soldiers are paid on time. Then, if the soldiers do not follow the commands of St. John, it should be brought to the princes' attention in such a way that the soldiers learn to be content with their pay and not inflict harm on the city folk with whom they are living.

These things that have been said about soldiers can be applied to all the court officials: they too should be content with their salaries. If they receive anything beyond their salary they should recognize the generosity of the prince and not take it as retribution owed them. Besides that, they should set an example of modesty, kindness, and justice to all other people who serve private inheritors and reside in private homes. It frequently happens that while the prince is modest and kindly, his court officials are arrogant and harsh. The prince insists on justice and does no injury to anybody, but his officials are not content with their own salaries; they lust after gifts and practically sell access to the prince or to other things that are part of their office. But vices of this sort, which can affect the prince's good reputation, can be easily headed off if the prince earnestly and frequently recommends household discipline to the chief steward of the palace and orders him to take care, either personally or through others, that nothing happen in the palace that might result in injury to God or to the prince's reputation.

It is also very important that the prince earnestly warn his relatives and court officials not to turn people who are involved in criminal or civil lawsuits over to public judges. They should not get involved in the distribution of government offices or magistracies. For this results in applying a certain pressure in law cases as long as the judges dare not ignore the recommendations of the prince's court; meanwhile, courtiers get rich from the goods of poor people. It also frequently happens that public offices are pretty much up for sale to greedy people. Ambitious men love this, to the great harm of justice for the people.

There remains one crime that is common to soldiers and court officials: that they easily flatter their prince. They praise to the skies anything he says or does, as if it were a statement of the highest wisdom or a most splendid deed. Like a sweet poison, this flattery slips easily into [the prince's] mind, unless he has a mind truly humble and fully submissive to God. It is beyond telling how numerous and serious are the troubles that arise when the poison of flattery takes over the prince's mind. For the person who gives ear to flatterers first reeks with pride and walks, as the Scriptures say, into great and marvelous things that are above him and thinks that everything is easy for him [Ps. 131:1]. He then scorns the advice of the wise or spurns them as timid, or if they happen to steer him away from deeds that are more dangerous than advantageous, he thinks they are envious of his glory. Against people of this sort we have the wonderful example of Canute the Great,

king of England and Denmark. I am going to insert here a passage that
Polydore Vergil wrote for the instruction of great princes:

> Therefore King Canute sometimes used to walk along the ocean shore
> to refresh his mind. There a solder who was serving him called out to
> him in the wind as he took his leisure, "O King of Kings, by far the
> most powerful of all, you command the lands and seas far and wide."
> Then the king was quiet; his mind suddenly alert to contemplating
> God's power so that he might refute the pompous assertions of his
> lords and soldiers by an argument. He took off his cloak and wrapped
> it in a ball and sat on it as near the water as possible when a strong tide
> was pushing in from above. He said, "I command you, O wave, not to
> touch my feet." When he said this, his men were wondering why he
> was doing this. The rising tide soaked everything. Then he stepped
> back a bit and said, "See, my lords, you call me the King of Kings who
> can command land and sea. But I was not able by my command to
> stop this little wave or slow it down. No mortal man is worthy of such
> a title. There is one King, the Father of our Lord Jesus Christ, with
> whom He reigns. All things are ruled by a nod [of His head]. Let us
> worship Him, let us call Him King, let us profess that He rules over
> the heavens, the earth and the sea." After this he went to Winchester
> and with his own hands placed the crown he used to wear on the head
> of the statue of Christ crucified that hung in the church of the
> Apostles Peter and Paul. After this he never used this sort of splendid
> ornament on his head.[16]

From this [story] godly princes can learn not only to disregard flatterers
but also to teach them. [They can also learn] to keep adulation from puff-
ing them up with pride and to make progress in humility and to rejoice in
the true glory of their only Lord.

Book 1, Chapter 21. *The Duty of a Prince toward his Equals.*
We have written with our usual brevity about the duty of a prince toward
his superiors and toward his inferiors. It now follows for us to reflect on
how princes should deal with their equals. By "equals" we refer to those
men who are not superior to or subject to one another, such as are all those
who are called independent princes. . . .

16. *Polydore Vergil's English History* (New York: Johnson Reprint Corporation,
1968, originally printed for the Camden Society, 1846) vol. 1, p. 277. Polydore
Vergil (1470?–1555?) was an Italian humanist summoned to the court of Henry VII
to write an elegant Latin history of the English kings. The story of Canute is especially famous. Canute (994?–1035) was king of England (1016–35), Denmark
(1018–35), and Norway (1028–35). He fought and won wars against English opponents and Sweden. He was a skilled, popular, and devout ruler.

First, a powerful prince should not, for any reason or on any pretext, oppress a weaker prince, even if he can do so easily. . . . So that we may warn
princes a bit more carefully about such an important matter, they should
take it for granted that it is not in any way permitted to oppress by war a
neighboring prince or any other person unless the conditions for a just war
are present. The four conditions [for a just war] usually listed are: legitimate
authority, a just cause, a good intention, and reasonable conduct.[17] Legitimate authority belongs to an independent prince. . . . Private citizens, if
they are injured by another citizen, must have a common judge to whom
they have recourse. But princes who are really independent do not have
[that option]. The cause of a just war is an injury received from another
prince or also from an independent republic that does not have a higher
[ruler]. . . .

But we have to give very close attention to this: the injury that is being
redressed by war should not be dubious or minor but certain and serious.
Otherwise there is danger that a war may cause more harm instead of the
good that was hoped for from the war. Hence it is not easy for a powerful
prince to make a judgment about the cause of a just war against a weaker
prince because a desire to increase his principality may drive him to think
he has a just cause for going to war when this is not really the case. In this
matter he should not trust too much in his own local professors but should
seek the advice of foreigners, those who are respected and highly skilled,
men not looking for money; lightweights and men with a superficial
knowledge of the common consensus should be ignored. For here there is
question of a grave sin that involves many other sins.

A good intention, which is the third condition, is extremely necessary for
a just war. When the purpose of war is peace and the tranquility of the
state, it is not enough to start a war (except in the interest of the common
good) simply because legitimate authority and just cause are not lacking. . . . Not only does the absence of this third condition make the war unjust, it makes it a bad war even if it is just. In this respect, the third
condition differs greatly from the two previous ones. If they are not present,
the war is not only bad but also unjust since it would clearly be contrary to
justice. But when a war is undertaken for a just cause and by the authority
of a prince but without a good intention, it is against charity but not
against justice.

This factor also deserves careful consideration here: when a war is going
to be started as a means for peace, the means are still very important and

---

17. Most Christian theologians have traditionally condemned war as evil but have
allowed Christian rulers to engage in war on certain conditions that allow them to
fight a legitimate or "just" war. Bellarmine here explains those conditions.

dangerous. It should not be started immediately; rather other, easier and better, means should be tried first, as that Moses pointed out in Deuteronomy, "When you approach a city to attack it, offer terms of peace to it" [Dt. 20:10]. . . .

There remains the last condition: how [the war is waged]. War should be fought in such a way that only those who justly deserve to be punished should be punished. First those who are not from the number of the enemies should be set aside—for instance those who are not citizens of the enemy state. Those soldiers who have mistreated, pillaged, persecuted, or captured people through whose land they were marching or those who when barracked among people often repaid their kind hospitality with evil deeds, should not be treated mercifully. Such soldiers cannot be excused because their salaries are not paid them on time, for soldiers have no right to the goods of people who have done them no harm. Neither should civilians and friendly peasants be made to pay up because the prince has not paid his soldiers their salaries. Next, young children, women, old men, and others who cannot bear arms are out of bounds. Still, these people who cannot fight can be captured and stripped if they belong to the hostile state. But they certainly cannot be rightly killed, unless somebody of this sort is killed by an unintentional accident, for instance when a soldier accidentally shoots an arrow into an enemy formation and by chance kills a boy or weak old man. God Himself ordered this of the Hebrews when they were waging war, that they were to spare children and women. Natural reason teaches the same thing. What purpose is served by killing many people who cannot fight, unless it be to show off one's beastly cruelty? Those passages in Scripture in which God Himself commands that neither children nor women nor cattle are to be spared should not be mentioned. God's command should be obeyed completely since nobody can ask Him, "Why are you doing this?" Finally, according to the law of the Church the following kinds of people are not to be harmed: priests, monks, converts, pilgrims, merchants, and peasants who are coming or going or living by agriculture and the animals used in plowing or in transporting seed to the fields—for they have a right to enjoy a proper security.

These are then the conditions of a just war. Without [these conditions] no prince should harass any other prince. Still less should a powerful prince harass a weaker one. Otherwise he should fear the judgments of God, who often brings it about that the weaker prince easily defeats the stronger one.

CHAPTER 8

JESUITS IN THE EYES
OF THEIR ENEMIES

INTRODUCTION

Few groups in history have inspired such enthusiastic praise or such bitter hatred as the Jesuits. Webster's dictionary gives two meanings for *Jesuit:* first, a member of the Society of Jesus; second, "one given to intrigue or equivocation, a crafty person." *Jesuit* and *Jesuitical* carry the same hostile connotations in most Western languages. During the 14th and 15th centuries, members of the Dominican and Franciscan orders were the favorite targets of the anticlericalism that was widespread in Europe. The Protestant reformers built upon this anticlericalism; their attacks on Catholic doctrine and practice tended to stress the sins of the clergy—the sloth, greed, ignorance, and promiscuity of priests and friars as well as the wealth, pride, and power of bishops and popes. Most of these accusations, however, did not fit the Jesuits very well. By contemporary standards, most Jesuits were well educated. The few who were promiscuous were expelled from the order. Few were greedy as individuals (though raising funds for their colleges did lead the Jesuits to cultivate favor with the rich and powerful). Jesuit priests were seldom accused of being lazy; on the contrary, they were accused of working all too hard for an evil cause. Both Protestants and Catholics, laypeople and clergy, often accused the Jesuits with excessive pride—and this charge usually stuck.

Luther and Calvin opposed all religious orders in principle. Protestants tended to see the Jesuits as the shock troops of the Counter-Reformation who preached and wrote books against Protestant teachings (as was illustrated in Chapter 4). An elite body within the order, called the Professed Fathers, took a special vow to go on missions if so ordered by the pope. (This group included less than 5 percent of the order under Loyola; the Professed Fathers' numbers grew after his death.) This vow was widely interpreted as a vow of blind obedience to the pope on all matters by all Jesuits. Many Protestants during the Reformation regarded the pope as the

Antichrist—as Satan's lieutenant on earth. To such Protestants the Jesuits were the most dangerous agents of the papal Antichrist.[1]

Catholic opposition to the Jesuits was also widespread. Many friars, especially many Dominicans, saw the Jesuits as upstart rivals. The Dominicans, the Order of Preachers, had long been the religious order that stressed scholarship and learning among its members. Now the Jesuits were not only enjoying great success as preachers but were also opening colleges all across Catholic Europe to train lay students, a ministry neglected by the Dominicans. This chapter traces opposition to the Jesuits by two of the most prominent Spanish Dominicans in the mid-16th century: the great theologian Melchor Cano (1509–60) and Juan Martìnez Silíceo, the archbishop of Toledo and primate of Spain.[2] It also records the hostility directed against the Jesuits by the ordinary people of Zaragoza.

As noted earlier the Jesuits, unlike other religious orders, did not recite or sing the Divine Office in common. Many monks and friars believed common recitation was central to the lifestyle of a religious order, and that, therefore, the Jesuits were not a legitimate religious order. Others criticized the extreme centralization of power in the hands of the Jesuit general, who was elected for life and appointed all other important superiors. Other orders were much more democratic and decentralized. Many Catholics regarded the Jesuits as proud, arrogant, and power-hungry.

The Jesuits' loyalty to the pope and the fact that Loyola and many of his first companions were Spaniards caused many non-Spanish Catholics to identify the Jesuits with the expansion of papal influence and the imperialistic ambitions of Philip II of Spain. This attitude was especially strong in France, the nation against which Spain fought seven wars in the 16th century. But it was also common in the Netherlands, which was fighting for independence from Spanish control after 1560, and in England, where

1. Two interesting, bitter, and yet humorous examples of Protestant anti-Jesuit literature were written in Jacobean England. The most popular play of the era was Thomas Middleton's *A Game at Chess* (1624), which opens with a dialogue between Error personified and Loyola, who is pictured as a disciple of Machiavelli: Thomas Middleton, *A Game at Chess,* edited by T. H. Howard-Hill (Manchester: Manchester University Press, 1993). John Donne, the leading preacher and poet of the age, wrote *Ignatius His Conclave,* edited by T. S. Healy (Oxford: Clarendon Press, 1969), which traces Loyola's descent into hell, his confrontation with Satan, and his appointment as Satan's top lieutenant.

2. Juan Martìnez Silíceo, O.P., studied at the University of Paris, where he published a book on mathematics in 1541. He then returned to Spain and taught at the University of Salamanca. He was made archbishop of Toledo in 1546.

Henry VIII had rejected the papacy and where Elizabeth I fought against Spain for some twenty years.[3] To most Englishmen, the English Jesuits were traitors. To many French, the Jesuits were undermining the special status and liberties enjoyed by the French church within Catholicism; and besides, the Jesuits were allied with the Spanish enemy. In France the enemies of the Jesuits held key positions at the University of Paris and in the Parlement of Paris. This chapter prints a selection from Juan Polanco's account of anti-Jesuit hostility among French university professors and the hostility of the bishop of Paris. It also includes part of the learned and lengthy attack on the Jesuits by Étienne Pasquier, a leading member of the Parlement of Paris. The popular hostile stereotype of the Jesuit is well captured by Jean Lacouture: "Devious in manner, modest in demeanor, but sly and vain in appearance, he went his way, from the confessional to bed-chamber, stage left, stage right—a stiletto concealed between the pages of his prayer book or between soutane and velvet hairshirt, all *ad majorem Dei gloriam* [for the greater glory of God]."[4]

This chapter closes with two attacks on the Jesuits published in 1601 by Christopher Bagshaw (1552–1625?) and William Watson (1559?–1603). These English Catholic secular priests felt that the Jesuits slandered and looked down upon diocesan priests. They accused the Jesuits of meddling in politics, of favoring the Spanish in England's war against Spain (which dragged on from 1588 to 1604), and of having too much influence with Archpriest George Blackwell (1545–1612), who had charge of English Catholics in the absence of Catholic bishops in England.

3. The best short introduction to anti-Jesuit writings in early modern Europe is Peter Burke's essay "The Black Legend of the Jesuits: An Essay in the History of Social Stereotypes," in *Christianity and Community in the West: Essays in Honor of John Bossy,* edited by Simon Ditchfield (Aldershot, UK: Ashgate, 2001), pp. 165–82. Burke stresses English attacks on the Jesuits. French attacks are reviewed in Jean Lacouture's *Jesuits: A Multibiography,* translated by Jeremy Leggatt (Washington, DC: Counterpoint, 1995), pp. 348–77. Similar attitudes abounded in 19th-century Europe—see Rósín Healy, *The Jesuit Specter in Imperial Germany* (Leiden: Brill, 2003) and Geoffrey Cubitt, *The Jesuit Myth: Conspiracy and Politics in Nineteenth-Century France* (Oxford: Clarendon Press, 1993). Americans shared this hostility: on May 6, 1816, former president John Adams wrote to former president Thomas Jefferson, "If ever there was a body of men who merited damnation on earth and in Hell, it is this society of Loyola's." *The Adams–Jefferson Letters: The Complete Correspondence Between Thomas Jefferson and Abigail and John Adams,* Lester Cappon, editor (Chapel Hill: University of North Carolina Press, 1959) vol. 2, p. 474.

4. Lacouture, *Jesuits: A Multibiography,* pp. 350–51.

Juan Polanco

Selections from *Chronicon*

[Chapter 2 of this book (on Jesuit education) includes selections from Polanco's
Chronicon *dealing with the pioneer Jesuit college at Messina; Chapter 6 con-*
tains selections from the Chronicon *illustrating special pastoral ministries. The*
passages from the Chronicon *offered in this chapter describe the opposition*
faced by the Jesuits in Spain. This opposition came from Melchor Cano, a Do-
minican; Archbishop Silíceo of Toledo; and the common folk living in
Zaragoza. These selections are followed by passages illustrating French opposi-
tion to Jesuits from the Parlement of Paris, the University of Paris, and the
bishop of Paris. These latter passages are arranged chronologically.[5]*]*

Opposition to the early Jesuits in Spain

The Year 1548: *260. Melchor Cano attacks the Jesuits.*

. . . There was a certain friar of the Order of Preachers in the illustrious
College of Saint Stephen; he was famous for his learning, as erudite in his
writings as he was famous for his preaching. He lectured in the chair (which
they call that of the first hour). He persuaded himself that the end times
were already at the door and that the Anti-Christ had been born. For various human reasons he was hostile to Father Ignatius, whom he had known
at Rome. The conviction that both Ignatius and his companions were the
precursors of the Anti-Christ began to become seated in his heart, and that
very solidly. He wanted the signs of the Anti-Christ and his ministers to fit
our men exactly. Hence he began to brandish these spears against the Society and its Institute and its members both in private conversations and in
his Lenten sermons so much that almost all his hearers recognized that he
was speaking about our men. Because of his reputation he so influenced the
people that they pointed out with their finger our men who were walking
the street and urged one another to beware of their tricks since they feared
[our men] as servants and supporters of the Anti-Christ. Respected men,

---

5. As in Chapters 2 and 6, each section is listed by year and number as found in the
volumes of the *Monumenta Historica Societatis Iesu* edition of Polanco's *Chronicon*.
The translations are *Year by Year with the Early Jesuits, 1537–1556: Selections from*
the Chronicon *of Juan de Polanco, S.J.,* edited and translated by John Patrick Donnelly, S.J. (St. Louis: Institute of Jesuit Sources, 2004), pp. 80–1, 107, 134, 184–5,
235–8, 291–3, 343–4, 386–7, 390–2. These passages are used with the permission
of the Institute of Jesuit Sources.

many of whom Doctor [Miguel] Torres[6] consulted, did not approve of the zeal or prudence of this sort of preacher. [Torres] had greeted the preacher himself politely before he attacked our men. Nonetheless he [Cano], both by himself and by another preacher of his Order whom he had perhaps won over to his viewpoint, wanted to drive out our men, who had not yet set foot in Salamanca. When finally Doctor Torres dealt with him face to face and kindly asked him to restore the wounded reputation of the Society, which the Apostolic See had approved, he did not make him any more fair minded toward Ours; rather on the contrary, [Cano] began to make this and that objection, and he asserted that the people should be forewarned so that they would not allow themselves to be deceived, and he said that nothing displeased him more than the fact that Doctor Torres was one of Ours—a man he said he thought well of. He asked a certain famous preacher of his Order, who is called Juan of Segovia, to join him in attacking the Society. After [Cano] had spoken at length to this purpose, [Juan] like a prudent man smiled and answered with a single word that it was not appropriate for him to condemn that Institute before the Church had condemned it.

261. Opposition to the Jesuits at Alcalá

. . . Some people who from the outset had not thought well of our Institute, so that they might be seen as having been good at divination, boasted that the Society would soon be destroyed. Moreover, the Archbishop of Toledo [Silíceo], who showed himself less than fair toward Ours, threatened that he was going to come to Alcalá and examine both our lives and our ceremonies and Institute. . . . Moved by these [anti-Jesuit accusations], as we have said, the Rector [of the University of Alcalá] called in Francisco de Villanueva [the Jesuit superior]; he satisfied the Rector by explaining everything in detail and asked him to convoke a meeting of the theology faculty and look into all the causes of this rumor and of the whole disturbance and make notes on those points about which they [the faculty] wanted to be satisfied. [Villanueva] would be most grateful if the truth were sought out with the greatest rigor and that, if it pleased the Rector, this examination should be entrusted to those who had showed themselves the most opposed [to the Society]. This last part pleased the Rector, and he turned the affair over to the three doctors who had in public shown themselves more jealous of the Society than the others. Villanueva went to them and satisfied all their doubts both concerning the Spiritual Exercises (about which they had harbored many

---

6. Torres (1509–93) was the superior at the Jesuit college in Salamanca in 1548. Loyola had great confidence in him and appointed him provincial superior of southern Spain (1554–55) and of Portugal (1555–61).

falsehoods in their hearts) and the rest of the things pertaining to our Institute and our way of proceeding.

The Year 1549: *461. Cano returns to the attack.*

One of the most prominent and noble ladies of that city, who regarded Ours with a great deal of charity, was just on the point of giving her daughter to a certain count with a dowry of 50,000 ducats when the daughter denied that she wanted to marry anybody. This so exasperated the mother that when she suspected that [her daughter's decision] had come from listening to the teaching of Ours, she began to think evil of and even speak out against Ours. That same religious of the Order of Saint Dominic [Melchor Cano], who on our first arrival warned people to avoid Ours like servants of the Anti-Christ, when he was about to leave Salamanca for the congregation of his Order, in his last lecture he warned his listeners over and over to be on guard against new teaching, not only in writings but also in behavior. Therefore God wanted Ours always to have some people who would put them to the trial lest Ours have their heads puffed up by prosperity and success and so that they might profit from contradictions.

The Year 1550: *218. The origins of the name* Jesuit.

At this time a certain Carmelite preacher, while explaining in the church of Saint Severinus the expression of Paul "brothers in Christ Jesus," at this point began to attack our Society because at Paris and Rome they had usurped for themselves the name *Jesuits,* as if they alone were brothers in Christ Jesus. He urged the people not to make much of this title since sometimes a book has a catchy title but has nothing good inside. Therefore just like that preacher at Salamanca [Melchor Cano], he urged his listeners, among whom were many professors, to beware. Our friends thought it worthwhile for Father Battista to meet with him, but he thought it better to defeat such words with patience.

. . . Nonetheless some members of the Order of Preachers, with a zeal that was perhaps not evil but was uninformed, kept attacking Ours, and it is certain that they tried to encourage the ministers of justice to visit our house to check on what books Ours owned. There was also a man who when preaching viciously attacked certain clerics who were considered holy. His statement was taken as applying exclusively to Ours. They achieved little, and some support from papal authority was sent from Rome against such troublemakers, and as we said above, letters patent from the General himself of the Order of Preachers imposed silence on detractors belonging to his Order.

The Year 1551: *354. More friction with Archbishop Silíceo.*

The same day Father Villanueva set out for Toledo with the plan that, if he was unable to please the Archbishop with good manners and arguments, he would go on to the Royal Council lest he allow force to be used against the Society contrary to the grants of the Holy See. Before going to Toledo, during his dealings with the court at Madrid, he presented the Apostolic Letters to the Council and asked it for a provision so that he could inform the Archbishop about the Apostolic Letters. But because such matters were not usually dealt with so quickly by the Royal Council, on the advice of the apostolic nuncio[7] and with a letter from him to the Archbishop and other people he went on to Toledo. The Archbishop did not hide his hostility toward the Society and put forward several arguments, namely that the Society had built our house at Alcalá without his permission, that it was called the Society of *Jesus,* that [Ours] were engaged in the ministry of preaching and hearing Confessions without his own permission, that the Spiritual Exercises, which he himself did not regard as evangelical, made people fools so that noblemen did not act like noblemen, and so forth. When Villanueva tried to answer each charge at length, he resorted to threats since his attitude rested not on reasons but on emotions. If anybody brought up the Apostolic Letters to him, he asserted that he would throw the person into prison. He said, "Here we don't need a Supreme Pontiff," and other things which would be better left unsaid. Finally he said he would be coming to Alcalá—his usual response when he intended to do nothing.

The Year 1552: *501. Still more troubles with Archbishop Silíceo of Toledo.*

We noted above how zealously in the name of the Supreme Pontiff his legate Cardinal Poggio dealt with the Archbishop of Toledo so that he would suspend his edict and prohibition about exercising its ministries that he had promulgated against the Society. Father Ignatius had also ordered that information be gathered and sent to Rome about the things which he had devised against the Society. Father Francisco Villanueva spent almost three months in this business, which forced him to make various trips, and he did not stop commending the Archbishop to the Lord in his own prayers and in those of the brethren. Earlier he alone was involved in this business; then Doctor [Miguel] Torres joined him, as we have said, but when he returned to Salamanca, Villanueva was left alone at the task in the end. At the start the reason for the edict could not be ascertained. Earlier a general edict of the Archbishop had gone out that nobody should

---

7. The apostolic or papal nuncios were the pope's diplomatic representatives, roughly equivalent to ambassadors, at the various royal courts of Europe.

administer the sacraments unless he had been examined by [the Arch-bishop's] visitors; hence [Villanueva] subjected himself and Ours to this edict lest he offend the Archbishop, and requested from his visitor, called Master Palacios, faculties for Ours. Nonetheless, an edict was issued against the Society by name and forbidding us to hear Confessions, preach, offer mass, and revoking all faculties given by his visitors.

503. Silíceo's opposition to Jesuits of Jewish ancestry.

The reason for the anger of the Archbishop [of Toledo] was then real-ized: namely that the Society had admitted some men [of Jewish ancestry] whom he himself had excluded from the church in Toledo by his edict. Thus the Archbishop had given this reason to Prince Philip and had writ-ten so that [Philip] himself would see to it that the Society would not admit men of the sort which he had excluded from his church. He then would favor the Society with his whole power. He also spoke well of the Society with other people, but he would not allow those of whom we spoke [to enter the Society]. It was understood that Cardinal Poggio had promised the Archbishop two things, first that none of that sort of person would be admitted to the college of Alcalá whom he himself had excluded in his edict from the church of Toledo and second that the Society would act toward him in the same way as the other Religious Orders. The Cardi-nal then promised these two things to the Archbishop, leaving Ours in total ignorance. Because some scholarly and noble men to whom some part of the Archbishop's edict applied wanted to enter the Society, and if they were sent elsewhere, other people would easily note it. The Cardinal replied that when this storm was blown over, Ours could make free use of their privileges and the purpose of their institute, seeing that his promise could not be binding on us without our consent.

516. Silíceo relents.

I will not omit that when the Archbishop of Toledo revoked that edict of his and laid down the opposite in favor of the Society he added these words: "Because they have submitted to our jurisdiction." Although in revoking his previous statement he seemed to have added this out of concern for his honor, still it seemed good to Ours that for our part these words should not be passed over in silence without some protest. Thus Father Pedro Tablares went to the royal court and protested before the notary of the Apostolic Nuncio that Ours were in no way submitting themselves to the power of the Archbishop. Indeed, this was done in the presence of the Legate himself and appeal was made from that phraseology. I add also that the Archbishop had been persuaded that all of Ours were new Christians [men of Jewish ancestry] and he said as much to Prince Philip. But when he realized that this was not the case, the main reason which had armed him against the So-ciety came to a halt. He also was convinced and objected against Ours that we had withdrawn ourselves from episcopal jurisdiction and that we wanted to enter the church of Toledo against his will. Then Father Araoz[8] showed him the letters patent of Father Ignatius in which he specified that with the consent and permission of the bishops we would undertake to hear Confessions and preach in their dioceses. The Archbishop received and read these letters and noted the signature of Father Ignatius and said that it was a welcome surprise for him to see this, for he would not have believed it without seeing it. He was so pleased by what was prescribed in those letters that he immediately ordered the Governor of Alcalá to proceed no further in a suit against the college of the Society which he had planned on since he was just about to receive a sentence to tear down the walls surrounding our garden, and as we recounted above, he offered to supply the needs of the Society. . . .

The Year 1555: *1062. Those at Zaragoza who receive the sacraments from Jesuits incur excommunication.*

Here is the tenor of the decree which the aforesaid Vicar General [Lope Marco] affixed to our doors: "Because some clergy, [acting] on their own authority and dismissing the fear of God, have said Mass, preached and administered the sacraments in a profane house, he was warning in advance all rectors and vicars to publicize this in their churches lest anybody go to any of the aforesaid ministries in the aforesaid house. If anybody acted otherwise, he would incur excommunication."

1068. The other religious orders at Zaragoza combine against the Jesuits.

When this decree was put into effect regarding Ours, all the rectors and vicars met together several times so they could work as one body against our college because Ours at Zaragoza were an annoyance to them. From this the people began to grow extremely obstreperous. It was said by many that our adversaries were stirring up the people, using means both public and secret.

1072. A gang of boys at Zaragoza stone the Jesuit house.

That same day some throngs of boys with a banner on which some devils and perhaps some of Ours were painted came armed with stones against our house and began throwing stones at it. But immediately some of the Viceroy's ministers raced there and grabbed two or three of those boys, who confessed that they had been encouraged to this by some clergy and also by some unknown monks. The royal treasurer and city proceeded against them. Immediately the monks and the pastors marched through the whole city for three days with a bell, marching along the public streets against our house and the crowd threw stones to scare us. They carried a crucifix facing

8. Antonio Araoz was Loyola's nephew and the Jesuit superior in Spain.

backwards and covered by a black cloth and chanted in public from the Psalm [Ps. 109:1], "Be not silent, O God of my praise," which contains so many curses. This business stirred up an amazing hostility, and the crowd was so excited against Ours that everything was full of shouting and some horrible things were said against Ours.

1073. Aragonese versus Castilians, common folk versus noblemen at Zaragoza.

On orders from the Archbishop [Hernando de Aragon] all those belonging to religious orders in the city (except for the [Order] of Saint Jerome) gathered together against Ours and no limit was set to the complaints, threats and false accusations. The people were otherwise pretty free and were stirred up by the Archbishop, churchmen and the Religious Orders. Most of our few men working in Zaragoza were Castilians, against whom the Aragonese usually harbored a prejudice. There was fear not only that the lives of Ours might be in danger but also that the nobles, who were favorable to Ours, might face a riot from the people. When the boys first attacked our house with stones, many noblemen were playing soccer on a nearby field or were watching the players. Half naked they rushed to our defense, although some went to the Viceroy, who himself came with great nobility. There were grounds to fear a major riot.

1074. Efforts for a compromise reach an impasse.

Before things went that far our adversaries sought concord, but they would not allow us to build anything or preach or administer the sacraments or say Mass in public. Had they allowed the last items, as regards Masses and Confessions, perhaps Ours would have agreed.

1075. The Archbishop ignores higher authorities.

Princess Juana[9] tried zealously to favor justice for Ours and wrote the Archbishop and his vicar, the abbot, and she ordered that they rescind whatever they had done against our privileges. The Supreme Council of Aragon in its decree ordered that our [papal] bulls be observed. But the Archbishop would not yield to anyone, nor was he willing to obey either the Apostolic Letters or the brief which the apostolic nuncio sent him regarding these negotiations.

1079. The Jesuits leave Zaragoza.

Generally [the city authorities] were quite pleased with our departure. Lest they seem to be expelling Ours when Ours were leaving of their own accord, one of the officials and one senator accompanied them when they left the city. But so great was the mob of those who lined the city streets to watch Ours that they seemed to be coming to some public spectacles.

---

9. Princess Juana was the sister of Philip II; during Philip's absences from Spain she served as regent. She pressured Loyola into allowing her to take secret vows as a Jesuit. She was the last female Jesuit.

They had done this at other times when Ours were going somewhere from their house. The people attacked Ours with loud shouts and even injuries, for it seemed that churchmen and religious had persuaded the common folk that Ours were the cause of this uproar and the interdict, especially when they saw Ours depicted as surrounded by devils, as we said above.

Opposition to the early Jesuits in France

The Year 1553: *646. Troubles with members of the Parlement of Paris.*

When on the day [February 2] of the Purification of Mary[10] [Paschase Broët[11]] visited many of the senators and asked them to favor our cause, some of them offered their help, but he offended some to a remarkable degree. There was one of them who said that the devil had dreamed up this Society and was its founder. Father Paschase responded to him that he believed that the Holy Spirit was its founder, not the devil, who is not usually worried about getting done all the good works which the Society devoted itself to throughout the whole world, even to the Indies. There was another [senator] who said that we were superstitious, proud and arrogant with such anger that good Father Paschase did not have any way to respond since the senator would not listen. Instead of responding, [Broët] armed himself with patience. But in the end [the senator's] anger passed away and the two went off as friends. In saying goodbye Father asked him to recommend our Society as the Lord inspired him to speak. The General Procurator of the King, normally a pious Catholic, honestly confessed that he could not bring himself to support a confirmation of our privilege. He went over several reasons which seemed to affect the good of the state which delayed expediting our cause. He clung to this position despite the pleas of the Bishop of Claremont.

647. The troubles continue.

When Father Paschase went to the first president and asked him to expedite our business, he asked that if the Parlement decided something against our Society, [the matter] should be referred to the King. But the president began to shout that there were enough religious orders and that, if we wanted to be religious, we should enter [the Order] of Saint Francis or the

---

10. Forty days after the birth of a firstborn male, Jewish women had to undergo a purification ceremony at the temple in Jerusalem (see Lev. 12:2–8). For Mary's purification, see Lk. 2: 22–39. The Christian feast day of the Purification was forty days after Christmas.

11. Broët was the Jesuit superior in Paris. He was also one of Loyola's first companions from their student days in Paris.

Carthusians or some other order.[12] When Father Paschase said that purpose
of our Institute was different, he answered with great anger, "You don't perform miracles, do you, or do you think you are better than the other [or-
ders]?" . . . Many people objected that we had usurped the name of the
Society of Jesus. They said, "Do we, who don't belong to your Institute, belong to the Society of the Devil?" I should add, however that the same person who said that the devil was the founder of the Society was not afraid to
say in the hearing of Father Paschase that the devil had been the leader of
the Council of Trent.[13] But all those people denigrated us only with words.
There was one man who thought that Ours should be punished with whips
and be expelled from the University of Paris.

    648. The Bishop and University of Paris attack the Jesuits.

    Eventually the Parlement reached a decision, entered a new path and
lifted the whole burden from its own shoulders—it transferred judgment
on this whole controversy to the Bishop of Paris [Eustace du Bellay] and the
Faculty of Theology. It seems quite clear that the Parlement did this to prevent the Society from gaining any advantage, since its members could easily
learn the attitude of the Bishop and the doctors of theology. Father
Paschase took the sentence of the Parlement along with our Apostolic Letters and privileges and the royal grant to the Bishop and the faculty of theology. When he first came to the Bishop, the Bishop sang the same old song
as the others, that there were already quite enough and more than enough
Religious Orders without Ours. When Father Paschase said that the
Supreme Pontiff had approved it and the Most Christian King [of France]
had also done so for his realm, [the Bishop] answered that the Supreme
Pontiff could give approval for areas subject to his own temporal jurisdiction but could not give approval for our Religious Order in the Kingdom of
France. The King could not approve a religious order since this was a spiritual question. So much for their first meeting. He added that he would
never allow that the Order of our Society be admitted, which was in his
power. On a second visit [Broët] found him more subdued, but [Broët]

---

12. The Order of St. Francis is the Franciscans, the largest religious order of Loyola's time. The Carthusians were an austere monastic order founded by St. Bruno in
1084.

13. The Council of Trent was the ecumenical council convoked by the popes to
deal with the theological challenges of Protestantism and to reform the Catholic
Church. It met periodically from 1545 to 1563. Since the council seemed to be
dominated by bishops from lands under Charles V and later Philip II, the French
kings Francis I and Henry II forbade French bishops to attend most of the sessions.
The Parlement of Paris refused to approve the council's reform decrees, notably that
of ratifying the papal approval of the Jesuits.

took care that some of our friends with considerable prestige (among them the Bishop of Claremont) should talk to the Bishop. Father Ignatius at Rome also had Cardinal Maffeo write to Cardinal du Bellay.[14] [Maffeo] kindly performed this act of charity and gave a splendid testimonial, as is clear from his letter.

653. Still more opposition in Paris.

These negotiations with the University were drawn out almost seven months, and meanwhile the Dean of the theologians tried to argue that the Society should seek only permission for setting up a college and that Ours could be admitted to the theology curriculum and receive the doctoral degree. But from Father Paschase, he knew that Ours were more concerned about preaching good and sound doctrine than in taking degrees of this sort. Some said that the Society was indeed behaving well now, but would later degenerate like the other Religious Orders. To these [charges] Father Paschase in his humility responded that through God's grace [the Society] could also persevere and that, although the question of whether it would degenerate in the course of time was in doubt, it would be good if the church used its ministry as long as it was doing well. He added that those to whom they wanted to subject Ours could themselves fall off just as easily as we could. Nonetheless they declared their opinion that our privileges should not be approved since the church, that is, an [ecumenical] council, had not approved them. The Dean said explicitly that a pope could not give a privilege against the hierarchical order and to the prejudice of bishops and pastors. When Father Paschase presented [contrary] arguments, they said that what had been laid down by the sacred councils should be observed.

The Year 1554: *690. More troubles with the Bishop of Paris.*

When the [Queen's] advisor Lord Dumont carried out his business with the Bishop about promoting [men] to sacred orders, the Bishop told him explicitly that he would act in a way that he would not seem to be approving of our Society if he admitted one of Ours to sacred orders. He added that the theologians had discovered more than forty errors in our apostolic documents, hence he concluded that our Society was a disgrace. It was not surprising that the apostolic letter had so little importance for him because when Father Paschase showed him the approbation of two popes he replied that the Supreme Pontiffs had done many things that were not good, implying that the approbation of our Society was among them. . . .

---

14. Cardinal Bernadino Maffeo, who worked at the Roman curia, was a good friend of the Jesuits. Cardinal Eustace du Bellay, the bishop of Paris, had a long history of hostility toward the Jesuits.

703. The theology faculty at the University of Paris issues the following decree:

"This new Society claiming for itself alone the unusual title of the name of Jesus admits anybody quite without restraint or discrimination, however criminal, illegitimate and shameful they be. It has no difference from secular priests in its outward garb, in tonsure, in saying privately the canonical hours or in singing them publicly in church, nor in observing cloister, silence, in its choice of foods and days, in fasting and in its various laws and ceremonies which distinguish and preserve the status of Religious. [The popes] have given it many and varied privileges, indults and liberties, especially regarding the administration of the sacraments of penance and the Eucharist, and that without regard for places and persons. [These privileges] in the office of preaching, lecturing and teaching are prejudicial to bishops and the hierarchical order. They are also prejudicial to other Religious Orders and even to temporal princes and lords. They are contrary to the privileges of universities and finally are a heavy burden on the people. [This Society] seems to violate the uprightness of the monastic life and weaken the zealous, pious, and very necessary exercise of virtues, abstinence and austerity; indeed it provides an opportunity to freely desert the other Religious Orders and detracts from proper obedience and subjection to bishops; it unjustly deprives both civil and ecclesiastical lords of their rights; it brings on trouble for both the [civil and ecclesiastical] community and jealousies and various schisms. Therefore in all these things and others which have been carefully examined and thought through, this Society seems to endanger the matter of faith, to disturb the peace of the Church, to overthrow the monastic and religious life, and to result in more pulling down than in building up. Issued by the command of the Dean, the Lords and the Main Masters of the Faculty of Sacred Theology at Paris."

The Year 1555: *871. Wild rumors at Paris against the Jesuits.*

Of the four professors who accompanied the Cardinal of Lorraine to Rome, one was Master Benoit of the Order of Saint Dominic, who had written all the arguments against the Society in the aforesaid decree. Another professor was [Claude] Despence, who showed himself much opposed to our Institute. As was seen, these returned from Rome with a far different attitude. Meanwhile some rumormongers boasted that the Society had lost its lawsuit against the theologians, yet in truth the Society had no plans to initiate a legal controversy. Some people said that our Institute was some sly contrivance and crafty deceit of the devil. The rumor was spread that the founder of our Institute had been a certain Jew who had instituted this form of religious life in expiation for his shameful crimes.

880. The Bishop and others at Paris attack the Society.

Such contradictions gave Ours more encouragement so that they hoped that if anywhere, the Society would have a glorious future at Paris since solid foundations were being laid through so much persecution. But the Bishop [of Paris Eustace du Bellay], whom Apostolic Letters had assigned as the Society's protector and as sort of bronze wall against calumnies,[15] stated that after he was informed of the censure of the Sorbonne he was convinced that the Society should be abolished. When he had Ours brought before a court of justice, and after they were indicted, his officials heaped on Ours countless insults and abuse. They added threats; they called [Ours] hypocrites, schismatics, members of conventicles, founders of new sects; they said that ecclesiastical censures, prison, and the secular power also would be employed against Ours if they in the future observed a form of religious life in accord with our Institute. They forbade Ours to say Mass, hear Confessions, or administer any sacrament. Ours appealed to the Pope, thus thwarting the hope of those who were trying to hale us before the Archbishop [of Lyons and Primate of France]. Thus did those who were preparing crosses for Ours began to find themselves crucified and troubled.

Étienne Pasquier

Le Catéchisme des Jésuites[16]

[In 1602 Pasquier (1529–1615) published the most learned attack on the early Jesuits. "But the only true begetter of Jesuitphobia, the man who raised the phenomenon to a new level of the literary genre (and export product) was

15. The fact that the pope's officials, who drew up the Apostolic Letters for him, appointed du Bellay, a long-standing enemy of the Jesuits, as protector of the Jesuits has two possible explanations. Either they were ignorant about du Bellay or they may have been following orders from the new pope (Paul IV, 1555–59) who, as Cardinal Giampietro Carafa, also had a long history of hostility toward the Jesuits.

16. Étienne Pasquier's masterwork was his *Le Catéchisme des Jésuites* (Paris: Chez Guillaume Grenier, 1602). Claude Sutto published a modern critical edition with a long scholarly introduction (Sherbrooke: Les Édition de l'Université de Sherbrooke, 1982), pp. 11–121. The translation here (completed by John Patrick Donnelly with the help of Joseph Mueller) is based on pp. 425–30 of Sutto's edition. Pasquier's book was rapidly translated and published in several languages. The English translation of 1602 is entitled *The Jesuites Catechisme. Or Examination of their doctrine. . . .* A modern photo reprint of that translation is available in the English Recusant Literature series, (Menston, UK: Scolar Press, 1975), vol. 264.

Étienne Pasquier." [17] *Pasquier was, for many years, a leading member of the Parlement of Paris, whose early opposition to the Jesuits was described in several passages from Polanco earlier in this chapter. Pasquier had a long history of opposing the Jesuits. In 1565 he defended the University of Paris' opposition to Jesuit efforts to gain university affiliation for Jesuit schools and argued that Jesuits should be entirely barred from teaching. Though these efforts failed, he was successful in blocking Jesuit integration into the University of Paris. He also published a short attack on the order in 1594.]*

Book 3

Chapter 24. That the sect of the Jesuits is no less dangerous for our Church than is the Lutheran sect.

This statement may seem paradoxical at first glace, but it is true. The arrangement of the hierarchical order of our Church conforms to, and corresponds with, the human body in a certain way. In it, the head exercises kingship over all the other members, among which there are certain noble parts such as the heart, liver, and lungs, without which neither the head nor the whole body would subsist. Were one to take away from the head, diminishing it to distribute to the other parts, or do the opposite and take away from the noble parts to give to the head, removing the proportion and correspondence that ought to exist among all the members, one would ruin the whole body. The same applies to our hierarchy. The head of the Church is our Holy Father the Pope; the noble parts under him are the archbishops, bishops, pastors, and priests. I will add the kings and universities. As for the rest of the people, they represent the other members of the human body.

Martin Luther was the first to offend the head so as to introduce a form of aristocracy into our Church and make all the bishops in and beyond their dioceses equal to the Holy See of Rome. [18] From this there emerged first the sect of the Lutherans and then that of the Calvinists. Several years later there arose Ignatius of Loyola, who defended the authority of the Holy See by a totally opposite proposition, but by wearing this out so much that he did not do less damage to our Church than they did. For pretending to uphold our Holy Father under better tokens than everybody else and attributing to [the Pope] unprecedented authorities to the prejudice of the

17. Lacouture, *Jesuits: A Multibiography,* p. 352. Lacouture discusses Pasquier's hostility toward the Jesuits on pp. 352–54.

18. Pasquier argues that Luther, by attacking the popes as agents of Satan, undermined their power and made all bishops equal, thereby replacing the monarchy of the popes with an aristocracy of the bishops.

bishops, he and his men obtained, successively, from one pope after another, such privileges, indults, and grants to the prejudice of prelates, monasteries, and universities that by allowing them to live in the midst of us, you are erasing the true face of our Church, universal and Catholic.[19] Remember what the Jesuit showed to you the other day, and you will find what I am saying to you is very true.[20] The difference, then, that existed between Luther and Ignatius was that the former troubled our Church by taking up arms against its head, and the latter by striking against the other noble parts. It is a vice to attach oneself to extremes; virtue is a rule in the middle between the two. For me, I believe that the true Catholic, Apostolic, and Roman Church is that which was in use starting from, and ever since, the passion of our savior and redeemer Jesus Christ. This is the one approved by all ancient Doctors of the Church, among whom the least had more Christian teaching and sentiment in his soul than Luther and his followers and than Ignatius and all his confidants. It is the Church in which all good and faithful Christians ought to live and die.

I will gladly add that I would rather falter with them than run the risk and hazard of my soul by joining up with these new people. But this would be to speak wrongly on a matter of such great worth. I will not say, therefore, that I would prefer them. But I will indeed say boldly that I would fear to falter. For to say that the Jesuit is the true sword to beat back the blows of the Lutheran or Calvinist—not only do I not think that; on the contrary, it is the main way to confirm them in their erroneous opinions. I know that when one of my friends was attending a sermon—out of curiosity and not devotion—a minister cried out to his audience, "My brother Christians, God has looked on us with a merciful eye. Although Martin Luther was strong enough to fight the papacy with flags flying, it is the case that Ignatius of Loyola has given us a great advantage, for he has undermined [the papacy] while pretending to support it. What better way is there to subvert a state than by internal factions and divisions? And what else do the Jesuits produce in the Roman Church? Since this [Jesuit] sect is its principal support, we

19. The popes of the 16th century issued various documents granting privileges to the Jesuits that put them under the authority of their own superiors, unlike diocesan priests who were under the authority of local bishops. Papal documents also gave Jesuit schools authority to grant academic degrees, something that Pasquier thought undermined the rights of older universities. Earlier popes had granted similar privileges to other religious orders.

20. The Jesuits very often defended their activity by showing their opponents copies of papal documents granting them certain rights and privileges. Pasquier would deny that the popes had the right to issue such documents since they curtailed the liberties of the French Catholic Church.

have captured the city. And unquestionably the head must be infinitely sick, if for the sake of sustaining itself, it ruins all the other noble parts by favoring this novel sect. But what is the cause of this disorder? The vow about going on an imaginary mission by which the Pope makes himself a sponsor of their quarreling. My friends, let us then praise God and say what Demea said of old to her brother Mitius in the comic poet [Terence], 'Whether he consumes, is ruined, and dies, it's not my problem.' "[21] These six or seven Latin words uttered against the Holy See are truly blasphemous. But this is the unbridled license used in various ways by those who mount the pulpits to preach, attributing all the shortcomings of their rage to the Holy Spirit. Although this harmful conduct did not move this minister in the least, it should acutely move the heart of any good Catholic who wants to live and die in the Apostolic and Roman Catholic Church. We all have an interest in ensuring that these gentleman ministers do not triumph in this and that their triumphs not be founded on our Jesuits. Consider whether they have a basis for saying this. For among the other points in the censure of our theologians in the year 1554,[22] it was said that the Jesuits would be seed-beds of schisms and divisions in our Christian Church and that they were brought in for its ruin and desolation rather than for building it up. If I have done wrong in saying that the Jesuit sect is no less dangerous to the true Church than the Lutheran ones, I have done this not without judgment, having as a guide in this the judgment of that venerable faculty of theology of Paris.

Chapter 25. Of the notorious enterprise of the Jesuit General against the Holy See of Rome and of that new sect [the Jesuits] which in time may be so dangerous to [the papacy].

When the venerable faculty of theology of Paris censured the sect of the Jesuits in 1554, they took into consideration only the inferior orders, both spiritual and temporal. But they did not investigate how this concerned the Holy See. It was also impossible for them, for they had not yet been given all the bulls or Constitutions [of the Jesuits]. Now that God by his holy grace has enlightened us over time, I do not hesitate to say that the image of Lucifer, who wished to make himself equal to God his creator, is represented in the person of the General of the Jesuits. So this man, who is the creature of the Pope, gives himself not only equal, but even greater power, and authority over his own men than the Pope has over the universal

---

21. "Consumat, perdat, pereat, nihil ad me attinet," Terence, *Adelphi,* I, ii, 134. Terence (c. 185–c. 159 B.C.) was, after Plautus, the most important writer of Latin comedies.

22. For the university's condemnation of the Jesuits see p. 244 of this chapter.

Church. In Rome [the Jesuits] broadcast that they obey the Pope absolutely, not only about going on a mission but also in all other commands. And on this pretext they have obtained, and are obtaining day after day, an infinite number of extraordinary privileges to the detriment, and (dare I say) to the shame of archbishops, bishops, religious orders, universities, and the whole ancient Catholic Church. Nonetheless, the truth is that, having two objects to revere, they give incomparably more honor to their own General than to the Holy See.

Ignatius of Loyola, a Spaniard and a descendant of a great and noble family, changed his life without changing his nature. . . . For it was he whom [his first companions] promised to go and meet on a certain day at Venice; he who gathered them later at Vicenza to deliberate whether they should return to Rome to set up their new sect; he who took charge of it as its head. This was the reason why, making sure that they would proceed to the election of a General of their Order, he could never fail to occupy this position; he ensured, before they left, that the General would exercise this office his whole life and would have total power over his men. . . .

Since then, the Order being approved at Rome and Ignatius elected General on this basis of absolute power, he who had been nourished as a youth in a military milieu, without [training] based on literature, introduced into the family of the Jesuits a tyrannical government, desiring that all his wishes and those of his successors as General would be absolutely held as good, just, and valid. For although they have pretended, since then, to make a similar vow of obedience to the Holy See and were on this basis authorized in Rome, it is the case that in all ways they give greater obedience to their General than to the Pope. I say not to their General only but to all the other superiors, such as their Provincials and Rectors; even in their vow to go on a mission their General has more power over them than the Pope does. All of this is as I have discussed it with you in more detail, speaking as much about the vow to go on a mission as about blind obedience. Therefore I conclude—and in concluding I will not be opposed by a soul who is not strongly prejudiced—that the command the Pope and the General hold over the Jesuits is sovereign in all matters, but is incomparably more precise in what concerns their General.

This makes me believe that if the Holy See ever suffered a breach, there would be no sect so damaging to [the papacy] as the [sect] of the Jesuits, seeing that their General is in Rome. We cry out against the Lutherans, and with a good reason, all the more so because they were the first in our century to disturb the peace of our Church. But for all that I do not think them a greater threat against the Holy See than the Jesuits. Some pedant or stupid schoolboy will say that I am a heretic for having sustained this view.

I don't give that any credit. Hear my argument. None of those who we in France now call those of the "pretended Reformed" or "new Religion" [i.e., Calvinists] have any settled or permanent head over them. If they were to have one, they would be contradicting their own claim to have removed the primacy from the Pope by bringing in another [primacy] over themselves. They live in an oligarchy, or better, an aristocracy. . . .

But I fear everything from the Jesuits, not only in France but also in Rome because their policy aims exclusively at establishing a tyranny over everybody, which they will achieve step by step if no one straightens this situation out. They have a General who is not elected for a set term but for his lifetime, just like the Pope. . . .

Their General serves for life; all the other officials of his Order are temporary. Under him are the Provincials, according to the division of provinces. Under them are the Rectors who have specific authority over their houses and schools and hence over the [professed] fathers and over the spiritual and temporal coadjutors and over the approved scholastics. As to the principals of the schools, they are mainly commissioned to watch over the lay students. These assignments are usually for three years; however, they may be lengthened or shortened at the pleasure of the General. He decides about temporal things without any counsel other than his own. He exercises an infinite number of prerogatives, which are not given even to our bishops.

English Catholic Attacks on the Jesuits

[The next two attacks on the Jesuits were written by English Catholic diocesan or secular priests. The first attack is excerpted from A Sparing Discovery of our English Jesuits, and of Father Parsons's Proceedings under the Pretext of Promoting the Catholic Faith in England, *published in London in 1601 by Christopher Bagshaw. The second attack is taken from William Watson's prefatory letter to John Mush's* A Dialogue betwixt a Secular Priest and a Lay Gentleman. *The title page of that book gives the place and date of publication as Reims, 1601.*[23]

23. The excepts from both Bagshaw and Watson are taken from the photo reprints of these two books in the English Recusant Literature series (Menston, UK: Scolar Press, 1970), vol. 39. The spelling, punctuation, and some of the wording have been modernized to make these two excerpts more readable. The excerpts from Bagshaw's book are from pp. 1–8. Unfortunately Watson's prefatory letter to the Mush book has no pagination. For further information about the books of Bagshaw, Mush, Watson, and other English anti-Jesuit tracts of the last years of Elizabeth I as well as the Jesuits' replies, see Peter Milward, *Religious Controversy of the Elizabethan Age: A Survey of Printed Sources* (Lincoln: University of Nebraska Press, 1977), pp. 116–24.

Both these works were part of a quarrel among English Catholics known as the Appellant Controversy, or Archpriest Controversy. The underground, and bishopless, Catholic Church in England needed a leader to unify English Catholics and to serve as a sort of substitute bishop. In 1598 Pope Clement VII appointed the secular priest George Blackwell as archpriest to serve as the leader of the English Catholic clergy.[24] Unfortunately many secular priests considered Blackwell as too much under the influence of the Jesuits and attacked both Blackwell and the Jesuits on a range of issues, many of which are raised here by Bagshaw and Watson. These authors argue that the Jesuits hold secular priests in contempt and slander them. To Bagshaw and Watson the Jesuits meddle in politics and stir up sedition, wars, and assassinations; are worldly priests who seek out positions of influence at royal courts, where they serve as spies for the Jesuit hierarchy; and cultivate an excessive reverence for the Spaniard Ignatius of Loyola. Both authors accuse the Jesuits of political hypocrisy: they supported Spanish imperialism and urged Philip II to attack England on several occasions (most notably the Spanish Armada of 1588); they dared to accuse and insult secular priests for meddling in politics. Finally, Bagshaw and Watson accuse the Jesuits with supporting Archpriest Blackwell, whom many secular priests distrusted.]

Christopher Bagshaw

A Sparing Discoverie of Our English Jesuits (1601)

We do not make this mention of religious men, as if we disliked those most holy and Religious Orders; we are truly persuaded that they were devised and founded by the Spirit of God. Some of them especially [devoted themselves] to contemplation and some to join therewith their prayers and travel for assisting us who are secular priests in the great work committed to us, but not to deal with us as our new masters the Jesuits do, to oppose themselves as a faction against us or to calumniate and slander us falsely, or to allure the people's hearts from us hypocritically, or to insult or tyrannize over us most proudly and disdainfully. For this is plainly pharisaical[25] and can no longer be well endured. It has already taken deeper root in a short time among us than many men think, and it will grow to be pernicious to the Catholic Church if they are not plucked up like pestilential weeds with greater foresight and diligence.

---

24. For information on Archpriest George Blackwell, see J. H. Pollen, *The Institution of the Archpriest Blackwell* (New York: Longmans, Green, 1916).

25. In the four Gospels, Jesus frequently accuses the Pharisee rabbis of being hypocritical. Bagshaw sees the Jesuits as acting in the same way.

Some of their followers have presumed by their directions to affirm in writing that the Jesuits are more free from error, more familiar with God, more individually illuminated in all their fitting rewards and more especially are endowed with the spirit of guiding souls than are secular priests in the harvest of God. And thereupon a warning is given to all Catholics to take diligent heed and beware of all priests in general that are not themselves Jesuits or are related to them and are in all their proceedings advised and guided by them.

And concerning women, some of them are admitted by our archpriest and the Jesuits into their secret councils, and both there and elsewhere among their groups they censure us in the depth of their great judgment very wisely. [These women] rail upon us of their charity very devoutly, and they condemn us before they hear us out. Their seducing guides do fawn upon them, flatter and praise them and that makes the poor souls to be so fond of them and to dote as they do and run riot after them.

We confess and thank God for it very heartily that as yet many sound and grave Catholics, both men and women, are not bewitched with the Sirens' songs of these new enchanters. . . . [26]

In this our rough draft to reveal in some sort unto you the contagion and practices of our English Jesuitism and Jesuits, we do first treat about them and such as they are more generally, and then we will be a little bold to claw Father Parsons[27] where he does not itch, as the man that has been and still continues the chief firebrand that has and does inflame so many hearts of both men and women with pride, disdain, and malice against us, [who are] their ancient, most loving, and faithful spiritual Fathers, who notwithstanding their unkindness toward us, do love them still sincerely and praying for them continually are ready every day to offer our lives for the honor of the Catholic Church and for the confirmation of their faith. Now for the first point, so that you may more truly discern what sort of fellows the Jesuits are who have thus bewitched many of you: we do refer you (the better

---

26. In Homer's *Odyssey*, the songs of the Sirens lure sailors to destruction. See Book 12, lines 39–52 and 158–198.

27. Robert Parsons, also Persons (1546–1610), was a leading English Jesuit during his last thirty years. He worked underground in England (1580–81) but returned to the Continent to train priests for the English mission. His frequent dealings with Philip II made him a traitor in the eyes of English Protestants and many Catholics. He wrote several controversial and devotional books. He was a friend and supporter of George Blackwell as archpriest until Blackwell was captured, imprisoned, and forced to take the Oath of Supremacy, which denied all papal authority in England and asserted that the English monarch was supreme head of the Church in England.

to ease our pains herein) to certain treatises which have been published to the world by various good Catholics, as they have professed themselves to be, against [the Jesuits] and their enterprises in other countries. . . .

The Order of that Society being approved by the Pope is to be honored by all good Catholics, and the men themselves are to be reverenced—we mean those who live according to their calling and first institution, which few of them do. For in recent years many of that Order behave as if religion were nothing but a mere political device, conceived, framed and upheld only by human wisdom and sleights of wit. And they were the men that by Machiavelli's rules are raised up to maintain [the Jesuit Order] by equivocations, detractions, dissimulations, ambition, contention for superiority, stirring up strife, setting kingdoms against kingdoms, raising up rebellions, murdering Princes, and we know not how many stratagems of Satan coming out of hell and tending to confusion.

The old saying was, "Let the shoemaker meddle with his slipper, the smith with his anvil, and the priests with their prayers." But the Jesuits like frank gamesters are into everything. He is not worth a straw among them who is not able to manage a kingdom. Matters of state, titles of princes, genealogies of kings, rights of succession, disposing of scepters and such affairs are their chief studies. Some fear that they are more knowledgeable [about the works of Pietro] Aretino, Lucian and Machiavelli than their breviaries. . . . [28] Assuredly they do not behave themselves like men of other Religious Orders. He that tells them to live in a cloister [would be wasting their time]; such a base kind of life is far unworthy of their excellence. There are few royal courts in Europe where some of their masterships do not reside with the purpose of receiving and passing to their General at Rome all that happens in those parts of the world. They dispatch this information to and fro by secret codes. They have either a Jesuit or someone altogether Jesuited in most of those royal Councils who for the good of the Society must without scruple deliver to them all known details about the secrets of their sovereigns.

It is true that all the other Religious Orders have a special esteem for their own founders, but the Jesuits have carried this whim beyond all limits. Since the inventor of their Order was a Spaniard and a soldier, all of his

28. Pietro Aretino (1492–1556) was an Italian writer known for his poisonous pen, which earned him the title of *Scourge of Princes*. He also wrote pornography. Lucian (c. 120–c. 190) was a Greek who wrote philosophical dialogues spiced with cynical humor. Niccolò Machiavelli (1469–1527) is best known for *The Prince,* in which he seems to encourage princes to practice deceit and ruthlessness to increase their power. The Jesuits were often seen as Machiavellian. Breviaries were the prayer books with which priests were required to pray daily.

disciples regardless of the country of their birth are in their hearts and practices altogether Spanish, breathing little but cruelties, confusions and troubles. They have in their writings, their sermons and by all their endeavors labored to persuade all Catholics that the king of Spain and our faith are so linked together that it becomes a point of necessity in the Catholic faith to put all Europe into his hands, or otherwise the Catholic religion will be utterly extinguished and perish. This is a ridiculous, nay, a wicked conceit, and like [the Jesuits] themselves it builds the faith of Saint Peter and his successors upon the King of Spain's monarchy, as if unless he does not have all, the Church must come to nothing.

But these courtly rabbis do think they may easily carry us poor secular priests after their shadows and make us admire whatsoever they tell us. How they labored in France (even the French Jesuits themselves) to have lifted the Spaniard onto the throne of that kingdom, with the consequent overthrow of their own native country, as you are not ignorant. This rang loudly through all Christendom to their perpetual shame. If they were only stained with these prodigious and more than heathenish practices and if the contagion of them had not infected the Jesuits who came among us here in England, it would much less have grieved all discreet English Catholics and especially us secular priests. But to our infinite danger it is far otherwise. For some of them strove mightily in Spain to persuade King [Philip II] to invade this our country (a plan containing in it the very ocean of all desperate calamities) giving the king many reasons why he was bound to undertake that enterprise [the Spanish Armada of 1588] and assuring him of great assistance here, if once his forces were landed. Since that time hardly anybody is ignorant about how they urged him to a second and to a third attempt.

William Watson[29]

"Preface to the Reader" in John Mush's *A Dialogue betwixt a Secular Priest and a Lay Gentleman*

Among many letters and treatises that have come into my hands concerning the matters in question between the secular priests and the Jesuits, one

---

29. Watson was arrested several times by the English government; he escaped three times from prison, only to be arrested as part of a plot to overthrow James I. He was executed December 9, 1603. His hatred of the Jesuits was a constant theme throughout most of his life and writings. A short account of his life, taken from the *English Dictionary of National Biography*, is reprinted in a collective biography of great British spies: *Secret Lives*, edited by M. R. D. Foot (Oxford University Press, 2002), pp. 25–30.

with the most importance, significance, and substance (in my opinion) is the discourse of the following dialogue. It much more merits my poor recommendation by adding to it a general preface because it is a sort of an abstract, compendium or brief for all the most important matters that are in controversy between us and the said Spanish or Jesuitical faction. For (omitting other particulars) you have here exquisitely handled the great contention about the superiority arrogated to the Jesuits over the secular priests. You have here discussed the question about schism and the unlearned and very malicious libels of Father [Thomas] Lister [1559–1628], the Jesuit secretly refuted.[30] You have here decided the case of obedience and disobedience and in what sort of ignorant disrespect the common sort of Catholics holds the secular priests, for they do not know this of themselves but from a forgery filled with Jesuitical lying lips which have given it a glaze of stainless dye in a senseless conceit of infallible truth to rest in the bare words of a wretch unworthy of naming because he has mightily prejudiced the honor of the priesthood. You have here set down the causes behind the Jesuits' double diligence in defending the Archpriest, together with their many dishonest, uncharitable, irreligious, unpriestly practices for [gaining] a supremacy. You have here insinuated to you the unspeakable pride, ambition, envy, malice, extortion, cruelty, and above all the intolerable backbiting tongues of the Jesuits against the people they hate—more than ever did Ovid, Horace,[31] or any other malignant detractor, scold, or cynical slanderer. In short, you have here explained the grounds of all the Jesuitical calumnies, defamations, and injuries. . . .

For what Catholic before the Jesuits got a footing in England would not have trembled at the heart to have called an anointed Catholic priest (however he had previously lived) a knave, a villain, a spy, a soothsayer, an idolater, a schismatic, a libertine, an apostate, an atheist, with the other most odious terms that the devil or malice is able to invent? And yet nothing is more common now than this everywhere among this lewd brood of the Jesuitical faction. Our common [Protestant] enemies even out of their own humanity and for civility's sake show a more reverent esteem and respect are to be given priests (at least for their learning, scholarship, moral virtues, and other good abilities noted in most of those whom that faction held in

---

30. Lister, who entered the Jesuits in Rome and earned a doctorate in theology in France, was sent by his superiors back to his native England in 1596. In the aftermath of the Gunpowder Plot of 1605—a failed attempt to blow up Parliament—he was exiled by King James I but returned to England in 1610. He wrote an unpublished tract that attacked the secular priests and defended Archpriest Blackwell.

31. Together with Virgil (70–19 B.C.), Ovid (43 B.C.–A.D. 17) and Horace (65–8 B.C.) were the leading Latin poets in the age of Emperor Augustus (27 B.C.–A.D. 14).

disgrace) than any of these new pestiferous Puritan Jesuitical sectarians will ever acknowledge. . . .

As for their other slanders: that the matter in contention was already decided in Rome and that they would therefore make the world believe the secular priests were seditious, turbulent, and factious persons, and also that the said priests are the only politicians and meddlers, politicizing more dangerously than they (the said Jesuits) do Hispanize or make Spanish, etc. the one and the other, are both most false, mere calumnies, forgeries and slanders without any truth in the report or documentation about them abroad. Very sensibly, prudently and learnedly are they here confuted, and their shameful dealings, treacheries and impieties are secretly discovered thereby together with the foisting of that poor simple fellow Master [George] Blackwell into an office and authority about whose meaning he knew little (God knows) or what treasonable practices he was expected to carry out.[32] Finally, here arise things to be carefully considered (as a point in my mind of as great import, moment and consequence as anything we have touched upon so far) the panegyrics of the Jesuits' praises, the causes that move them to send forth their spirits to course over sea and land with bugle blasts of the bloody menaces of the goddess of war to all that dare to contradict a Jesuit. There is also that extreme folly, madness, lunacy, or what I do not know how to call it in various Catholic laymen, yea, and in the more unlearned and less experienced sort of priests who will believe every word of an oracle that falls from a Jesuit's lips. It goes so far that one person once said that if such a priest, a follower and supporter of the Jesuit faction, should bid him to hang himself, he would do it. They cannot be persuaded otherwise [from believing] that all the whole Church and commonwealth of Christendom depend upon their impotent aspirations. . . .

32. Watson and Bagwell, leaders of the secular priests known as the Appellants, despised Archpriest Blackwell because they saw him as a simpleton and tool of the Jesuits.

INDEX

Page numbers in italics refer to illustrations.

Acepsemas, 161
Acquaviva, Claudio (superior general of the Jesuits), xvii, xviii, 110, 160, 193–98, *196*, 208–10, 216–22
Adams, John, 233n3
Alexander the Great, 110
Alvarez, Baltasar, 174
Alvarez, Francisco, 23
Ambrose, St. (Church Father), 146, 147, 153
Anabaptists, 155
Anjiro (Japanese convert), 66
Anthony, St., 161
Aphraates, 161
Aquinas, St. Thomas (medieval Dominican theologian), 41, 42, 123, 124, 144, 157
Aragon, Hernando de (archbishop of Zaragoza), 240
Araoz, Antonio, 2, 32, 33, 239
Aretino, Pietro (Renaissance satirist), 253
Arians, early heretics, 171
Aristotle, 42, 124
Artiguaye, Miguel, 115–17
assassination of kings, 208, 210–16
Attila the Hun (leader of Mongol warriors), 154n31
Augustine, St., 144, 146, 149, 150, 153, 157, 162, 164, 169
Augustus (Roman emperor), 58, 169, 255

Bagshaw, Christopher (English diocesan priest), 233, 250–51, 256; *A Sparing Discoverie of Our English Jesuits* (anti-Jesuit literature), 251–54
Barma, Juan Bautista de, 205, 207

Barreto, João Nunes (Jesuit patriarch of Ethiopia), 21–6
Beira, Juan de, 129
Bellarmine, St. Robert (Jesuit cardinal and theologian), xvi–xviii, 12, 158, 175, 179–87, *182*, 208; *de Controversiis Christianae Fidei (Controversies of the Christian Faith)*, 143–55
Bellay, Eustace du (bishop of Paris), 242, 243, 245
Bellini, Isidore, 50
Benedict, St. (founder of Benedictine Order), 159
Benedictines, 157
Benoit, Jean, 244
Bermudes, João, 30
Bernard, St. (medieval preacher), 159
Berze, Gaspar, 85
Bible as the sole norm of doctrine, 143–55
Blackwell, George (archpriest over English Catholics), 233, 251, 252, 255, 256
Bonaventure, St. (medieval Franciscan theologian), 180
Borgia, St. Francis, 32, 47
Boroa, Diego de, 119
Brébeuf, St. Jean de, 65, 121–30
Brenz, Johann (Lutheran theologian), 145, 155
Broët, Paschase, 241, 242
Buddha, Gautama, 96–8
Buddhism, 93, 95–100
bullfighting, opposition to, 205, 206
Bunny, Edmund (English Protestant writer), 175

Calvin, John (Protestant reformer of
    Geneva), xi, xvi, 131, 144, 148,
    155, 162, 231
Campion, St. Edmund, 132, 138–43,
    141
Canisius, St. Peter, 2, 49, 50, 132,
    133, *137,* 209
Cano, Melchior (Dominican theolo-
    gian), 232, 234–36
Canute (king of England), 228
Cardona, Didaco de, 47, 49
Carneyro, Melchior, 22
Casini, Giovanni Filippo, 53
caste system in India, 104–11
Catherine of Siena, St. (late medieval
    mystic), 127
censorship, 134–36
Charles V (Holy Roman Emperor), 2,
    7, 16, 17, 19–21, 34, 48, 132, 209,
    222, 242
Charles IX (king of France), 214
Chastel, Jean, failure to assassinate
    Henry IV, 211n3
Chemnitz, Martin (Lutheran theolo-
    gian), 151, 155
Chronicon (selections), by Polanco,
    189–93, 205–7, 234–45
Chrysostom, St. John (Church
    Father), 146, 151, 152, 161n8,
    162
Claudius (Ethiopian emperor), 22,
    30
Clavius, Christopher, 88, 91
Clement, Jacques (assassin of Henry
    III), 212–14
Coelho, Francisco, 77
Columbus, Christopher, xi
Confucius, 92
Constantine (Roman emperor), 161
Contreras, Juan Augustín, 118
*Controversiis Christianae Fidei, de,
    (Controversies of the Christian Faith)*
    by Bellarmine, 143–55
Contzen, Adam, 211
Coudret, Annibal de, 49, 50, 52, 53
Crashaw, Richard, 175

Criminali, Antonio, 78, 79
Cyrus the Great, 150

Delrio, Martin, 199
Decem Rationes, by Edmund Cam-
    pion, 139
Despence, Claude, 244
Diocletian (Roman emperor), 56
Divine Office, recitation of, 232
Doménech, Jerónimo, 192
Dominic, St., 5
Dominicans, 157, 198, 231, 232,
    234, 236, 244
Donne, John (Anglican preacher and
    poet), 175, 232
drama in Jesuit colleges, 55–63

Ebionites, 153
Elizabeth I (queen of England), 142,
    233
Emerson, Ralph, 138
Epictetus, 94, 96
Erasmus, Desiderius, 39, 156, 157
Euclid, 50, 91
Eusebius (early church historian),
    152–54

Fernandez, Juan, 83, 84
Ferdinand I (Holy Roman Emperor),
    xvi, 17, 34, 132–38, 209
Filippo, Giovanni, 192
Francis of Assisi, St. (founder of Fran-
    ciscans), 5, 159
Franciscans, 157, 188, 231, 241
Francis I (king of France), 17, 242
Freux, André des, 49, 50
Fumo Can (early Chinese convert),
    91, 93, 94

Gesù, the (mother church of Jesuit
    Order), *9*
Gonçalves, Luís Câmara de, 2, 3, *218*
Gregory the Great (saint and pope),
    146, 147
Gregory XI, 127
Gregory XV, 102

Guarani Indians, 111–20, 209
Guérer, Jean, 211
Guise family of French dukes, the,
    212, 213, 244

Henry II (king of France), 17, 132, 242
Henry III (king of France), 212–14
Henry IV (king of France), 211, 212
Henry VIII (king of England), 232
Herbert, George, 175
Hinduism, 101–8
Homer, 252n26
Hopkins, Gerard Manley, 158
Horace, 255
hostility toward Jesuits, 231–56: in
    England, 250–56; in France, 241–
    50; in Spain 234–41; in the United
    States, 233
Huron Indians, 65, 121–27

Ignatius of Loyola. *See* Loyola, St.
    Ignatius of
Inquisition, xiii, 135, 198
Irenaeus, St. (early Church Father),
    146, 153

James I (king of England), 254
Jefferson, Thomas, 233n3
Jerome, St. (early Church Father and
    biblical scholar), 146, 153, 169
Jewish ancestry, Jesuits of, 238, 244
John III (king of Portugal), 21, 23,
    30, 33, 65, 74
John Climachus, St., 180
John of Avila, St. (Spanish friend of
    early Jesuits), 164
Juana (princess of Spain), 240
just war, theory of, 228–30

Koran, the, 154

La Puente, Luis de, xvii, 156, 158,
    174–79
Ladislaus IV (king of Poland), 208
Landini, Silvestro, 189, 190
Lannoy, Nicholas, 133

Lao-Tzu (founder of Taoism), 98
lay brothers, 163n18
Leo I (saint and pope), 153, 172
Leo X (pope), 145
Lippomano, Andrea (Venetian bene-
    factor of Jesuits), 34
Lister, Thomas, 255
Lombard, Peter (medieval theolo-
    gian), 42
Lopez, Ignatius, 47
Louis XIV (king of France), 56
Loyola, St. Ignatius of, xii–xviii, 1–
    10, *3*, 22, 23, 32, 33, 35, 37, 38,
    46–8, 51, 52, 54, 64, 65, 80–8, *82*,
    130–38, 157, 163, 165, 166, 188,
    191, 209, 231, 232, 246–48, 249,
    251, 253; Autobiography of, 2–8;
    correspondence of, 2, 16–31, 132–
    37; on education, Jesuit colleges, 32,
    37–45; Jesuit Constitutions, xvi, 1,
    5, 8, 10, 37–46, 64, 167; hatred of
    Protestantism, 132–38; life of, xii–
    xiv, 2–8; missionary strategy of, 21–
    31; politics of, 16–21, 131–37; *Spir-
    itual Exercises,* xiii, 1, 8–16, 131,
    157, 158, 165, 180
Lucian, 253
Luther, Martin, xi, xii, xvi, 131, 144,
    145, 148, 149, 162, 231, 246, 247

Machiavelli, Niccolò, 131, 222, 232,
    253
Maffeo, Bernadino (cardinal), 243
Manichees, 155
Mansilas, Francisco de, 67
Maracaná, Roque (Guarani Indian
    chief), 114–17
Marco, Lope (Vicar General at
    Zaragosa), 239
Marquette, Jacques, 121
Mariana, Juan de, xviii, 208–16; *On
    a King and the Education of a King,*
    210–16
Maximus the Confessor, St. (early
    Church Father), 153, 154
Medina, Bartolomé de, 197

meditations, meditation technique, 8–15, 157, 166–79
Melanchthon, Philip, 39, 148
Messina, Jesuit college at, 32, 33, 46–54
Middleton, Thomas (English Jacobean dramatist), 232
Minas (emperor of Ethiopia), 22
Micer Paolo, 67
missionary work overseas: Canada, 121–30; China, 64, 66, 83–5, 88–101; Ethiopia, 21–31; India, 64, 66–79, 97, 101–11; Japan, 80–7; South America, 65, 111–21
Mohammed, 154
Montoya, Antonio Ruis de, 65, 111–21, 209
Muslims, 16–21, 155; *see also* Turks

Nadal, Jerome, xvii, 2, 16, 49–51, 156–58, 163, 166–74; *On the Night of the Lord's Birth: The Nativity of Christ,* 168
Nicene Creed, 171, 172
Nobili, Roberto de, 64, *105; The Report on the Customs of the Indian Nation,* 101–11

Oath of Supremacy, 252
Oecolampadius, Johann (Swiss Protestant theologian), 148
Origen (early Church Father), 146, 154
Osiander, Andreas (Lutheran theologian), 148
Otello, Girolamo, 52, 53
Ovid, 255
Oviedo, André de, 22

Palmio, Benedetto, 49, 50, 52
Parlement of Paris, 211, 233, 234, 241, 242, 246
Paris Method, xiii
Parsons, Robert. *See* Persons, Robert
Pasquier, Étienne, 233, 245–46, 245n15; *Le Catéchisme des Jésuites,* 245–50

Passeri, Giovnni Battista, 50
Paul III (pope), xiv, 1, *7,* 22, 48, 49, 65
Paul IV (pope), 245
Pelagius (early heretic), 162
Persons, Robert, 138, 175, 250, 252
Philip II (king of Spain), 210, 232, 238, 240, 242, 252, 254
Philip III (king of Spain), xviii, 208, 211
Philip IV (king of Spain), 111, 112, 121, 209
Pindar, 180
Plantin, Christopher (Belgian publisher), 166, 180
Plato, 96, 180
Plotinus, 180
Poggio, Giovanni (cardinal), 237, 238
Polanco, Juan (Loyola's secretary), xvi, xvi, 16, 32–4, 46, 47, 188–93, 197, 232, 234–46; *Chronicon* (selections), 189–93, 205–7, 234–45
politics, Jesuit involvement in, xvii, xviii, 16–21, 132–38, 140, 208–30
Polo, Marco, 89
preaching, 194–96
Prester John (legendary king of Ethiopia), 23–6, 28
prostitution, helping prostitutes, 190–93
Protestantism, Jesuit opposition to, xvi, xvii, 131–55
Pythagoras, 93, 96

Quirinius, 169

Ratio Studiorum, 193–97
Ravaillac, François, 211
reductions, 112, 118, 119
Regis, St. Jean François, 194
Ribadeneira, Pedro, 2, 131, 162, 211
Ricci, Matteo, 64, 86, 88–101, *95; The True Meaning of the Lord of Heaven,* 95–101

Rodrigues, Simão (Simon) de, 65, 73–6, 81, 82, 87, 129, 208
Rodriguez, Alfonso, xvii, 156, 158–66
royal confessors, xviii–ix, 209, 222–25; "Rules for the Confessors of Princes" (Claudio Acquaviva), 216–25
Ruffinus, Tyrannius (fourth-century Christian writer), 153, 154
Ruggieri, Michele, 88
rural missions to peasants, 193–98

Scibani, Carlo, 211
Sebastian (king of Portugal), 208, *218*
Segneri, Paolo, 194
Seneca, 56
seminaries for training priests, 136–38
Silíceo, Juan Martìnez (archbishop of Toledo), 232–35, 237, 238
Simons, Joseph, 55–63
soldiers, their duties to their king, 225–28
Soto, Pedro de (Dominican theologian), 145
Southwell, Robert, 175
Spee von Langenfeld, Friedrich (Friedrich Spee), xvii, 198–205
Spiritual Exercises, by Loyola, xiii, 1, 8–16, 131, 156–58, 160, 167, 180, 193
Spiritual Exercises, xv, 8, 10–16, 32, 111, 158, 197, 220, 236, 237
Stephan I (saint and king of Hungry), 222
Suárez, Francisco, 174
Suleiman the Magnificent (Ottoman Sultan), 17, 20

Tablares, Pedro, 238
Tanner, Adam, 199
Taoism, 98
Terence, 42, 53, 248
Teresa of Avila, St. (Spanish mystic), 130

theology faculty at the University of Paris, 244
Thomas à Kempis, 156
Torres, Cosme de, 83, 84
Torres, Miguel de, 235, 237
Trent, Council of, xi, 151, 242
Trigault, Nicholas, 89–94
Turks, xiii–xiv, 16–21, 23n25, 132, 222
tyrannicide, 210–16

University of Paris, xiii, 33, 70, 71, 131, 242–44, 248
Urtasun, Martín, 113, 114

Valens (Roman emperor), 161
Vasco da Gama, xii, 67
Vega, Eleonora de, 49, 191
Vega, Fernando de, 52
Vega, Juan de (Spanish Viceroy of Sicily), 32, 48, 49, 51–3, 191, 193, 208
vendettas, 189–90
Vergil, Polydore, 228
Villanueva, Francisco de, 235, 237
Vinck, Antoine, 50, 52
Virgil, 60, 96, 255
Vives, Juan Luis (leading Spanish humanist), 53

war, *see* just war, theory of
Watson, William, 233, 250–51, 254; "Preface to the Reader" (anti-Jesuit literature) 254–56
Whitaker, William (English Protestant theologian), 144
Wierix brothers, 166, *168*
witch persecution, xvii, 188, 198–205

Xavier, St. Francis, xiii, 64–88, *82, 87,* 97n37, 128, 129, 130, 163, 166
Xu Guanqi (Chinese Christian scholar), 91n28

Zwingli, Huldreich (Protestant reformer at Zurich), xi, 148